Graphic Thinking
for Architects
& Designers

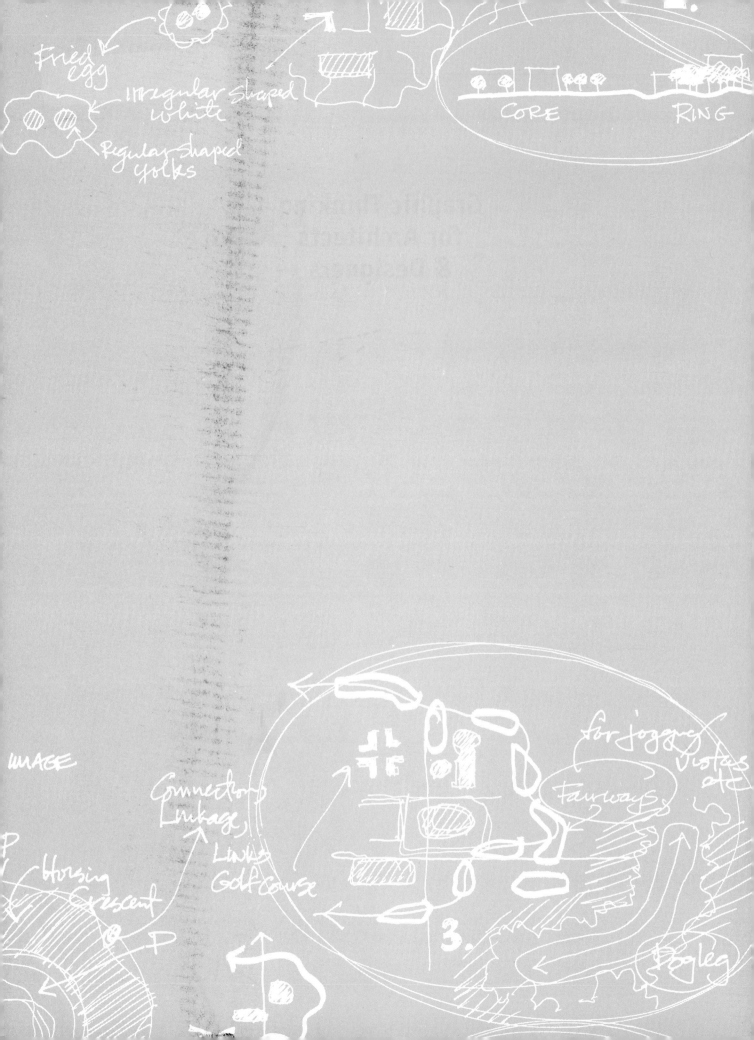

THIRD EDITION

Graphic Thinking for Architects & Designers

PAUL LASEAU

JOHN WILEY & SONS, INC.

New York   Chichester   Weinheim   Brisbane   Singapore   Toronto

Published simultaneously in Canada.

Interior Design: David Levy

This publication is designed to provide accurate and author-itative information in regard to the subject matter covered. It is sold with the understanding that the publisher is not engaged in rendering professional services. If professional advice or other expert assistance is required, the services of a competent professional person should be sought.

Library of Congress Cataloging-in-Publication Data:

Laseau, Paul, 1937-
    Graphic thinking for architects & designers / Paul Laseau.—3rd. ed.
        p.   cm.
    Includes bibliographical references and index.
    ISBN 0-471-35292-6 (paper)
    1. Architectural drawing.   2. Communication in archi-tectural design. 3. Architecture—Sketch-books.
4. Graphic arts.   I. Title.

NA2705 .L38   2000
720'.28'4—dc21   99-086809
Printed in the United States of America.

10 9 8

Contents

Foreword

Paul Laseau proposes two related ideas: the first is that of "graphic thinking"; the second is graphic thinking as a device for communication between the designer and the designed for. The following brief remarks are addressed to the relationship between the two ideas.

Historically, building design was not so indifferent to human well-being that "communication with the people" became an issue until the act of drawing was divided into two specialized activities. The first was design drawing, in which the designer expressed his or her ideas. The second was drafting used to instruct the builder.

Design drawing began as and remains a means of generating ideas, for tapping initial concepts to be sorted out and developed, or simply as an enjoyable activity. Drafting is an eight-hour task performed daily, filling sheets of paper with precise lines dictated by others.

Long ago, when the work of individual craftsmen became larger and more complex, when a cathedral rather than a chair was to be designed, dimensions had to be established so that the work of a single craftsman could be coordinated with the work of many. Drawing was introduced as a creative device for planning work.

Craftsmen have always used drawings to help them visualize their ideas as they made adjustments in the continuous process of fitting parts together. Drawing under these conditions is inseparable from the work itself. Some historians say that the working drawings for the great churches of the twelfth and thirteenth centuries were drawn on boards that were later nailed into the construction.

But drawing also has other purposes. The division of labor increases productivity. Artifacts requiring several weeks of work by a single skilled craftsman are divided into smaller standardized work tasks. Production is increased as skill is eliminated. The craftsman's expression of material, design sense, and sketches are banished from the workplace. Drawings and specifications predetermine all facets of the work.

Design decisions are given to a new class of workmen who do not work with the material but instead direct the actions of others and who communicate their decisions to those who work through drawings made by draftsmen. Designing, as a separate task, has come into being. The professional designer, the professional draftsman, and the assembly line occur simultaneously as related phenomena.

This all occurred some time ago, but the momentum of the change from craftsmanship to draftsmanship, brought about by the peculiar form of industrialization we have chosen to adopt, persists. It now extends to the division of labor in the designer's office. The building of great buildings is no longer the creation of master craftsmen led by a master builder but of architectural offices organized along the lines of industrial production. The task of the architect has been divided and subdivided into an assembly line of designer, construction manager, interior designer, decorator, structural, electrical, and mechanical engineers, and draftsmen. Design decisions once made by the designer on the drawing board are now made by the programmer on computer printouts.

There are those of us who believe that industrialization could have been achieved without destroying the craftsman's skill, love, and respect for material and the joy of building. We find it even less desirable that the joy of creativity and graphic thinking that accompanies that activity should leave the designer's office for the memory bank of a computer.

The built world and artifacts around us are evidence of the almost fatal error of basing design on the mindless work of the assembly line. To develop programming and operational research based on mindless design would be to continue a disastrous historic continuum.

Graphic thinking is of course necessary to help rejuvenate a moribund design system. But communication "with the people" is not enough. Creativity itself must be shared, and shared with everyone from dowel knocker to "Lieber Meister." The need for graphic thinking is great, but it is greater on the workbenches of the assembly lines at River Rouge than on the desks of the chief designers of Skidmore, Owings & Merrill.

—FORREST WILSON, 1980

Preface to the Third Edition

Twenty years have passed since the first publication of this book. The events of the intervening years have served to reinforce my initial assumptions and the points made by Forrest Wilson in the Foreword.

The accelerated developments in personal computers and their application to architectural design and construction have raised more forcefully the question of the role of individual thought and creativity within processes that are increasingly complex and specialized. Will individuals experience more opportunities for expression and contribution or will their contributions be devalued because of the speed and precision of computer–driven processes?

Although the Internet/web has dramatically increased individual access, two major philosophical camps still guide computer development and applications. One camp sees the computer as a way to extend and improve traditional business organization, with its segmentation of tasks and reliance on specialists. The other camp sees the computer as a way to revolutionize business by broadening the scope and impact of the individual to the benefit of both the individual and the organization. One view is of individuals supporting information; the other is of information supporting individuals.

A premise of the first edition of this book was that individual, creative thinking has a vital role in a present and future society that must cope with complex, interrelated problems. Addressing such problems depends upon a comprehensive understanding of their nature rather than shoehorning them into convenient, simplistic, theoretical models. And visual communication provides an important tool for describing and understanding complexity. Increased comprehensive, rather than specialized, knowledge in the possession of individuals should benefit both the organization and the individual. In their book, *In Search of Excellence,*[1] Peters and Waterman illustrated that the effectiveness of organizations depends upon an understanding of values, aspirations, and meanings that is shared by all members. We are also becoming more aware that the mental and physical health of individuals is a valid as well as practical concern of organizations.

Preface to the First Edition

In the fall of 1976, while participating in a discussion group on design communication at the University of Wisconsin–Milwaukee, I had the occasion to mention my book *Graphic Problem Solving*. Essentially, that book was an attempt at convincing architects to apply their freehand concept-gathering skills to nontraditional problems dealing more with the processes than the products of architecture. During the discussion, Fuller Moore stated that the graphic skills I had assumed to be part of architectural training were being neglected in the schools and that a more basic book on drawing in support of thinking was needed. Soon after, I had the chance to talk to several architects about the sketches they use to develop designs in contrast to the "finished drawings they use in presentations." Most creative architects had developed impressive freehand sketching skills and felt comfortable sketching while thinking. Some architects drew observations or design ideas in small sketchbooks they carried with them at all times. Both the architects and the educators I interviewed expressed concern over the apparent lack of freehand graphic skills in people now entering the profession.

As I began to collect materials for this book, I wondered about the relevance of sketching in architecture. Could sketching be better applied to designing as practiced today? The answer to this question depends on an examination of the present challenges to architectural design:

1. To be more responsive to needs, a problem-solving process.
2. To be more scientific, more reliable, or predictable.

The response to these challenges was suggested by Heinz Von Foerster:

...the language of architecture is connotative language because its intent is to initiate interpretation.

The creative architectural space begets creativity, new insights, new choices. It is a catalyst for cognition. This suggests an ethical imperative that applies not only to architects but also to anyone who acts on that imperative. Act always so as to: increase, enlarge, enhance the number of choices.[1]

Relating these ideas to the challenges enumerated earlier, I see two corresponding imperatives:

1. Architects should solve problems *with* people instead of *for* them by helping them understand their needs and the choices of designs that meet those needs. This is done by bringing those who use the buildings into the process of designing those buildings.
2. Architects must better understand science and how much it has in common with architecture. Jacob Bronowski pointed out that the creative scientist is more interested in exploring and expanding ideas than in establishing fixed "truths." The unique quality of human beings lies in the increase rather than the decrease of diversity.

Within this context, sketches can contribute to design, first by facilitating the exploration and diversity of each designer's thinking. Second, sketches can help open up the design process by developing communication *with* people instead of presenting conclusions to people.

The notion of *graphic thinking* grew out of the recognition that sketching or drawing can and should support the designer's thinking. I realize that some readers would be more comfortable with a book about either thinking or drawing, but I felt it was critical to deal with their interaction. Pulling them apart seemed to be like trying to understand how a fish swims by studying the fish and the water separately. I hope you will be able to bear with the rough spots in this book and find some things that will help in your work.

Acknowledgments

This book is dedicated to those architects who generously took time to discuss their use of drawings in design during my original and subsequent research. Many of them also provided sketches to illustrate the text. Their dedication to creativity in architecture, enthusiasm for drawing, and comments about their design processes were a great help and inspiration for my work. Among these architects, I am especially indebted to David Stieglitz, Thomas Beeby, Morse Payne, Thomas Larson, Michael Gebhart, Romaldo Giurgola, James Tice, Norman Crowe, Harry Egink, Kirby Lockard, and Steven and Cathi House.

Recognition is due the following people for their particularly important contributions to this effort:

Fuller Moore for first suggesting the idea.

Robert McKim for his insights to visual thinking and his encouragement.

Jim Anderson for vital comments on graphic communication.

Karl Brown for comments and other valuable assistance.

Michele Laseau for technical assistance.

Jack Wyman, Ken Carpenter, Juan Bonta, Charles Sappenfield, and other present and past colleagues at the College of Architecture and Planning, Ball State University for comments and moral support.

A special thanks to Forrest Wilson for his enthusiastic support at the humbling outset of this effort.

Finally, thanks must be given to my wife, Peggy, and children, Michele, Kevin, and Madeleine, for their great patience and sacrifices while I struggled with revisions.

Previously published drawings were photographed by Jerry Hoffman and Steven Talley.

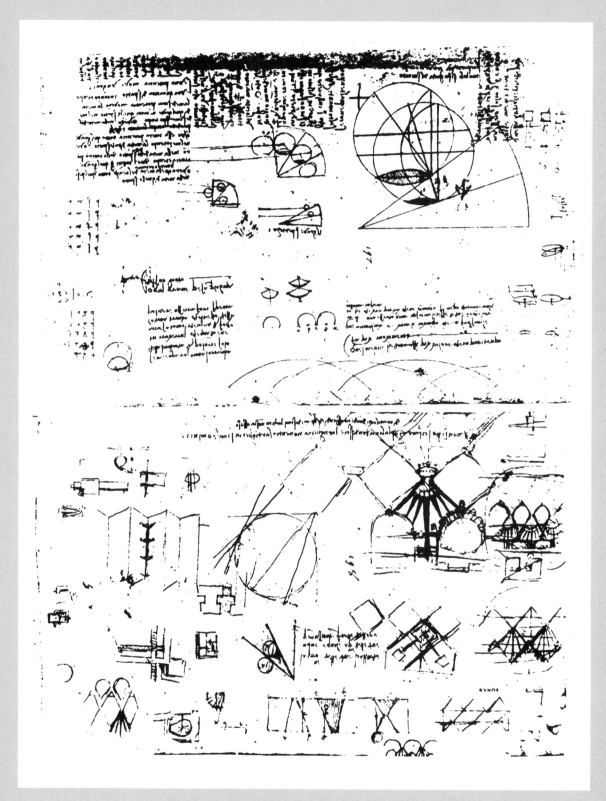

Figure 1-1 By Leonardo da Vinci. Studies of fortifications.

1 Introduction

Graphic thinking is a term I have adopted to describe thinking assisted by sketching. In architecture, this type of thinking is usually associated with the conceptual design stages of a project in which thinking and sketching work closely together as stimulants for developing ideas. Interest in this form of thinking is promoted by a reexamination of the history of architectural design, the impact of visual communication in society, and new concepts of the role of design and designers.

There is actually a very strong tradition of graphic thinking in architecture. Looking through reproductions of the notebooks of Leonardo da Vinci, we are struck by the dynamic thinking they reflect. It is impossible to really understand or appreciate da Vinci's thinking apart from his drawings because the graphic images and the thinking are one, a unity. A closer look at these sketches reveals certain features that are instructive for anyone interested in graphic thinking.

1. There are many different ideas on one page—his attention is constantly shifting from one subject to another.
2. The way da Vinci looks at problems is diverse both in method and in scale—there are often perspectives, sections, plans, details, and panoramic views on the same page.
3. The thinking is exploratory, open-ended—the sketches are loose and fragmented while showing how they were derived. Many alternatives for extending the ideas are suggested. The spectator is invited to participate.

What a marvelous example! Here is a mind in ferment, using drawings as a means of discovery rather than as a way to impress other people.

Although it is often difficult to find records of developmental sketches in historical documents, there is enough surviving evidence to indicate that the use of sketches for thinking was common to architects throughout history. Depending on the dictates of the building trades or customs, the drawing conventions varied from plan to section to elevation. For almost two centuries, the Ecole des Beaux Arts in Paris used the plan *esquisse* as the foundation for its

Figure 1-2 By Edwin Lutyens. Castle Drogo and British Pavilion 1911 Exposition, Rome.

Figure 1-3 By Edwin Lutyens. Castle Drogo and British Pavilion 1911 Exposition, Rome.

training method. With the establishment of large architectural firms in the United States, three-dimensional scale models gradually replaced drawing for the purposes of design development. The use of designing sketches further declined with the advent of professional model makers and professional renderers.

Figure 1-4 By Alvar Aalto.

There has, of course, been an intense interest in architects' drawings rekindled by exhibits like the Beaux-Arts and 200 Years of American Architectural Drawings. But the emphasis is mostly on communication of the final fixed product, and these presentation drawings tell us practically nothing about the way in which the buildings were designed. The thinking sketches are necessary to understand the step-by-step process. Yet even when the thinking sketches are available, as in the documents of the work of LeCorbusier, they are usually overlooked in favor of the renderings or photos of the finished work. We are just beginning to appreciate the importance LeCorbusier placed on sketches. As Geoffrey Broadbent notes, "All the internal harmony of the work is in the drawings.... It is incredible that artists today should be indifferent (even hostile) to this prime mover, this 'scaffolding' of the project."[1]

Figure 1-5 By Thomas Larson. The Grandberg Residence.

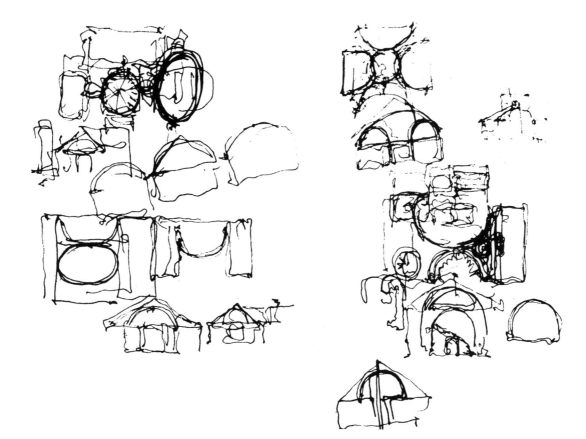

Figure 1-6 By Thomas Beeby. House of Virgil.

Among modern architects, Alvar Aalto has left us probably one of the best models of the graphic thinking tradition. His sketches are rapid and diverse; they deftly probe the subject. Hand, eye, and mind are intensely concentrated. The sketches record the level of development, proficiency, and clarity of Aalto's ideas. There are many other architects whose work we can turn to, particularly here in the United States, where we are experiencing a resurgence of sketching. Their drawings are inventive, diverse, and provocative. Whether they are making notes in a sketchbook or turning over concepts in the design studio, these creative designers are looking for something special over and above solving the design problem, like the gourmet who is looking for something more than food. They enjoy the *eureka* experience, and they enjoy the search as well. This book is really about finding things, about seeing new ideas, about discovery, and about sharing ideas and discoveries.

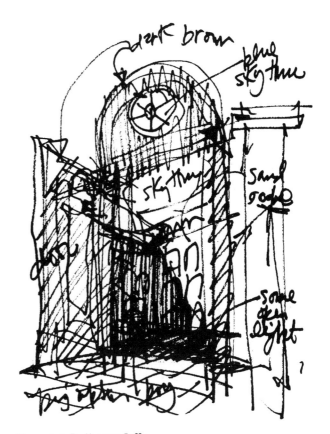

Figure 1-7 By Norman Jaffe.

Figure 1-8 Battle of Cety I with the Cheta.

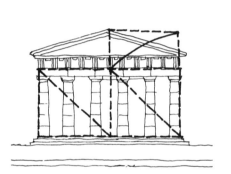

Figure 1-9 Greek geometry

Figure 1-10 Exploration map.

Figure 1-11 Constellation of stars

VISUAL COMMUNICATION THROUGH TIME

Throughout history, vision has had an important impact on thinking. Starting with the caveman, drawings were a way of "freezing" ideas and events outside of him and creating a history. In many ways, the "second world" man created through his images was critical to the evolution of thinking. Man was able to separate the here and now from what could be imagined, the future. Through images, the world of the spirit, the ideal world of mythology, and compelling utopias became immediate and real. The ideals of an entire culture could be contained in one picture; the unspeakable could be shared with others. From earliest times, this visual expression of thinking has been communal. Once a concept, such as the notion of man being able to fly, was converted to an image, it was free to be reinterpreted again and again by others until the airplane was invented.

Man used signs and symbols long before written languages were adopted. Early written languages, such as Egyptian hieroglyphics, were highly specialized sets of symbols derived from pictures. The development of geometry, combining mathematics with diagrams, made it possible to think of structure and other abstractions of reality. This led to the construction of objects or buildings of monumental scale from designs. In addition to trying to make sense of his immediate surroundings, man used drawings to reach out into the unknown. Maps reconstituted from notes and sketches of explorers sparked the imagination and stimulated new discoveries about our world and the universe.

In spite of the ascendance of written language, visual communication continues to be an essential part of the way we think. This is revealed in these phrases that liberally sprinkle our everyday conversation: "I see what you mean; take another look at the situation; put this all in perspective." Although research opinion varies, it seems generally accepted that 70 to 80 percent of what we learn is through sight. Sight seems to be the most rapid and compre-

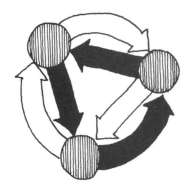

Figure 1-12

Figure 1-13

Figure 1-14

Figure 1-15

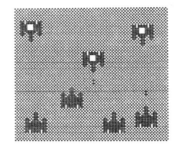

Figure 1-16

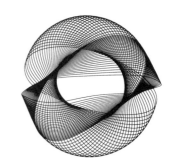

Figure 1-17

hensive of our senses for receiving information. Through centuries of conditioning, we rely on vision for an early warning of danger. Not only have we come to depend on sight as a primary means of understanding the world, but we have also learned to translate information picked up by the senses into visual clues so that, in many ways, sight is actually used as a substitute for the other senses.

There is ample evidence that visual communication is becoming an even more powerful force in our lives. The most obvious example is television, through which we can explore the skies, the oceans, and the societies of our shrinking planet. We rely heavily on graphics to explain and persuade. Cartoons have become a very sophisticated means of distilling and reflecting our culture. But the most significant revolution is the shift of visual communication from the realm of specialists to that of the general public. Instantly developing film and video recorders are just the beginning of the visual tools that will become as common as the PC and the calculator.

The potential of visual communication will be tested as we begin the twenty-first century. Two overriding features are the deluge of information that we must absorb and the increasingly interactive nature of the problems we must solve. As Edward Hamilton put it, "Up...to the present age we have absorbed information in a one-thing-at-a-time, an abstract, lin-

ear, fragmented but sequential way.... Now, the term *pattern*...will apply increasingly in understanding the world of total-environmental stimuli into which we are moving."[2] We seek patterns, not only to screen for significance of information, but also to illustrate processes or structures by which our world operates. The emerging technology for collecting, storing, and displaying different models of reality holds exciting promise. Computer-constructed satellite maps, video games, computer graphics, and the miniaturization of computing and recording equipment will open up a new era in visual communication.

The full use of this new capability will be directly related to the development of our own visual thinking. "Computers cannot see or dream, nor can they create: computers are language-bound. Similarly, thinkers who cannot escape the structure of language, who are unaware that thinking can occur in ways having little to do with language, are often utilizing only a small part of their brain that is indeed like a computer."[3] This observation by Robert McKim points out the critical issue of man–machine interaction. The new equipment is of no value in itself; it is only as good as our imagination can make it. If we are to realize the potential of visual technology, we must learn to think visually.

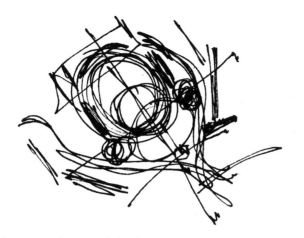

Figure 1-18 Conceptual sketches.

VISUAL THINKING

The study of visual thinking has developed in major part from the study of creativity within the field of psychology. The work of Rudolph Arnheim in the psychology of art has been particularly significant. In his book, *Visual Thinking,* he laid a basic framework for research by dissolving the artificial barrier between thinking and the action of the senses. "By cognitive, I mean all mental operations involved in receiving, storing, and processing of information: sensory perception, memory, thinking, learning."[4] This was a new way of understanding perception, namely, an integration of mind and senses; the focus of the study of creativity shifts from the mind or the senses to the interaction of both. Visual thinking is therefore a form of thinking that uses the products of vision—seeing, imagining, and drawing. Within the context of designing, the focus of this book is on the third product of vision, drawings or sketches. When thinking becomes externalized in the form of a sketched image, it can be said to have become graphic.

There are strong indications that thinking in any field is greatly enhanced by the use of more than one sense, as in doing while seeing. Although this book's focus is on architectural design, it is my hope that other readers will find the explanations and examples useful. The long history of architectural design has produced a great wealth of graphic techniques and imagery in response to highly complex, comprehensive, quantitative–qualitative problems. Today, architectural design attempts to deal with our total man-made environment, a problem that is personal and pressing for everyone. The graphic thinking tools used by architects to solve problems of interaction, conflict, efficiency, and aesthetics in buildings have now become important to all parts of society with its own increasingly complex problems.

Figure 1-19 Conceptual sketches.

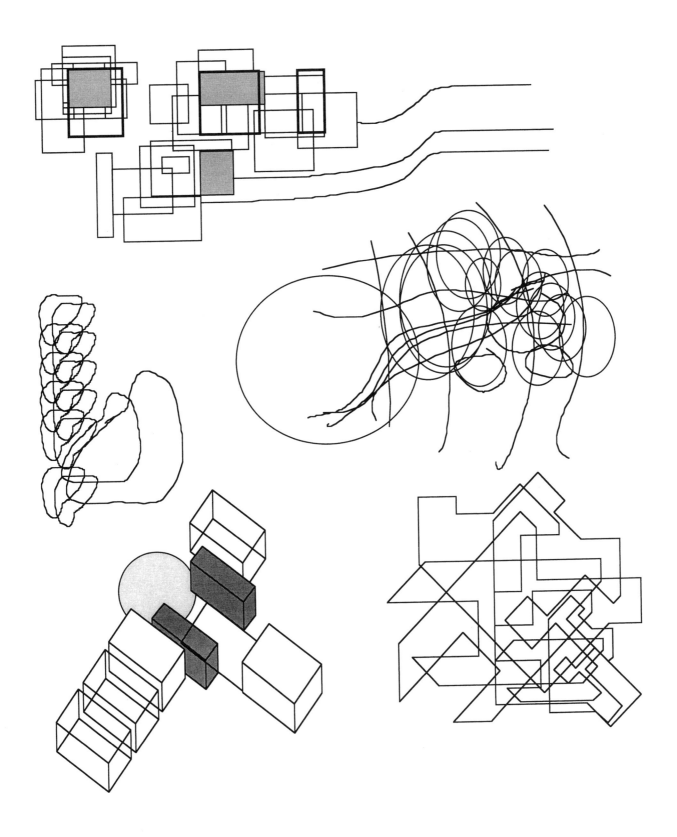

Figure 1-20 Conceptual sketches using digital media.

Figure 1-21 Graphic thinking process.

GRAPHIC THINKING AS A COMMUNICATION PROCESS

The process of graphic thinking can be seen as a conversation with ourselves in which we communicate with sketches. The communication process involves the sketched image on the paper, the eye, the brain, and the hand. How can this apparently closed network generate ideas that are not already in the brain? Part of the answer lies in the definition of an idea. The so-called new ideas are really a new way of looking at and combining old ideas. All ideas can be said to be connected; the thinking process reshuffles ideas, focuses on parts, and recombines them. In the diagram of the graphic-thinking process, all four parts—eye, brain, hand, and sketch—have the capability to add, subtract, or modify the information that is being passed through the communication loop. The eye, assisted by perception, can select a focal point and screen out other information. We can readily accept that the brain can add information. But the other two parts, hand and sketch, are also important to the process. A difference often exists between what we intend to draw and what actually is drawn. Drawing ability, materials, and our mood can all be sources of change. And yes, even the image on paper is subject to change. Differences in light intensity and angle, the size and distance of the image from the eye, reflectivity of paper, and transparency of media all open up new possibilities.

The potential of graphic thinking lies in the continuous cycling of information-laden images from paper to eye to brain to hand and back to the paper. Theoretically, the more often the information is passed around the loop, the more opportunities for change. In the sequence of images opposite, for example, I started with a sketch of cartoon-like bubbles to represent spaces in a house that is yet to be designed. Depending on my experience, interests, and what I am trying to do, I will see certain things in the sketch and ignore others. The resulting perceptual image segregates special-use spaces, the living room and kitchen, from several other more private or support spaces. Next, I form a mental image to further organize the spaces and give them orientation based on what I already know about the site or a southern exposure for the living room and kitchen. When this mental image is transferred to paper once more, it goes through yet another change in which the special spaces begin to take on distinctive forms.

This is, of course, an oversimplification of the process. Graphic thinking, like visual communication with the real world, is a continuous process. Information is simultaneously darting all over the network. When graphic thinking is most active, it is similar to watching a fantastic array of fireworks and looking for the one you really enjoy. Not only is it productive, it is fun. In Arnheim's words, "Far from being a passive mechanism of registration like the photographic camera, our visual apparatus copes with the incoming images in active struggle."[5]

Visual thinking and visual perception cannot be separated from other types of thinking or perception. Verbal thinking, for example, adds more to the idea of a kitchen or living room with such qualifiers as bright, open, or comfortable. Obviously, graphic thinking is not all you need to know in order to solve problems or think creatively, but it can be a basic tool. Graphic thinking can open up channels of communication with ourselves and those people with whom we work. The sketches generated are important because they show how we are thinking about a problem, not just what we think about it.

Image on Paper

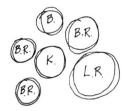

Perceptual Image

Mental Image

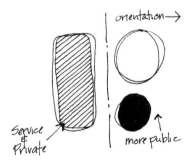

New Image on Paper

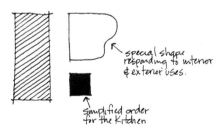

Figure 1-22 Evolution of images.

Multiple Messages

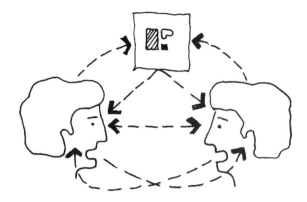

Figure 1-23 Dialogue.

Graphic thinking takes advantage of the power of visual perception by making visual images external and explicit. By putting them on paper, we give visual images objectivity outside our brain, an existence of their own over time. As Robert McKim points out, graphic thinking, as externalized thinking:

has several advantages over internalized thought. First, direct sensory involvement with materials provides sensory nourishment—literally 'food for thought.' Second, thinking by manipulating an actual structure permits serendipity—the happy accident, the unexpected discovery. Third, thinking in the direct context of sight, touch, and motion engenders a sense of immediacy, actuality, and action. Finally, the externalized thought structure provides an object for critical contemplation as well as a visible form that can be shared with a colleague.[6]

To the person who must regularly seek new solutions to problems, who must think creatively, these qualities of immediacy, stimulation, accident, and contemplation are very important. To these qualities I would add one more special attribute of graphic thinking, simultaneity. Sketches allow us to see a great amount of information at the same time, exposing relationships and describing a wide range of subtleties. Sketches are direct and representative. According to Arnheim, "The power of visual language lies in its spontaneous evidence, its almost childlike simplicity.... Darkness means darkness, things that belong together are shown together, and what is great and high appears in large size and in a high location."[7]

Figure 1-24 By David Stiegletz. Development sketches on back of a placemat, Siegler Residence.

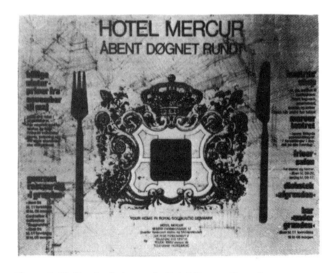

Figure 1-25 Front of placemat, Hotel Mercur, Copenhagen.

EFFECTIVE COMMUNICATION

A standard story that many architects delight in telling describes how the most basic concept for a multimillion-dollar project was first scribbled on the back of a restaurant napkin. I have wondered why both the teller and the listener always seem to derive amusement from such a story. Perhaps the story restores confidence in the strength of the individual designer, or maybe it is the incongruity that decisions on such important matters are being made in such a relaxed, casual manner. Viewing this story in the context of graphic thinking, it is not at all surprising that inspired, inventive thinking should take place at a restaurant table. Not only are the eyes, minds, and hands of at least two persons interacting with the images on the napkin, but also they are further stimulated by conversation. Besides, these persons are separated from their day-to-day work problems; they are relaxing in a pleasant atmosphere, and with the consumption of good food, their level of anxiety is significantly reduced. They are open, ready, prepared for discovery; indeed, it would be surprising only if the most creative ideas were not born in this setting.

To be effective communicators, architects must:

1. Understand the basic elements of communication—the communicator, the receiver or audience, the medium, and the context—and their role in effectiveness.
2. Develop a graphic language from which to draw the most effective sketches for specific communication tasks.
3. Never take for granted the process of communication and be willing to take the time to examine their effectiveness.

Basic communication theory stresses the communication loop between the communicator or sender and the receiver in order to attain maximum effectiveness. Response from the audience is essential to a speaker who wants to get his message across. The information coming from the receiver is as important as what the sender, the architect, transmits. And so we must pay very close attention to those persons with whom we hope to communicate. The best approach is to try to place oneself in their shoes. What are they expecting? What are their concerns? Equally important, we should be aware of our motivations and concerns. Do we have an unconscious or hidden agenda?

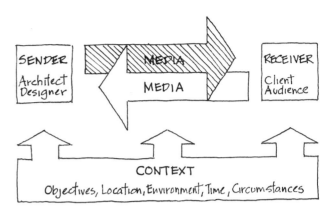

Figure 1-26 The structure of communications.

As further chapters review the many ways graphic thinking is used in the practice of architecture, it is critical to remember that individuals cannot really be cut off from their environment or their society. The graphic thinking of one person thrives in the presence of good company and a supportive atmosphere. Seek both enthusiastically.

Although the medium with which this book deals is principally freehand sketches, the basic methods are applicable to many graphic media. But each specific medium has some unique characteristics that have special effects on communication. Experimentation with different media is the fastest route to using them effectively. Although there are books on the use of these media, there is no substitute for practice, because we all have different needs and abilities.

The context for communication includes such things as location, time, duration, weather, and type of space, what took place before the communication, what will take place after. We may be able to control some of these context variables, but we cannot afford to ignore them.

Figure 1-27 Gym, St. Mary's College, C. F. Murphy Associates, architects.

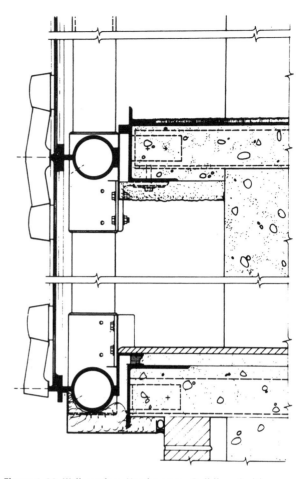

Figure 1-28 Wall section, Headquarters Building, Smith, Hinchman & Grylls Associates, Inc.

THE ROLE OF GRAPHIC THINKING IN ARCHITECTURE

To realize the potential of graphic thinking in architecture, we must understand today's prevailing attitudes on the design process and the use of drawings in that process. In the early 1960s, A. S. Levens was able to write with confidence that:

> One source of confusion in thinking about design is the tendency to identify design with one of its languages, drawing. This fallacy is similar to the confusion which would result if musical composition were to be identified with the writing of notes on a staff of five lines. Design, like musical composition, is done essentially in the mind and the making of drawings or writing of notes is a recording process.[8]

Today, we have broader concepts of how and where design takes place, but drawings are still normally thought of as simply representations of ideas; their purpose is to explain to other people the products of our thinking, the conclusions. Training in architectural schools has been primarily geared toward the attainment of finished presentation skills, while in architectural offices, the emphasis has been on turning out working drawings that clearly present the necessary directives for the contractors.

In response to Levens' analogy, graphic thinking treats drawings more like a piano than a score sheet. Like composition, design is possible without an instrument to provide feedback, but for most designers this is not very productive. Design thinking and design communication should be interactive; this implies new roles for graphics. As we anticipate the potential of computers and other evolving communication technologies, the concept of feedback will be key to effective use of media.

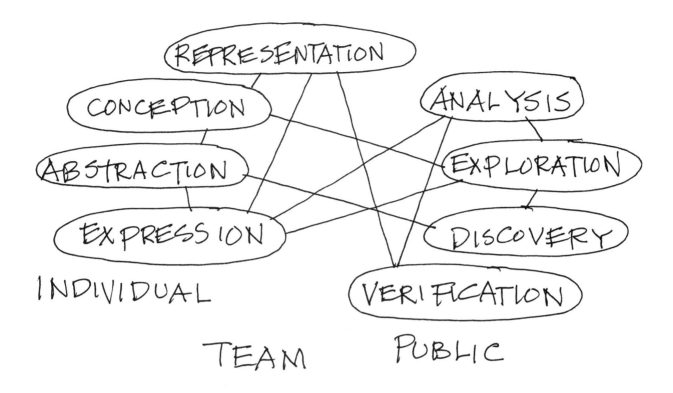

Figure 1-29

ORGANIZATION OF THE BOOK

The first major section of the book is devoted to the basic graphic thinking skills of *representation* and *conception*. The section includes four chapters dealing with *drawing*, the use of *conventions, abstraction,* and *expression*. My aim is to promote an awareness of the rich variety of graphic tools available for adding productivity and enjoyment to thinking activities.

The second section of the book addresses the application of graphic thinking to design processes. Its four chapters discuss *analysis, exploration, discovery,* and *verification*. Although there are some obvious applications of these uses to a number of design process models, I have purposely avoided promoting a specific design process. One of the problems with design process models is their acceptance in too simplistic a way; types of thinking or behavior are categorized, and the intermeshing of processes and ideas is ignored. Instead of categories, we need flexibility. Manipulation of graphic images, for example, might be used at many stages of designing. I still would not attempt to guess where it would be handy for a specific project. Manipulation of the stereotypes for a

building could get designing started. Distortion of an elevation might reveal a new approach to detailing. Reversal of a process diagram might suggest a modification of the building program.

The third section of the book considers graphic thinking as communication in three design contexts: *individual, team,* and *public*. The emphasis is on better communication so that ideas can be shared.

This book is a collection of images, ideas, and devices that I hope are helpful and enjoyable. The approach is eclectic rather than discriminating, inclusive not exclusive, expectant not conclusive. The intent is not simply to describe examples but to convey the excitement of graphic thinking and even make it contagious. We all have special, unique capacities for thinking, which, if unlocked, could make great contributions to the solution of problems we face. Arnheim emphasizes that "Every great artist gives birth to a new universe, in which the familiar things look the way they have never before looked to anyone."[9] This book is written in anticipation of a time when many of us will be able to give birth to our own universes.

BASIC SKILLS

Figure 2-1

2 Drawing

This chapter's focus is on the basic representation skills helpful to graphic thinking methods as presented in the remainder of this book. Developing freehand drawing skills is necessary to the attainment of graphic thinking and perceptual skills. Some might say, "I really admire good drawings and those designers who have a quick hand, but I have accepted the fact that I will never be that good." Bunk! It just is not so! Anyone can learn to draw well. If you don't believe me, take the time to talk to people who draw very well. You will find that their first drawings were tentative. They probably took every opportunity to draw. With time and hard work, they gradually improved and never regretted the effort they made.

There are two important conditions to keep in mind when trying to develop any skill:

1. Skill comes with repetition.
2. The surest way to practice any skill is to enjoy what you are doing.

Because of the heavy emphasis on rationalization in formal education, many people mistakenly think that they can master a skill, such as drawing, simply by understanding concepts. Concepts are helpful, but practice is essential.

The orchestra conductor Artie Shaw once explained why he refused all requests by parents to audition their children. He felt that the worst thing you can do to a talented child is to tell him he has talent. The greats in the music business, regardless of natural talent, became successful through hard work and a commitment to their craft. They believed in themselves but knew they would have to struggle to prove themselves to others. The focus of energy, sense of competition, and years of hard work are essential to becoming a fine musician.

The knowledge that drawing and thinking are important to architecture is not sufficient. Natural drawing talent is not enough. To sustain the necessary lifetime effort of learning and perfecting graphic thinking, we need to find pleasure in drawing and thinking. We must be challenged to do it better than those architects we admire do. Morse Payne of The Architects Collaborative once noted the influence of Ralph Rapsin on many talented designers: "To watch Ralph knock out one of his beautiful perspectives in fifteen minutes was truly inspiring. It set a goal for us that was very challenging."[1] Fortunately, there is still a lot of respect within the architectural profession for high-quality drawing. The person who can express himself both graphically and verbally on an impromptu basis is highly valued. When hiring, offices often look for ability to communicate over ability to be original. They know that your ability to develop ideas with them is much more important in the long run than the idea that you initially bring to them.

It is possible to be an architect without having well-developed graphic thinking skills. A barber or a bartender can surely cut hair or serve drinks without being able to carry on a conversation. But the job is a lot easier if you enjoy talking with people, and you will probably do more business. I believe that graphic thinking can make design more enjoyable and more effective.

Four types of basic skills support graphic thinking: observation, perception, discrimination, and imagination. Although these are considered to be primarily thinking skills, in this chapter I have tried to show how graphic means may be used to promote these skills and attain a fundamental integration of graphics and thinking. The sequence in which the skills are addressed reflects my assumption that each thinking skill supports those that follow.

Figure 2-2 By Lisa Kolber.

Figure 2-3 By Lawrence Halprin.

THE SKETCH NOTEBOOK

Frederick Perls held that, "People who look at things without seeing them will experience the same deficiency when calling up mental pictures, while those who...look at things squarely and with recognition will have an equally alert internal eye."[2] Visual imagery is critical to the creative designer; he must rely on a very rich collection of visual memories. The richness of these memories depends on a well-developed and active visual perception. The sketch notebook is an excellent way of collecting visual images and sharpening perception, for it promotes seeing rather than just looking. Architects who have gotten into the sketch notebook habit quickly discover its usefulness. All I can say is to try it; you'll like it.

A sketch notebook should be small and portable, able to fit into a pocket so it can be carried anywhere. It should have a durable binding and covers so it won't come apart. Carry it with you at all times and leave it next to your bed at night (some of the best ideas come to people just before going to sleep or right upon awakening). As the name implies, it is a book for notes as well as for sketches and for reminders, recipes, or anything else you can think about. Combining verbal and graphic notes helps unite verbal and visual thinking.

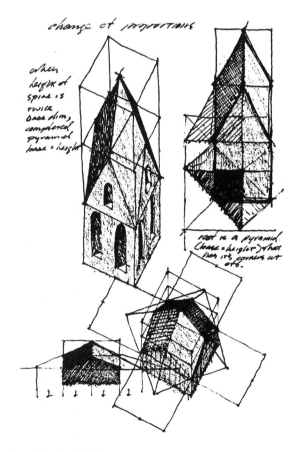

Figure 2-4 By Karl Brown.

Figure 2-5 By Karl Mang.

Figure 2-6 By Ronald Margolis. Old Main Building,
Wayne University.

Figure 2-7 By Patrick D. Nall.

Figure 2-8 Spanish Steps, Rome.

OBSERVATION

The thousands of students who pass through architectural schools are usually told that they should learn to sketch freehand and, to a certain degree, how. Rarely are they told what they should sketch or why. Drawing cubes and other still-life exercises are an attempt to teach sketching divorced from thinking. Most students find it boring, and it drives some away from sketching for the rest of their lives. I prefer to start students with the sketching of existing buildings because:

1. They are drawing subjects in which they have a basic interest and are ready to discuss.
2. The eye and mind as well as the hand are involved; perception becomes fine-tuned, and we begin to sort out our visual experiences.
3. One of the best ways to learn about architectural design is to look closely at existing buildings and spaces.

The clearest way to demonstrate the value of freehand sketching for developing graphic thinking skills is to compare sketching with photography. Although a camera is often a useful or expedient tool, it lacks many of the attributes of sketches. Sketches have the ability to reveal our perception, therefore giving more importance to certain parts, whereas a photo shows everything with equal emphasis. In the sketch of the Spanish Steps in Rome, the focus is on the church, ellipse, and steps as organizing elements for the entire exterior space. The significant impact of the flowers in the photo has been eliminated in the sketch. The abstraction can be pushed further until there is only a pattern of light and dark, or we can focus only on certain details, such as lamp posts or windows. This one scene alone is a dictionary of urban design. But you do not have to wait until you get to Rome to get started; there are lessons all around us. Become a prospector of architectural design; build your own collection of good ideas while you learn to sketch. It is a lot of fun.

Figure 2-9 Spanish Steps, Rome.

Figure 2-9a Spanish Steps, Rome.

Figure 2-10 Window Detail.

Figure 2-11 Street lamp detail.

Structure   Tones

Figure 2-12a House drawing structure.   Figure 2-12b Tones.

BUILDING A SKETCH

In his book *Drawing Buildings,* Richard Downer presented the most effective approach to freehand sketching I have ever come across. "The first and most important thing about drawing buildings is to realize that what you intend to draw should interest you as a subject."[3] Next, it is important to select a vantage point that best describes your subject. Now you are ready to build the sketch by a three-step process of sketching basic structure, tones, and then details. The basic structure sketch is most important. If the parts are not shown in their proper place and correct proportions it makes no difference what is drawn from then on; the sketch will always look wrong. So take your time; look carefully at the subject; continually compare your sketch with what you see. Now add the tones. These represent the space-defining elements of light, shadow, and color. Again, look carefully at the subject. Where are the lightest tones; where are the darkest? The sketch is becoming more realistic. The details are added last. At this point everything is in its place, and you can really concentrate on the details one at a time. It is no longer overwhelming; you can relax and enjoy it.

Figure 2-13a Bowl drawing structure.   Figure 2-13b Tones.   Figure 2-13c Finished bowl drawing.

Figure 2-12c Texture and color.

Texture / Color

Figure 2-12d Finished house drawing.

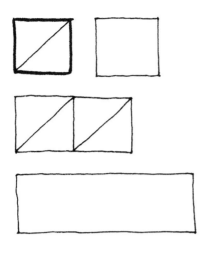

Figure 2-14

Figure 2-17

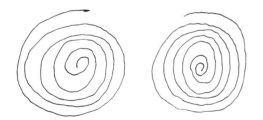

Figure 2-15

Figure 2-16

Structure Sketch

The most important part of a sketch, the basic line drawing, is also the most difficult skill to master. It requires a lot of practice, but I have a few suggestions that should help:

1. To help sharpen the sense of proportion needed for sketching, practice drawing squares and then rectangles that are two or three times longer on one side than on the other. Now try to find squares in a scene you are sketching. (At the beginning, this could be done with tracing paper over a photograph.)

2. Use a cross or a frame to get the parts of the sketch in their proper place, or maybe a prominent feature of the scene or subject can act as an organizer for the other parts of the sketch.

3. Although pencil can certainly be used for sketching, I prefer felt-tip or ink pens because the lines they produce are simple and clear. If a line is in the wrong place, it is quite evident. Because the line cannot be erased, it must be redrawn to get it right. This process of repetition and checking against the subject develops skill. Drawings that are so light they can be ignored or erased deny the designer the feedback essential to his improvement.

4. To gain more control over line making, try some simple exercises similar to our "idle moment" doodles. The spirals, like those above, are drawn from the outside toward the center, both clockwise and counterclockwise. Try to make them as fast as possible without letting the lines touch each other; try to get the lines close to each other. Straight hatching can be done in several directions, always striving for consistency.

Figure 2-18

Figure 2-19

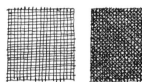

Figure 2-20

Tones

Tones can be represented with different densities of hatching or combinations of cross-hatching. The lines should be parallel and have equal spaces between them. Always remember that the main purpose of the cross-hatching is to obtain different levels of gray or darkness. Use straight strokes as if you were painting the surfaces with a brush. Erratic or irregular lines draw attention to them and distract the eye from more important things. There is no strict rule for applying tones on a sketch, but I have some preferences that seem to work well. Horizontal hatching is used on horizontal surfaces, diagonal hatching on vertical surfaces. When two vertical surfaces meet, the hatching on one is at a slightly different angle from the hatching on the other surface.

Apply tones in a three-step process:

1. Indicate any texture that appears in the surface, such as the vertical boards on a barn.
2. If the texture indication does not provide the level of darkness of the subject, add the necessary additional hatching over the entire surface.
3. Now apply more hatching where any shadows fall. To show gradations of shadow, add a succession of hatches at different angles.

The refinement of tones in a drawing is achieved by looking carefully at the subject and by getting more control over the consistency of the lines.

Several alternative techniques for sketching in tones are illustrated throughout this book. The one shown at the right above is a rapid method using random strokes. Designers usually develop techniques with which they feel most comfortable.

Figure 2-21

Figure 2-23

Figure 2-22

Details

Details are often the most interesting or compelling aspect of buildings. The window is an excellent example. There, the details can be the result of a transition between two materials—brick and glass—or between two building elements—wall and opening. The wood window frame, brick arch, keystone, and windowsill make these transitions possible, and each of these details tells us more about the building. On a regular basis, I have students sketch windows, doors, or other building elements so they gain an understanding and appreciation of the contribution of details to the qualities and functions of the building. Details tell us something of needs and materials as well as our ingenuity in relating them. The sketch of the metal grating around the base of the tree explains both the needs of the tree and the use of the surface under the tree where people walk.

In most architectural scenes, there are details close to us and others farther away. We can see more of the close detail and should show in the sketch such things as screws or fasteners or fine joints and textures. As details recede in the sketch, fewer and fewer of the pieces are shown, until only the outline is visible.

Figure 2-25 Montgomery, Alabama.

Figure 2-24 San Francisco, California.

Combining Observations

With practice, structure, tones, and details can be effectively combined to capture the complete sense of a subject. Older houses of different styles are suitable subjects for practicing and developing observation skills. They are usually readily accessible and provide a variety of visual effects that can sustain your interest. Try visiting favorite houses at different times of day in order to view the impact of different lighting conditions. Walk around, approach, and retreat from the subject to capture a variety of appearances.

Building a Sketch • **27**

Figure 2-26a Original sketch.

Figure 2-26b Overlay sketch.

Figure 2-26c Final sketch.

TRACING

Tracing existing graphic material is another way to build sketching skills. Making an overlay of your own drawings with tracing paper is an obvious but underused device. Rather than overwork a drawing that is headed in the wrong direction, make an overlay showing the elements that need to be corrected and then, in another overlay, make a whole new sketch incorporating the changes. You will learn more from your mistakes, and the final sketch will be better and fresher. Tracing can also be done by laying a transparent sheet with a grid over a drawing or photo, drawing a larger grid, and then transferring the drawing square by square. A third technique uses a slide projector and a small mirror to project images of a convenient size for tracing on your drawing table. The large sketch on page 31 was done in this way.

No matter the reason you thought copying was improper or illegal, forget it. Master draftsmen such as Leonardo da Vinci copied other people's work when they were learning to draw. No tracing is ever the same as the original. You will pick out some details and simplify other parts. Tracing forces you to look closely at the original sketch or photo and better understand the subject.

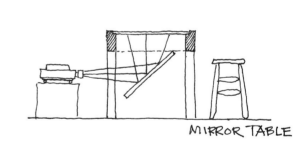

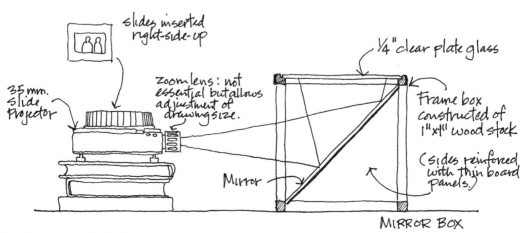

Figure 2-27 Projection table and projection box.

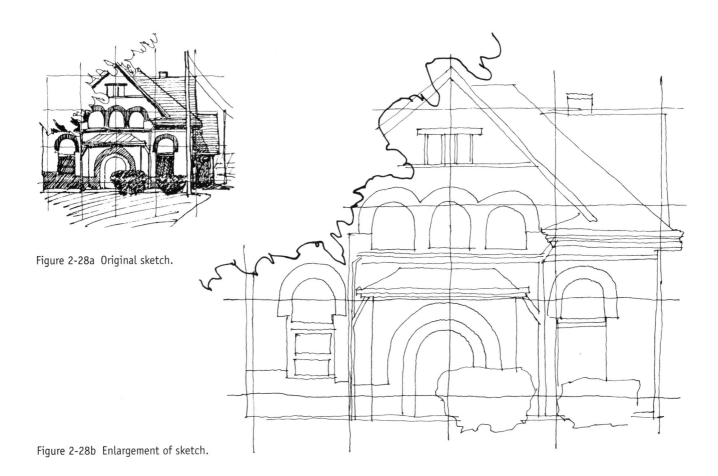

Figure 2-28a Original sketch.

Figure 2-28b Enlargement of sketch.

Figure 2-29 Tracing after Ray Evans.

Figure 2-30 Tracing after Ray Evans.

Figure 2-31 Sketch of Athens, Ohio.

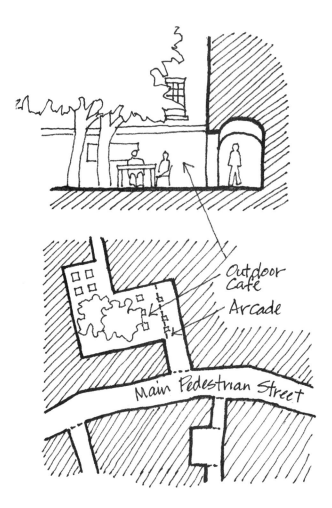

(a)

Figure 2-32 Sketch of Athens, Ohio.

Figure 2-33 Sketch of Athens, Ohio.

Figure 2-34 a (opposite), b (above) Plan, section, and perspective of garden-court restaurant, Salzburg, Austria.

PERCEPTION

Many architects have become methodical about sketch and note taking. Gordon Cullen, the British illustrator and urban design consultant, had a major influence on the use of analytical sketches. His book *Townscape*[4] is a wonderful collection of visual perceptions of the urban environment. The sketches are clear and comprehensive, impressive evidence of what can be discovered with graphic thinking. Using plans, sections, and perspectives, the sketches go beyond the obvious to uncover new perceptions. Tones are used to identify major organizers of space. (In the book, many of these tones are achieved mechanically, but they are easily rendered in sketches by hatching with grease pencil or large felt-tip markers.) The verbal categorization of urban phenomena through short titles helps to fix the visual perceptions in our memories; verbal and graphic communications are working together. And these are not complicated sketches; they are within the potential of most designers, as shown in the sketches opposite, which apply Cullen's techniques to the analysis of a small midwestern town.

As John Gundelfinger puts it:

> *A sketchbook should be a personal diary of what interests you and not a collection of finished drawings compiled to impress with weight and number...a finished on-the-spot drawing...shouldn't be the reason you go out, for the objective is drawing and not the drawing. I often learn more from drawings that don't work out, studying the unsuccessful attempts to see where and why I went off...can learn more...than from a drawing where everything fell into place.... The drawings that succeed do so in some measure because of the failures I've learned from preceding it, and so certain pitfalls were unconsciously ignored while drawing.*[5]

Figure 2-35 Waterfront, Mobile, Alabama.

Each subject may reveal new ways of seeing if we remain open to its special characteristics. It may be the redundancy of forms or a pattern of shadows; it may be an awareness of the special set of elements and circumstances that produces a particularly interesting visual experience. A sketch of the interior of a cathedral can uncover the exciting play of scale and materials. The act of drawing can dramatically heighten your visual sensitivity.

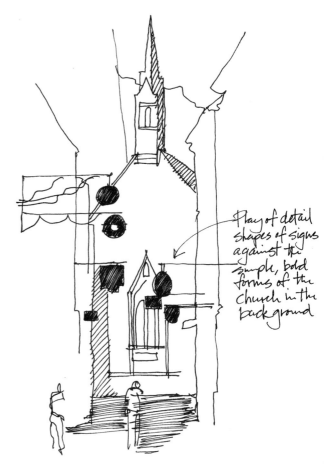

Play of detail shapes of signs against the simple, bold forms of the church in the background

Figure 2-36 Salzburg, Austria.

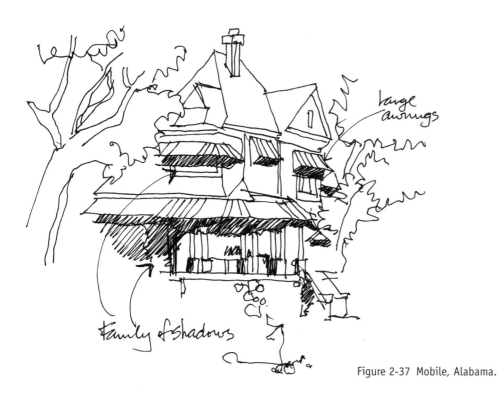

large awnings

Family of shadows

Figure 2-37 Mobile, Alabama.

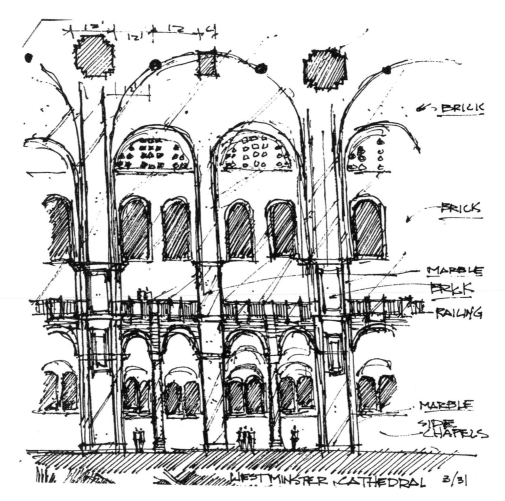

Figure 2-38 By Todd Calson. Westminster Cathedral.

Figure 2-39 Ohio University Quad, Athens, Ohio.

Figure 2-40 Cartoon style sketch, after Rowland Wilson.

Figure 2-42 After Saul Steinberg.

Figure 2-41 After Saul Steinberg.

Figure 2-43 After Saul Steinberg.

DISCRIMINATION

Cartoons are an important source of sketching ideas. My favorite sources are *The New Yorker* and *Punch* magazines, but there are many other sources. Cartoonists convey a convincing sense of reality with an incredible economy of means. Simple contour lines suggest detail information while concentrating on overall shapes. Michael Folkes describes some of the discipline of cartoon drawings:

> *...simplicity refers to the need to make the clearest possible statement.... Avoid all unnecessary detail.*

Make the focal point of your picture stand out. Refrain from filling every corner with objects or shading.... Train your hand and eye to put down on paper rapidly recognizable situations...in the fewest possible strokes. One significant detail is worth far more than an uncertain clutter of lines that don't really describe anything. Make dozens of small pictures...drawing directly in pen and ink so that the pen becomes a natural drawing instrument and not something that can only be used to work painfully over carefully prepared pencil lines.[6]

The cartoon is selective or discriminating; it helps you seek out the essence of an experience.

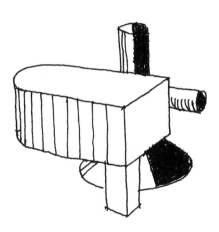

Figure 2-44 Sketch extending a view derived from the painting, Giovanni Arnofini and His Bride, by Jan Van Eyck.

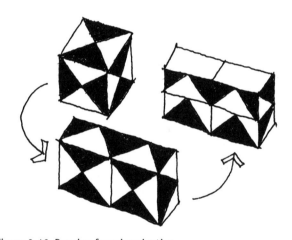

Figure 2-45 Drawing from imagination.

Figure 2-46 Drawing from imagination.

IMAGINATION

To move from graphics in support of observation toward graphic thinking that supports designing, you must develop and stretch imagination. Here are some simple exercises to start:

1. Find a drawing, photograph, or painting of a room that shows a part of a space. On a large sheet of paper, draw the scene depicted and then extend the drawing beyond its original frame to show those parts of the room accessible only through your imagination.

2. Draw a set of objects and then draw what you believe to be the view from the backside.

3. Sketch a simple object such as a cube with distinctive markings. Then imagine that you are cutting the object and moving the parts. Draw the different new configurations.

Figure 2-47 Game using cut-out shapes.

Figure 2-48 Sketching game.

Half of a Carpenter Center.

Winslow house sitting on top of its roof.

Top of AT&T building.

Figure 2-49 Doodles.

Visual–Mental Games

An entertaining way to improve hand–eye–mind coordination and promote an ability to visualize is to play some simple games.

1. Show a few people four or five cutouts of simple shapes arranged on a piece of paper (above, left). Out of view of the others, one person moves the cutouts while verbally describing the move. The others attempt to draw the new arrangement from the description. This is repeated a few times to see who can keep track of the position of the shapes. After mastering this exercise, have the persons drawing try to form a mental picture of each new arrangement and then try to draw only the final arrangement. In a second version of this game, an object is substituted for the cutouts, and it is manipulated, opened, or taken apart.

2. Form a circle with a small group. Each person makes a simple sketch and passes it to his right.

Everyone tries to copy the sketch he has received and in turn passes the copy to the right. This continues until the final copy is passed to the creator of the original sketch. Then all sketches are arranged on a wall or table in the order they were made. This game illustrates the distinctiveness of individual visual perception (above, center).

3. Doodles, using an architectural or design theme, are another form of puzzle. Here, the objective is to provide just enough clues so the subject is obvious once the title is given (above, right).

There are many visual puzzles that exercise our visual perception. Try some of those shown opposite; look for more puzzles, or invent some of your own. In the sketches opposite, an arbitrary diagram is given and the challenge is to use it as a parti for different buildings by seeing it as standing for a section or plan view for starters.

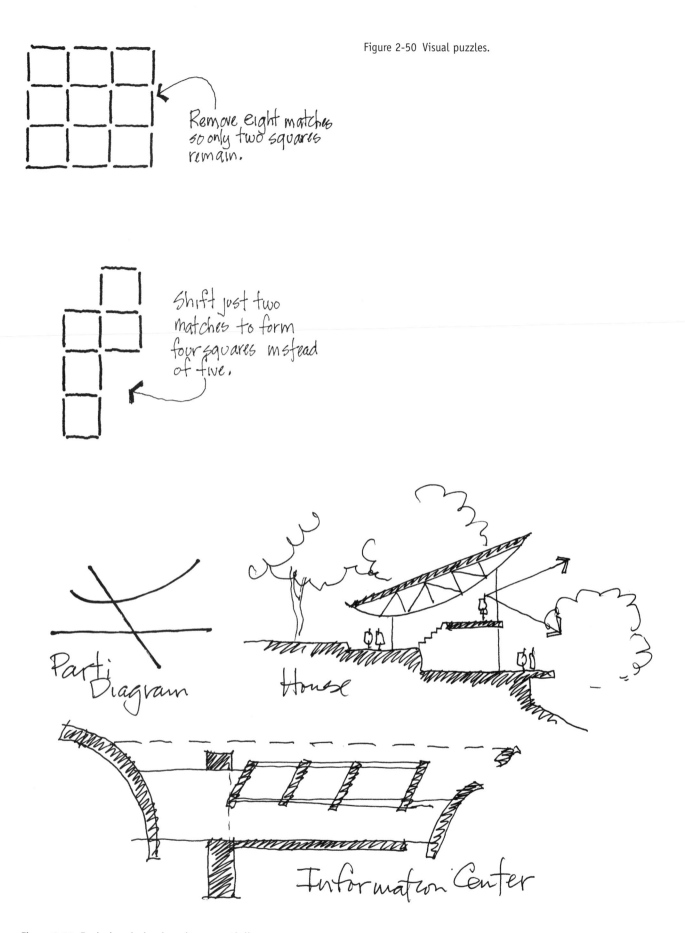

Figure 2-50 Visual puzzles.

Remove eight matches so only two squares remain.

Shift just two matches to form four squares instead of five.

Parti Diagram

House

Information Center

Figure 2-51 Exploring design based on a parti diagram.

Figure 3-1 By A. J. Diamond. Student Union Housing, University of Alberta at Edmonton.

3 Conventions

Represent: Call up by description or portrayal or imagination, figure, place, likeness of before mind or senses, serve or be meant as likeness of...stand for, be specimen of, fill place of, be substitute for[1]

Throughout history, representation and design have been closely linked. The act of designing grew directly out of man's desire to see what could or would be achieved before investing too much time, energy, or money. To create a clay pot meant simply working directly with your hands until the desired result was achieved. But making a gold pot required expensive material, much preparation, time, and energy. A representation, a design drawing, of the gold bowl was necessary before starting the project. Design became an important part of architectural projects simply because of their scale. Representing the imagined building permitted not only a view of the final result but the planning for labor and materials to assure completion of the project.

The representational capacity of sketches is limited. We must recognize that even with the most sophisticated techniques drawings are not a full substitute for the actual experience of an architectural environment. On the other hand, the capacity of sketches as thinking tools extends well beyond what is actually contained in the sketches. Drawings, as representations, should be seen as extensions of the person(s) who uses them to aid in thinking. As Rudolf Arnheim says:

The world of images does not simply imprint itself upon a faithfully sensitive organ. Rather, in looking at an object, we reach out for it. With an invisible finger we move through space around us, go out to distant places where things are found, touch them, catch them, scan their surfaces, trace their borders, explore their texture. It is an eminently active occupation.[2]

I find a great variation in the degree to which architects rely on drawings to visualize designs. One probable explanation for this is experience in visualizing and with the building of these designs. For example, when architecture students look at a plan view of a room, they likely see just an abstract diagram, but some experienced architects can visualize a perspective view of the same room without having to draw it.

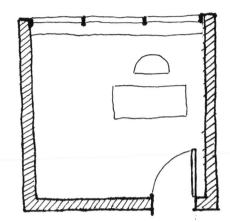

Figure 3-2

Figure 3-3

Some basic types of representation sketches, which I feel architects should be able to understand, are discussed in this chapter. I do not intend to present a comprehensive explanation of the construction of basic drawing conventions. There are already several good books on that subject. Rather, the emphasis will be on freehand techniques without the use of triangles, scales, and straightedges, allowing for rapid representation.

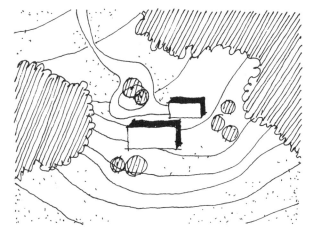

Figure 3-4 Site plan.

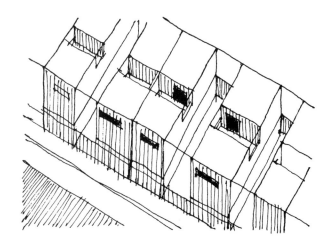

Figure 3-5 Axonometric.

Figure 3-6 Partial elevation.

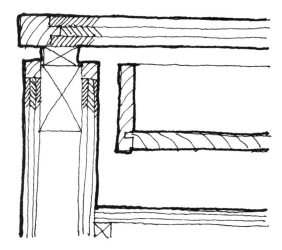

Figure 3-7 Detail section.

There are a great number of things we can represent about a space or a building and many ways to represent them. The sketched subjects can range in scale from a building and its surrounding property to a window or a light switch. We might be interested in how it looks or how it works or how to put it together; we may be searching for clarity or character. Variations in drawings range from the concrete to the abstract, and the conventions include section or cut, elevation, perspective, axonometric, isometric, and projections. Media, technique, and style account for many of the other variations. Many of these variations are covered in later chapters.

The elementary forms of representation discussed at this point are:

1. *Comprehensive views*—To study designs as complete systems, we must have models that represent the whole from some viewpoint.
2. *Concrete images*—Dealing with the most direct experience. Abstraction is covered in Chapter 4.
3. *Perceptual focus*—Trying to involve the viewer in the experience signified by the drawing.
4. *Freehand sketches*—Decision-making in design should include the consideration of many alternatives. Representation of alternatives is encouraged by the speed of freehand sketching, whereas the tediousness of "constructed" hard-line drawings discourages it.

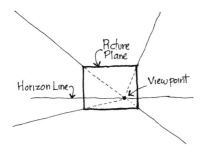

Figure 3-8a Setting the picture plane and viewpoint.

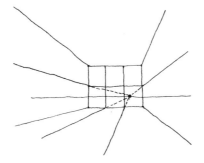

Figure 3-8b Starting grids.

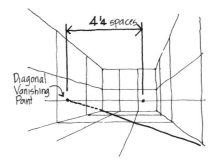

Figure 3-8c Setting cross-grids.

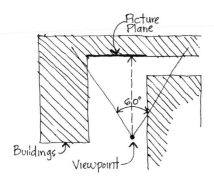

Figure 3-9a Setting the picture plane and viewpoint, plan view.

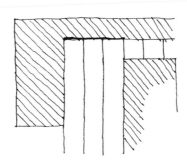

Figure 3-9b Setting one grid, plan view.

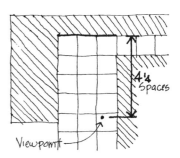

Figure 3-9c Setting the cross-grids, plan view.

PERSPECTIVE

Perspective sketches have an equal standing with plan drawings, the starting point of most design education. One-point perspective is the easiest and therefore, I feel, the most useful of perspective conventions. I have found the following three-step method to be most successful:

1. Indicate the picture plane in both elevation and plan; it is usually a wall or another feature that defines the far limits of the immediate space to be viewed. Locate the point from which the space is to be viewed, or viewpoint (V.P.). Vertically, this point is usually about 5.5 feet from the bottom of the picture plane. Horizontally, it can be placed just about anywhere in the space with the understanding that parts of the space outside a 60-degree cone of vision in front of the viewer tend to be distorted in the perspective. The horizontal line drawn through the V.P. is called the *horizon line.*

2. Establish a grid on the floor of the space. Draw the square grid in plan and count the number of spaces the viewer is away from the picture plane. Then, in the perspective, locate the diagonal vanishing point (D.V.P.) on the horizon line at the same distance from the viewpoint. Draw floor grid lines in the perspective in one direction coming from the viewpoint; draw a diagonal line from the diagonal vanishing point through the bottom corner of the picture plane and across the space. Where the diagonal intersects the floor grid lines running in the one direction, horizontal lines can be drawn to show the other direction of the floor grid.

3. Indicate the structure of the basic elements of the space. Continue the grid on the walls and ceiling (if appropriate). Using the grids as quick reference, place vertical planes and openings as well as significant divisions of the planes.

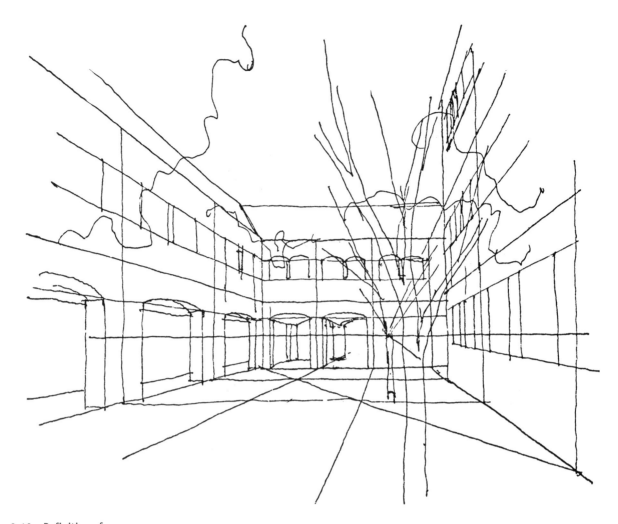

Figure 3-10a Definition of space.

Sketching straight lines freehand is an important skill to master for all types of graphic thinking, and practice makes perfect. Once you begin to rely on a straightedge, the work slows down. Start by concentrating on where the line begins and ends rather than on the line itself. Place a dot at the beginning and a dot where the line should end. As you repeat this exercise, let the pen drag across the paper between the two dots. This sounds pretty elementary, but it is surprising how many people have never bothered to learn how to sketch a straight line.

With the basic perspective and plan completed the values, or tones, can now be added. The actual color of objects or planes, shade, or shadows can cause differences in values; indicating these changing values shows the interaction of light with the space, providing spatial definition. Conventions for casting shadows are presented when plan drawings are discussed. For now, it is enough to note that shadows are first cast in plan and then added to the perspective,

using the square grid as a reference. Shade appears on objects on the side opposite to the sun or other source of light where no direct light falls; shaded surfaces are generally lighter in tone than shadows. As in sketching existing buildings, I prefer to use parallel hatch lines to show tones (see Building a Sketch in Chapter 2).

Finally, details and objects can be added. People are most important because they establish the scale of the space and involve the viewer through identification with these sketched figures. Simplicity, realistic proportions, and a sense of movement are basic to good human figures such as these. The square grids help in coordinating the placement of human figures and other objects in plan and perspective. Be sure to place people and objects where they would really be; the purpose of the sketch is to understand the space, not to camouflage it.

Figure 3-10b Adding tones and shadows.

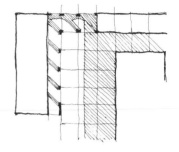

Figure 3-11 Casting shadows in plan.

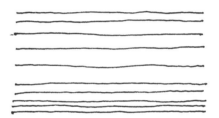

Figure 3-12 Practice drawing straight lines.

Figure 3-10c Completing details.

Figure 3-13 Practice drawing people.

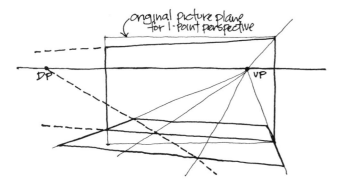

Figure 3-14 Modification of a one-point perspective.

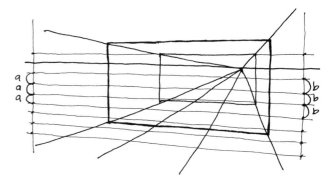

Figure 3-15 Organization of a modified perspective, after Lockard.

QUALITATIVE REPRESENTATION

At this point we are not interested in the qualities of drawing expression, such as style or techniques; this is covered in Chapter 5. By qualitative representation, I mean the representation of the qualities of a space. In his book *Design Drawing* William Lockard makes a very convincing argument for the superiority of perspectives as representational drawings. "Perspectives are more qualitative than quantitative. The experiential qualities of an environment or object can be perceived directly from a perspective...The qualities of the space/time/light continuum are much better represented and understood in perspective (than by other conventions)."[3] Perspectives have the advantage of showing the relationship of all the elements of a space in a way most similar to how we would experience it when built. Although it is true that buildings are not experienced only through perspectives, it is the best way of showing a direct visual experience of a specific space.

Lockard's chapter on representation has probably the best explanation of the use of perspective sketches for representation. Lockard illustrates a perspective view that is close to one-point perspective; it involves an imaginary second perspective point added at some distance from the sketch (see Figure 3-15). Lines running the width of the one-point per-

spective, parallel with the horizon line, are now slightly slanted in the direction of the imaginary second point. To make the transition from one-point perspective, the top and bottom lines of the picture plane can be given a slight slant and a new plane is established; by drawing a new diagonal, the new diagonal vanishing point can be set. A grid can also be applied to this type of perspective to help in placing objects in the space.

To represent the qualities of an imagined space, we have to know something about the qualities of spaces. Though this seems obvious, it is often ignored. As architects, we have to look for what gives spaces their special character, the different kinds of light, color, texture, pattern, or shapes possible and how they are combined. Continual sketching in a sketch notebook is one sure way of learning about the qualities of spaces. When this knowledge is applied to the representative perspective, we must remember to convey the three-dimensional experience of the space onto a two-dimensional surface, the paper. To do this, we need to illustrate the effects of depth or distance upon those things that give the space its qualities. With an increase in depth, light seems to produce fewer gradations of tone; detail is less evident; texture and color are less vivid; outlines or edges are less sharp. Depth can also be conveyed through overlap of object or contour.

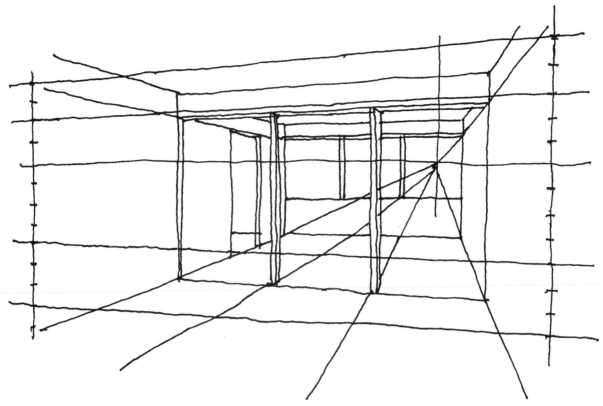

Figure 3-16a Setup of sketch perspective based on Lockard method.

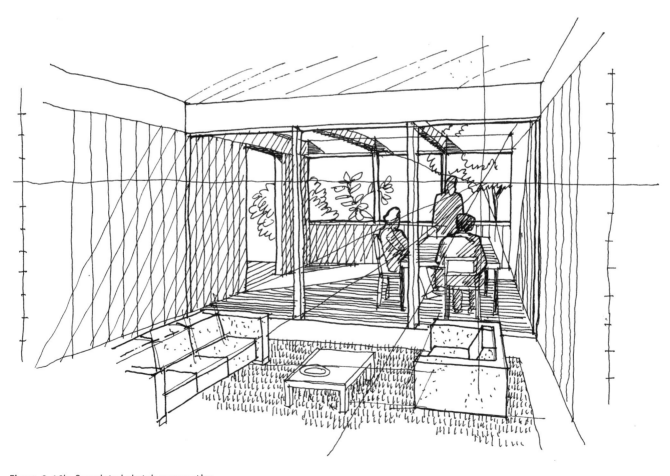

Figure 3-16b Completed sketch perspective.

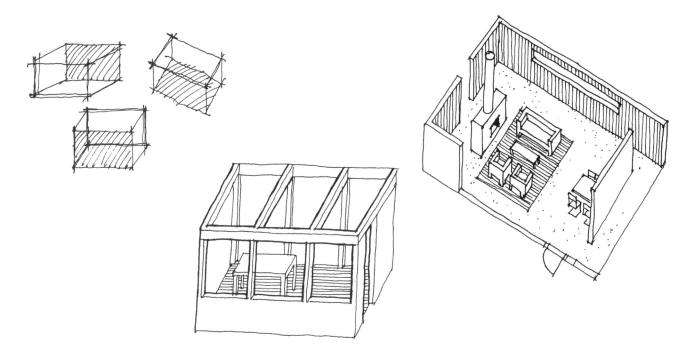

Figure 3-17 Parallel projections.

PARALLEL PROJECTIONS

Currently in common use, the axonometric sketch is an important alternative to the perspective, plan, and section. The axonometric is simply a projection from a plan or section in which all parallel lines in the space are shown as parallel; this is in contrast to a perspective where parallel lines are shown as extending from a single point. The axonometric technique is traditional in Chinese drawings. Instead of placing the viewer at a single point from which to view the scene, it gives the viewer the feeling of being everywhere in front of the scene. The axonometric has the additional advantage of representing three-dimensional space while retaining the "true" dimensions of a plan and section.

This last characteristic makes an axonometric easy to draw because all three dimensions are shown at the same scale. Axonometric projections forward or backward from plans or sections are conventionally made at angles of 30, 45, or 60 degrees, but in a sketch the exact angle is not important as long as the projected lines remain parallel.

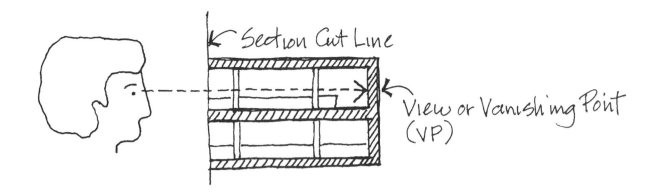

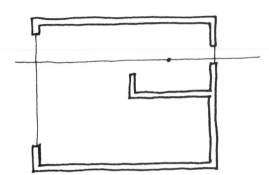

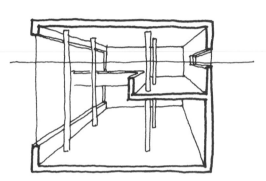

Figure 3-18 Section.

VERTICAL SECTION

A vertical cut through a space is called a *section*. What was said about the plan sketch also applies to the section sketch, except for the casting of shadows. With sections, we can show depth of space by applying the one-point perspective conventions explained earlier. Imagine you are looking at a cut model of the space; the point at which you look directly into the model is where the viewpoint (V.P.) will be placed. The viewpoint is used to project the perspective behind the section.

Human figures are also important for section sketches. Many designers sketch in view lines for the people; this seems to make it easier to imagine being in the space and gives some sense of what can be seen from a particular position in the space. Shadows can be indicated to see the effect of sunlight within the space.

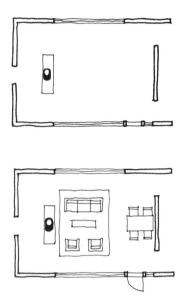

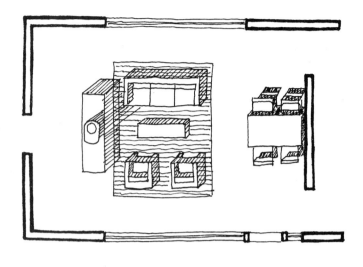

Figure 3-19 Plan.

PLAN SECTION

Abstract plan diagrams such as the one above have many uses in the early conceptual stages of design. This is covered in depth in Chapter 4. However, many architecture students make the mistake of trying to use these plan diagrams to represent the more concrete decisions about the formation of space. Plan sketches of designed spaces must show what is enclosed and what is not, including scale, height, pattern, and detail. A plan is basically a horizontal cut or section through the space. Things that are cut, such as walls or columns, are outlined in a heavy line weight. Things that can be seen below the place where the plan was cut are indicated in a lighter line weight. Things such as a skylight that cannot be seen because they are above the level of the cut can be shown with a heavy dashed line if desired.

The first stage of a representative plan is the heavy outlining of walls clearly showing openings. In the second stage, doors, windows, furniture, and other details are added. The third-stage sketch includes shadows to show the relative heights of planes and objects. The prevailing convention for shadows casts them on a 45-degee angle, up and to the right. The shadows need only be as long as necessary to clearly show the relative heights of the furniture, walls, etc. Finally, color, texture, or pattern can be added to explain further the character of the space.

OTHER REPRESENTATIONS

A variety of sketches based on the conventions of perspective, plan, section, and axonometric are shown on the next page. By means of sketches, we can cut open, peel back, pull apart, reconstruct, or make concrete objects transparent to see how they are arranged or constructed. These are just a few of the possible extensions of representation. As we use sketches to visualize designs, we should always be ready to invent new tools as needed.

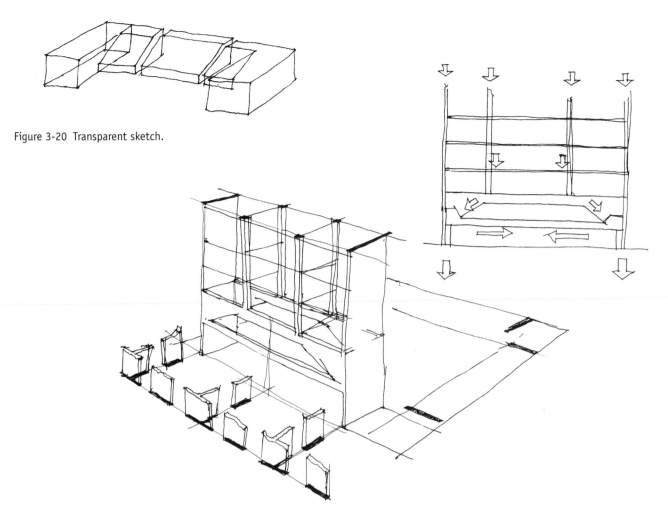

Figure 3-20 Transparent sketch.

Figure 3-21 By Thomas Truax. Structural systems illustrations, Boston City Hall, Kallman, McKinnell & Knowles, architects.

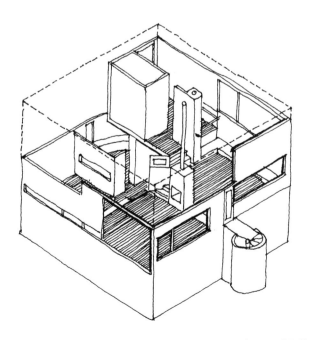

Figure 3-22 Cut-away view, the Simon House, Barbara and Julian Neski, architects.

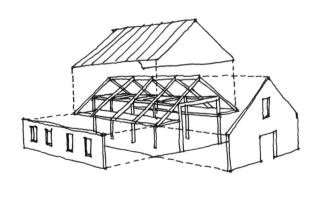

Figure 3-23 "Explodametric" drawing of a barn.

Figure 3-24 By Helmut Jacoby. Boston Government Service Center, Paul Rudolph, coordinating architects.

SKETCH TECHNIQUE

Many architects have developed their own sketching styles in an attempt to quickly represent structure, tones, and detail with a minimum of effort. An especially effective technique is that of Helmut Jacoby, an architectural delineator of international reputation.[4] The quick preliminary studies he uses to plan the final renderings provide remarkable clarity of spatial definition with an economy of means. Notice how, with a range of tight and loose squiggly lines, he can define surfaces and the rapid way that he suggests people, trees, textures, and other details. The underlying structure of the sketch is usually quite simple, with white areas used to help define space and objects. Jacoby is very aware of variations in tone and the effects of shade and shadow with respect to the surrounding trees as well as the building.

Michael Gebhardt sketches with an emphasis on tones and textures, defining space more through contrasts than line work. With a looping stroke, he is able to establish a consistency that pulls the drawing together and directs attention to the subject rather than the media. In establishing your own style, be sure to examine closely the work of others that you admire; there is no need to start from scratch. Also keep in mind that the objective in sketching is speed and ease.

Figure 3-25 By Helmut Jacoby. Ford Foundation headquarters, Dinkerloo and Roche, architects.

50 • *Conventions*

Figure 3-26 By Brian Lee. Automatic drawing done without looking at the paper. It encourages fluidity of line and naturalness of expression.

Figure 3-27 By Michael F. Gebhardt. Johns-Manville World Headquarters, The Architects Collaborative.

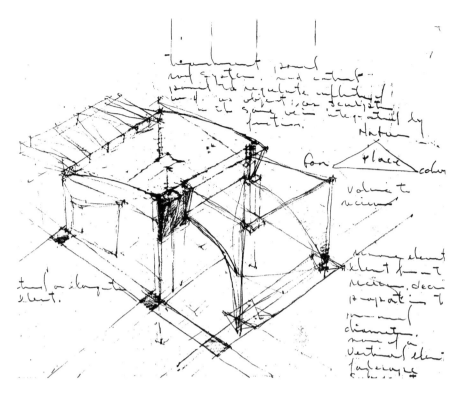

Figure 3-28 By Bret Dodd.

Designing depends heavily upon representation; to avoid disappointment later, the designer wants to see the physical effects of his decisions. It is inevitable that a student will tell me that he is waiting until he has decided what to do before he draws it up. This is backward. In fact, he cannot decide what to do until he has drawn it. *Nine times out of ten indecisiveness is the result of lack of evidence.* Furthermore, a decision implies a choice; recognizing that there is more than one possible design solution, it makes no sense whatsoever to try to determine if one isolated solution is good. Instead, the question should be whether this is the best of the known alternatives. To answer this question, we must also be able to see the other designs. The graphic thinking approach emphasizes sketches that feed thinking and thoughts that feed sketches; one is continually informing the other. For the beginning designer, these points cannot be overemphasized.

There is no way to avoid the intense, comprehensive job of representation or modeling in design. The only choice left is whether to make the job easier throughout a professional career by becoming a competent illustrator now.

Having said that, I would add the warning that drawing and thinking must be always open to growth. Cliches in drawing lead to cliches in thinking. As John Gundelfinger says:

I never know what a drawing will look like until it is finished. Once you do, that's security, and security is something we can all do without in a drawing. It comes from working in a particular way or style that enables you to control any subject or situation you encounter, and once you're in control, you stop learning. The nervousness and anxiety that precede a drawing are important to the end result.[5]

Architects who have been able to find adventure and excitement in drawing will readily attend to the great boost it gives to their design work and their thinking.

Finally, I want to stress two of my prejudices regarding representative drawing. First, freehand ability is vital for effective use of representation in architectural design. You must be able to turn over ideas rapidly; to do this requires the spontaneous graphic display that rapid sketching provides. Second, attention should be paid to making the sketches faithfully represent design ideas. Avoid adding things to a drawing simply to improve the appearance of the drawing. Changes should reflect conscious changes in the design. Kirby Lockard cautions, "Remember, the best, most direct and honest persuasion for a design's acceptance should be the design itself, and all successful persuasion should be based on competent and honest representations of the design."[6]

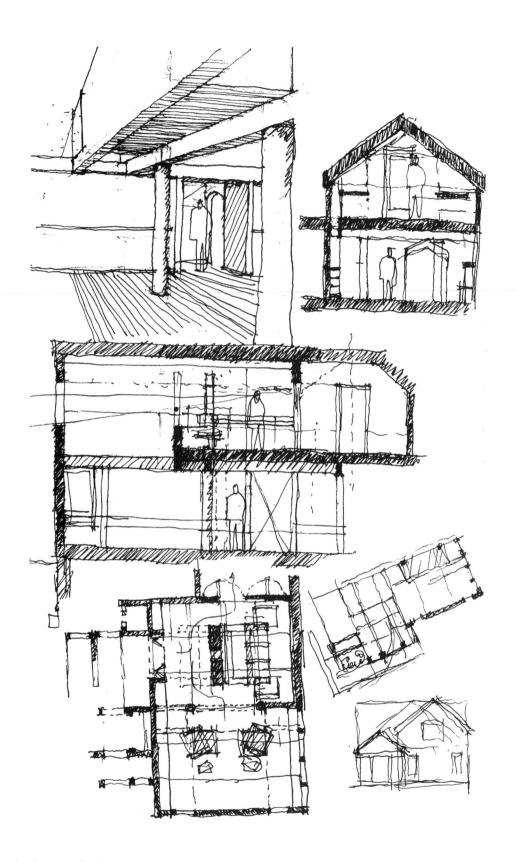

Figure 3-29 Design development sketches.

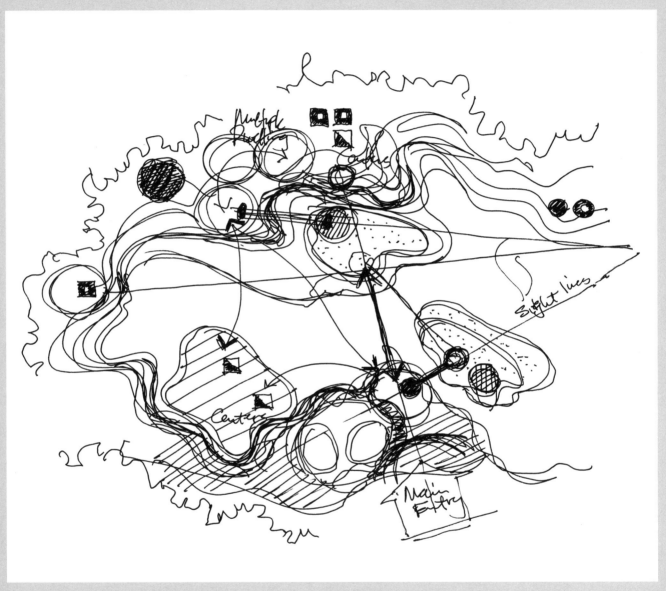

Figure 4-1 Site study.

4 Abstraction

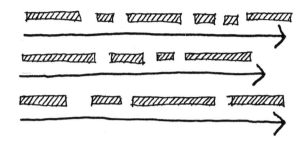

The design process can be thought of as a series of transformations going from uncertainty towards information. The successive stages of the process are usually registered by some kind of graphic model. In the final stages of the design process, designers use highly formalized graphic languages such as those provided by descriptive geometry. But this type of representation is hardly suitable for the first stages, when designers use quick sketches and diagrams...It has been accepted for years that because of the high level of abstraction of the ideas which are handled at the beginning of the design process, they must be expressed necessarily by means of a rather ambiguous, loose graphic language—a private language which no one can properly understand except the designer himself...the high level of abstraction of the information which is handled must not prevent us from using a clearly defined graphic language. Such a language would register the information exactly at the level of abstraction it has, and it would facilitate communication and cooperation among designers.[1]

—JUAN PABLO BONTA

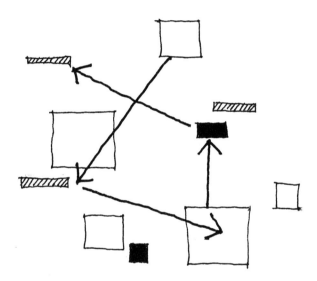

Figure 4-2

My own version of a graphic language is based on experience with students in the design studio and research in design process communications. It is presented here because I am convinced that a clearly defined graphic language is important both to design thinking and to communication between designers.

As Robert McKim pointed out, "A language consists of a set of rules by which symbols can be related to represent larger meanings."[2] The difference between verbal and graphic languages is both in the symbols used and in the ways in which the symbols are related. The symbols for verbal languages are largely restricted to words, whereas graphic languages include images, signs, numbers, and words. Much more significant, verbal language is sequential—it has a beginning, a middle, and an end. Graphic language is simultaneous—all symbols and their relationships are considered at the same time. The simultaneity and complex interrelationship of reality accounts for the special strength of graphic language in addressing complex problems.

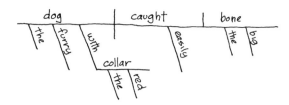

Figure 4-3a Sentence diagram.

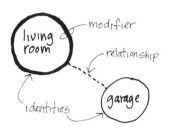

(c)

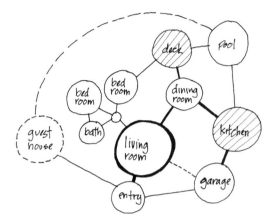

Figure 4-3b Graphic diagram.

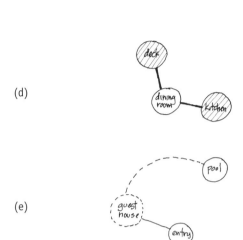

(d)

(e)

Figure 4-3c, d, e Graphic "sentences."

GRAMMAR

The graphic language proposed here has grammatical rules comparable to those of verbal language. The diagram of the sentence (Figure 4-3a) shows three basic parts: nouns, verbs, and modifiers such as adjectives, adverbs, and phrases. Nouns represent identities, verbs establish relationships between nouns, and the modifiers qualify or quantify the identities or the relationships between identities. In the graphic diagram (Figure 4-3b), identities are shown as circles, relationships are shown as lines, and modifiers are shown by changes in the circles or lines (heavier lines indicate more important relationships and tones indicating differences in identities). In the sentence diagram, the verb shows a relationship that the subject has to the object: the dog caught the bone. The line in the graphic diagram is bi-directional; it says that the living room is connected to the kitchen and that the kitchen is connected to the living room.

Thus the graphic diagram contains many sentences as:

1. The very important living room has a minor relationship to the garage (Figure 4-3c).
2. The dining room must be connected to the special spaces, the kitchen and the deck (Figure 4-3d).
3. The future guesthouse will be related to the entry and indirectly to the pool (Figure 4-3e).

There are other ways of drawing "graphic sentences"; three alternatives are shown here:

1. *Position*—An implied grid is used to establish relationships between identities; the resulting order sometimes makes the diagram easier to read (Figure 4-4a).
2. *Proximity*—The degree or intensity of the relationships of identities is indicated by the relative distances between them. A significant increase in distance can imply that no relationship exists. This type of diagram has more flexibility than the preceding type (Figure 4-4b).
3. *Similarity*—Identities are grouped by common characteristics such as color or shape (Figure 4-4c).

These alternatives may also be combined to form other grammatical variations (Figure 4-4d), but care should be taken to retain consistency. To communicate clearly, the grammatical rules should be immediately evident. According to Jerome Bruner, "The binding fact of mental life in child and adult alike is that there is a limited capacity for processing information—our span, as it is called, can comprise six or seven unrelated items simultaneously. Go beyond that and there is overload, confusion, forgetting."[3] One of the reasons for adopting some basic grammatical rules in graphic diagrams is to avoid confusion by reducing the number of variables that have to be handled at one time.

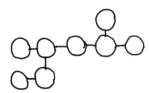

Figure 4-4a Structuring a graphic "sentence" by position.

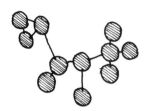

Figure 4-4b By proximity.

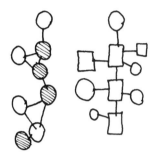

Figure 4-4c By similarity.

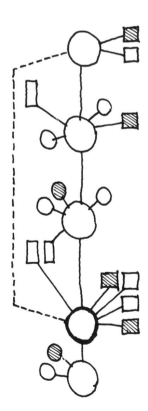

Figure 4-4d Combination of "sentence" structures.

Building a diagram.

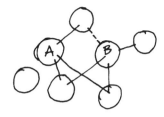

Figure 4-5a Basic identities and relationships.

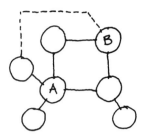

Figure 4-5b Reduction to simple ordering structure.

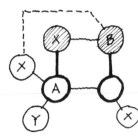

Figure 4-5c Second level of information.

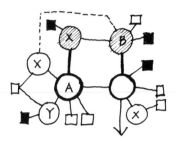

Figure 4-5d Tag-ons.

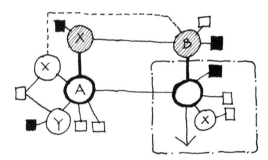

Figure 4-5e Segmenting.

One of the most useful qualities of graphic communication is that information can be transmitted and received on several levels simultaneously. Artists recognized this long ago. Successful paintings usually appeal to the viewer as overall compositions, renderings of detail, and technique with media, just to name a few of the levels. These levels of communication can also be used to good advantage in a graphic diagram. The basic process for building a diagram (shown above) is as follows:

1. Try to illustrate the basic identities and their relationships in a rough diagram.
2. Reduce the diagram to its simplest structure by applying rules of graphic grammar.
3. Modify the diagram to indicate a second level of information, using tones or heavy lines.
4. Add other levels of information as tags attached to the basic diagram.
5. If the diagram becomes too complicated, break it into segments by grouping or placing a boundary around identities.

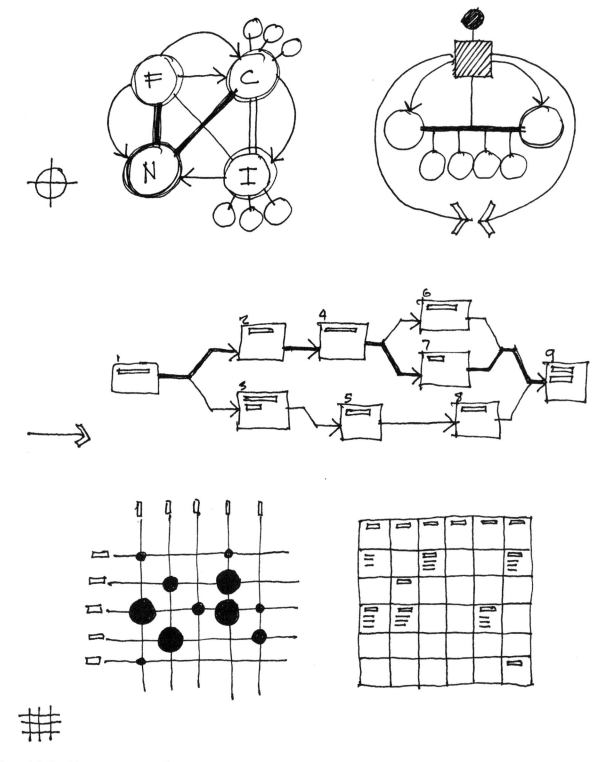

Figure 4-6 Graphic grammar conventions.

Alternate Grammars

The basic graphic grammar discussed so far is most commonly expressed in what are known as bubble diagrams. It is probably the most broad-based, versatile grammar. Other conventions may qualify as grammars, or rules for relating graphic elements so as to communicate. Two of the more prominent grammars are the network and the matrix. The basis for the grammar of networks is time or sequence. Although it is normally assumed that the sequence proceeds from left to right or top to bottom, arrows are often used to clarify the order or subtleties of the sequence. The most familiar type of network uses verbal descriptions of tasks or events, but graphic symbols could be used as well. The matrix diagram incorporates the other type of grammar. Its convention assigns identities to rows and columns and represents the relationships of identities with graphic symbols at the intersections of the rows and columns.

VOCABULARY

The meaning of words or symbols in any form of language must be consistent and shared in order to support human communication. This consistent set is called a *vocabulary*. Basic verbal vocabulary within our native language is normally acquired in childhood through association, while grammar is learned formally. Literacy is achieved over several years of education. The acquisition of graphic language is not a common component of a general education. In a formal sense it is more often a part of education in design and art curricula. However, there are some graphic "languages" to which the general public is exposed. Among those are international road signs, road map legends, music notation, and mathematical symbols.

The accessibility of graphic languages is heavily dependent on associations with familiar objects or experiences. These associations can be made through naming graphic items or by using symbols that are readily recognized as abstractions of familiar objects.

Identities

There are a great number of ways to symbolize an identity. The more common symbols are represented here in horizontal rows. The identity of these different possible groups is achieved by contrast. Usually all variables are held constant except for one. The number in each group is limited because most of us are unable to deal with more than five or six variations in one graphic diagram. The elementary symbols can be supplemented or replaced by numbers, letters, or other symbols. By judiciously combining different groups of symbols, it is possible to have several levels of information in a graphic diagram without sacrificing clarity. Sometimes identities are best shown with a more tentative quality using dotted and irregular lines. Later chapters further explain this less definite need.

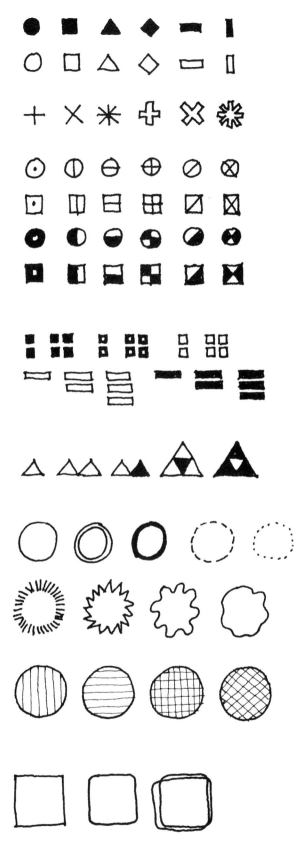

Figure 4-7 Graphic grammar conventions.

Figure 4-8

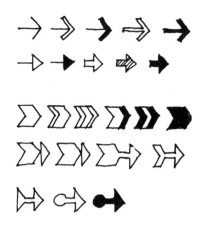

Relationships

As with identities, different relationships are best represented by sets of line types. These line types can also be used as borders for grouping identities as a means of segmenting a diagram or of showing special relationships.

The arrow is a very special device for indicating relationships. As a symbol of movement, Arnheim holds that it has compelling qualities: "...any movement in the environment automatically attracts attention because movement means change of conditions, which may call for a reaction."[4] Arrows combined with lines can indicate a one-way relationship, a sequence of events, or a process. Separate arrows can be used to mark important parts of a diagram or to show dependencies and the feed-in of supplementary information.

Modifiers

Identities and relationships are modified according to a hierarchical system. In this manner, the significance of parts and the different levels of intensity in the relationship between parts are expressed. Hierarchy can be shown by different line widths, multiple lines, or the relative size of dashes and spaces in dashed lines (Figure 4-9a). Graded tones and the accumulation of parts are also useful devices (Figure 4-9b).

Modifiers can also create emphasis, principally through contrast in terms of size, tone, contour, or detail. Emphasis is used to signal a special identity or relationship, segregate interwoven diagrams, or indicate special points or steps in a process (Figure 4-9c).

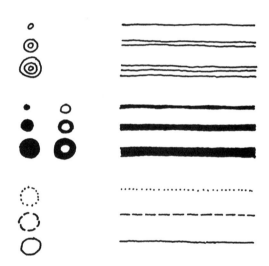

Figure 4-9a Modification by size.

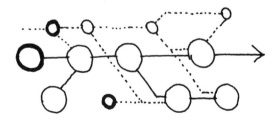

Figure 4-9b Indicating emphasis.

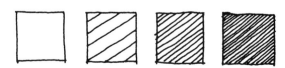

Figure 4-9c Modification by tone.

60 · *Abstraction*

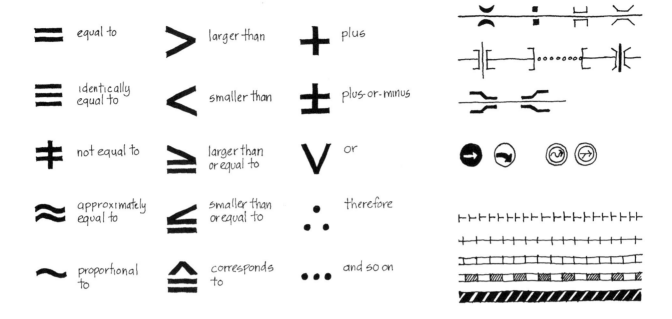

Figure 4-10 Mathematical language symbols.

=	equal to	>	larger than	+	plus
≡	identically equal to	<	smaller than	±	plus-or-minus
≠	not equal to	≥	larger than or equal to	V	or
≈	approximately equal to	≤	smaller than or equal to	∴	therefore
~	proportional to	≙	corresponds to	⋯	and so on

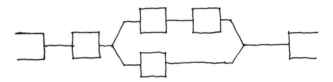

Figure 4-11 Graphic language elements from cartography.

Other Graphic Vocabulary

Several disciplines have developed their own short-hand symbols to facilitate rapid communication. Many of these symbols have a wide enough understanding to be useful in graphic thinking. Some of the most useful symbols, taken from the disciplines of mathematics, systems analysis, engineering, and cartography, are shown here and on the following pages.

Operations research and the analysis of communication systems led to the study of processes, which, in turn, led to many applications of process management. With the study of more complicated processes, a diagrammatic language was developed to properly describe these processes (Figure 4-12a). On the basis of a few symbols and a set of rules for using them, very elaborate processes can be readily explained in graphic terms. Some of the symbols shown to the right are useful in describing architecturally related processes, such as project plans, construction organization, and programmatic functions (Figure 4-12b).

Figure 4-12a Process diagram.

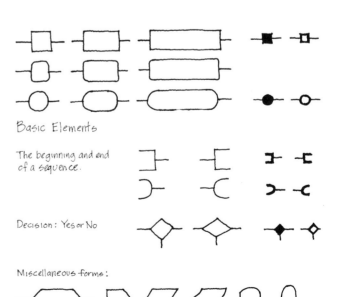

Figure 4-12b Process symbols.

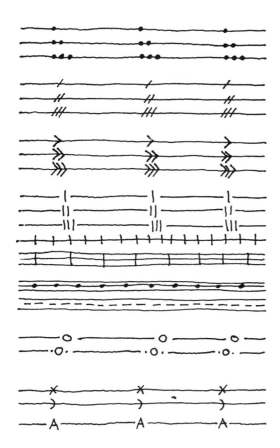

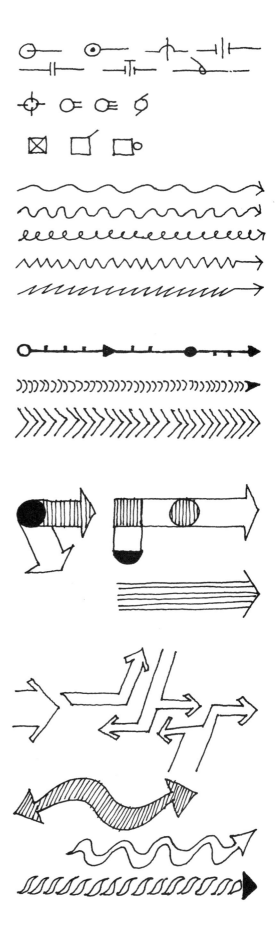

Figure 4-13 Graphic language elements from other areas of the building industry.

On this page are several symbols used in electrical, mechanical, and transportation engineering that can further extend our graphic vocabulary. Opposite are symbols from cartography and other symbol systems.

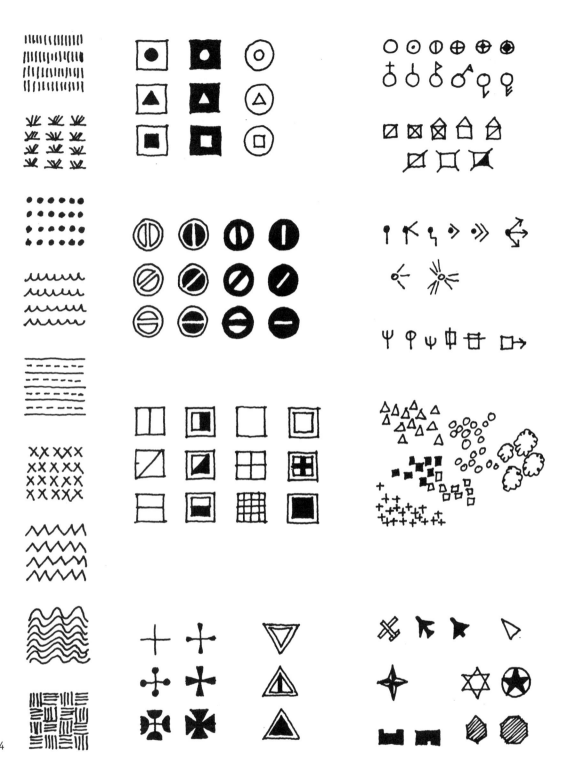

Figure 4-14

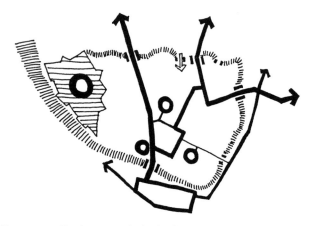

Figure 4-15 City image analysis, Quebec.

Applying Graphic Language

When the conventions of a graphic language are applied to different communication and thinking contexts, they can produce a wide variety of expressions. In each case effectiveness depends upon an explicit grammar and a consistency in its use. For an extensive explanation of the uses of graphic language, consult the second edition of my book *Graphic Problem Solving.*

Jerome Bruner stresses the point: "Unless detail is placed into a structured pattern, it is rapidly forgotten.... Detailed material is conserved in memory by use of simplified ways of representing it."[5] The graphic "vocabulary" just presented was selected because the symbols are commonly accepted, simplified ways of representation. Since our graphic vocabulary will continue to expand graphic communication, we must use commonly understood symbols and a clear grammatical structure as a context for the vocabulary to be effective. The obvious corollary is our need to become graphically "literate." We need to become familiar with a range of graphic languages. "The thinker who has a broad command of graphic language not only can find more complete expression for his thinking but can also re-center his thinking by moving from one graphic language to another...in effect he uses language to expand the range of his thinking."[6] This last point by McKim is extremely important to a full use of the material presented in this book. Communication and thinking are intertwined processes; we need to focus on how they assist each other rather than ask which is more important.

Graphic language can also have pitfalls, as identified by Robert McKim:

1. Lack of skill or inappropriate choice of language, which can be damaging to tender new concepts.
2. Mistaking graphic images for reality.

Figure 4-16 Neighborhood analysis.

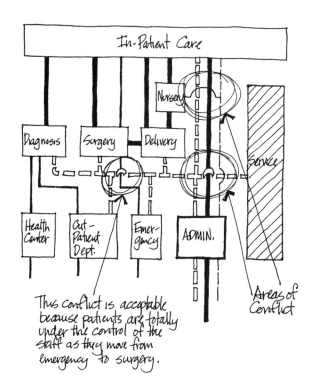

Figure 4-17 Hospital circulation analysis.

3. Glamorizing an idea.
4. Concealing what should be revealed.
5. Habitual use of a few languages, avoiding some types of mental operation.

Figure 4-18 Pedestrian traffic intensity.

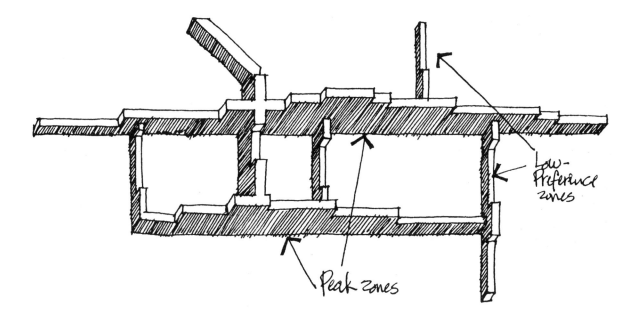

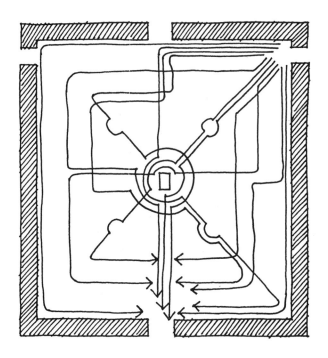

Figure 4-19 Circulation choices, Place des Vosges, Paris.

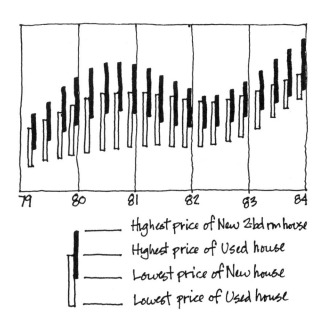

Figure 4-20 Housing price analysis.

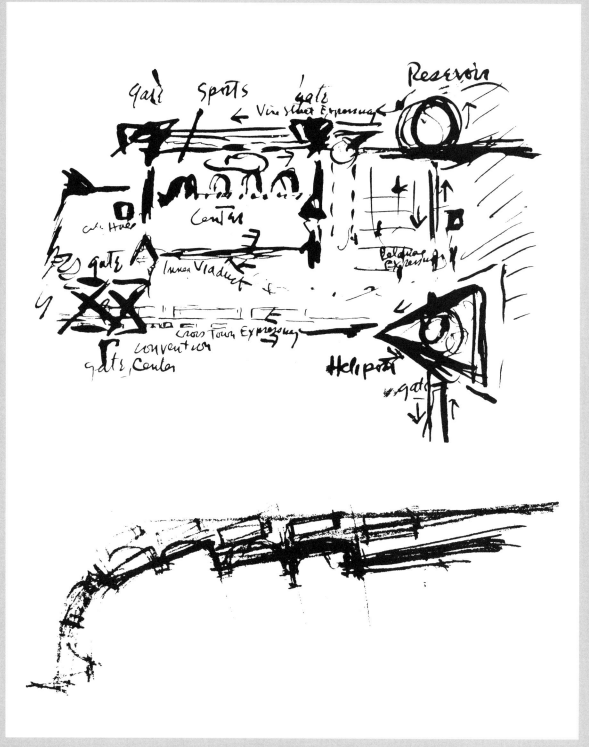

Figure 5-1 *(top)* By Louis Kahn. Concept sketch for central Philadelphia.
Figure 5-2 *(bottom)* By David Stieglitz. Buffalo Waterfront Redevelopment Project.

5 Expression

The designer who wishes to take advantage of expression, the second level of communication (the first level being the content of the drawing), should become aware of the range of qualities that can be communicated and useful techniques for doing so. The sketches in this chapter are offered as examples of what can be discovered. Each sketch conveys more than one quality, but I have tried to group the sketches according to their most significant qualities.

This chapter concentrates on some of the attitudes and priorities architects and designers convey by the manner in which they draw. It seems obvious that you can tell something about designers through their drawings. Care in drawing often indicates care in thinking. In my experience, clients, consultants, contractors, and others with whom architects work are greatly influenced by drawings, which set the tone for the work. The drawings are a way of telling people what you demand of yourself and provide a clue to what you expect of them.

IDENTITY

The drawings on these first two pages are significant for their strong sense of identity, a presence that says they are important and we ought to take time to look at them more closely. How does the way the sketches were drawn account for this quality? Both the style and the high contrast are important, but the fluidity of the sketches tells us about the intensity and confidence of the architect. We can almost see or feel the architect's hand moving over the paper.

CONSISTENCY

Discipline in drawing is sometimes associated with stiff or Spartan-looking drawings. But, as you can see, quality need not limit expression. These drawings have their internal consistency in common. It might be compared to the differences in car designs. The Porsche and the Rolls Royce are immediately recognized as two very different cars, but both have an expression of high quality and craftsmanship. Given the basic concept of each car, the designers have given every part of the car a feeling that it belongs to that, and only that, car.

Figure 5-3 By Edwin F. Harris, Jr. Assisi.

Figure 5-4 By Theodore J. Musho. Santa Costanza.

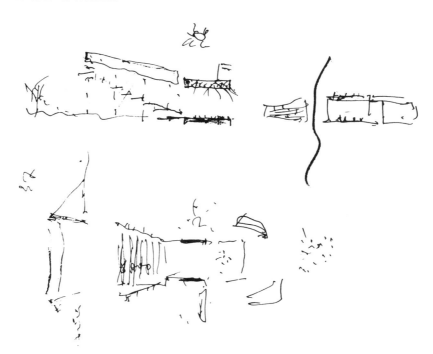

Figure 5-5 By LeCorbusier. Baghdad Gymnasium.

STYLE AND SELECTIVITY

Architects often develop certain "trademarks" in their drawings as their careers develop. The resulting style of the sketches can be seen as a reflection of the designer's personality: tentative lines might indicate a willingness to remain open to new ideas, whereas more deliberate delineation might show the designer's preference for deliberateness and quick closure on decisions.

Style is also formed by the architect's consistent selection of what he wants to show in his sketches and what he wants to leave out. His choices are often a reflection of what he feels are important design concerns in most projects.

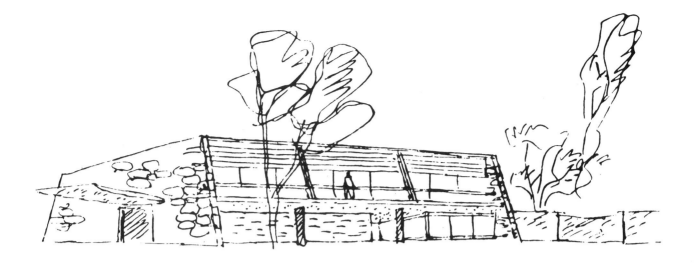

Figure 5-6 By Oscar Niemeyer. Capanema Residence.

Figure 5-7 By Jim Anderson. Country Side YMCA, Landplus West Inc., Landscape Architects.

Figure 5-8 By Lawrence Halprin. Lovejoy Plaza and Cascade, Portland, Oregon.

Figure 5-9 By Edwin F. Harris, Jr. Pisan Group.

ENERGY AND VITALITY

Sketches such as the ones shown here project the enthusiasm and intensity of the act of putting the images on paper. The design and realization of a building can be a taxing experience, particularly for the client. We know that the architect can help by instilling confidence and a sense of optimism. Vitality in sketches can do a lot to reinforce what we say to clients or others working on a project.

CREATIVITY AND REFRESHMENT

If we accept the premise that architects are creative in solving problems and open to new ways of seeing environment, the importance of a creative quality in our drawings should be obvious. As much as people strive to make decisions on an informed, rational basis, information is sometimes incomplete and there is usually a degree of risk-taking involved in design. Risks are taken on the basis of expectations partially conveyed by the way the architect expresses himself in his sketches.

Figure 5-10 By Gerald Exline.

Figure 5-11 By Thomas Larson. South Station, Boston.

Figure 5-13 By Romaldo Giurgola. City Council room, Boston City Hall Competition.

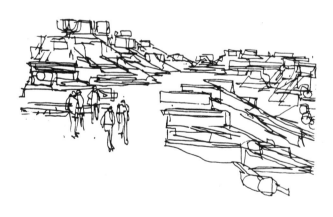

Figure 5-12 By Gerald Exline.

Figure 5-14 By Michael Gebhardt. Hockey Arena/Auditorium, Soldiers Field, Harvard.

DIRECTION AND FOCUS

A team of creative people working on a design problem needs to have an understanding of the general direction and parameters of their efforts while being given a sense of freedom and flexibility to contribute fully to the success of the project. Some architects are able to meet these needs in preliminary conceptual sketches. Tom Larson explains it this way: "These drawings are not yet 'architecture' intentionally. I am beginning to carve out negative space, to begin to understand the organizing spaces of the project. These are quick drawings."[1]

Figure 5-15 By Thomas Larson. Grandberg Residence.

Figure 5-16 By Lawrence Halprin. Lovejoy Plaza and Cascade, Portland, Oregon.

Figure 5-17 By Hugh Stubbins. Mount Holyoke College dormitories.

Figure 5-18 Paddack Residence study.

Figure 5-19 By Jim Anderson. Sidewalk zone development, Terre Haute Urban Development Action Program, Landplus West Inc., Landscape Architects.

CHARACTER AND MOOD

For many architects, one of the most difficult problems in design is the representation, the "capturing" of the intended character of a space or object. Here again, the way sketches are drawn can be of great help. On these two pages, I have tried to gather exam-

ples of a wide range of moods communicated by way of sketches. The skills that are demonstrated here and in the preceding pages are those of observation as much as manual skills. Sketching is supported by thinking and emotion, and the sketches reflect these experiences.

Figure 5-20 By Lisa Kolber. Byzantine church, Mystra, Greece.

Figure 5-21 By Lisa Kolber. Byzantine church, Mystra, Greece.Figure 5-21 By Patrick D. Nall. Ahmed Ibn Toulon Mosque, Cairo.

ECONOMY

As in verbal communication, we appreciate someone who can find just the right means to convey the essence of an experience. The sketches on these pages are by architectural students who were so inspired by what they encountered on their field trips that they spent much time drawing and developing an educated eye.

Figure 5-22 By Lisa Kolber. Gateway at Mystra, Greece.

Figure 5-23 By Lisa Kolber. Gateway at Mystra, Greece.

Figure 5-24 By James Walls. Trinity Church, Boston.

Figure 5-25 By Thomas Cheesman. Sienna, Italy.

Figure 5-26 By Patrick Nall. Roadside restaurant, Cairo.

Figure 5-27 By Patrick Nall. Temple of Luxor, Egypt.

AESTHETIC ORDER

Both in building design and in drawings, most of us are sensitive to the role of composition in achieving a sense of unity or synthesis. Unity in environments is also achieved through aesthetic order, characteristic shapes, patterns, or details shared by the elements that constitute these environments. Through sketching we can develop an awareness of aesthetic order that carries over to our drawings, endowing them with a similar sense of order.

Figure 5-28 By Barry Russell. Prague.

Figure 5-29 By Lisa Kolber. Knossos Pavilion, Crete.

APPLIED SKILLS

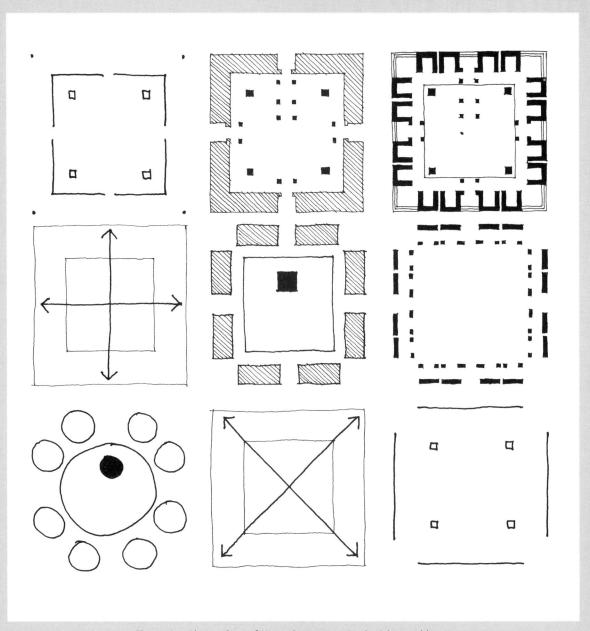

Figure 6-1 Abstractions of Hurva Synagogue, Louis Kahn, architect.

6 Analysis

According to Gordon Best, the analysis of design problems is fundamental to design process. "Practical design problems are variable and idiosyncratic. They generate a variety so great that it is nearly impossible to describe such problems let alone understand them. Despite this, practicing designers must interpret these problems if they are going to deal with them."[1] Architects must simplify problems, reduce them to their essential elements. This is the process of abstraction, the exposure of the underlying structure or pattern of a whole system. As we will see, graphic communication is well suited to the task of abstraction. The simultaneous view of the abstract sketches keeps the whole structure of a system up front.

A discussion of a system and its analysis is helpful to understand the functions of abstract sketches. Design problems are generally caused by poor function or breakdown of a system. If I can't get my car started on a winter morning, I know the cause could be a frozen gas line, a malfunctioning starter, worn-out spark plugs, the distributor, the battery, or even an empty gas tank. A car is a system of parts, all of which must interact properly for the engine to start. The system extends beyond the car parts to include routine maintenance, the manufacturer's inspection of parts, keeping moisture out of gas station storage tanks, and my checking the gas gauge regularly. To solve the problem with the car that does not start, we must understand it as an organized system. If the distributor is not the cause of the problem, no degree of inspection of the distributor can solve the problem.

In design, this understanding of the whole system is referred to as *holistic analysis*. As Geoffrey Broadbent put it:

The whole must be subdivided if we are to analyze it.... If we choose the wrong kind of subdivision, then the whole will be destroyed, whereas other kinds of subdivision may throw its structure into relief. Angyal considers four ways of subdividing a whole, such as a plant, an animal or some inanimate object. One could cut it at random, thus producing a collection of unrelated parts. One could divide it according to some preconceived and fixed principle that failed to take its inherent structure into account, which would represent a rational approach. One could abstract distinguishable properties from it, such as size, shape, color, consistency and so on, which would represent an empirical approach. Or one could divide the whole according to its structural articulation.[2]

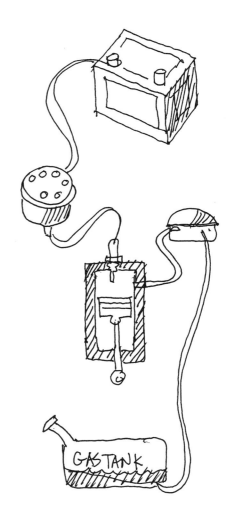

Figure 6-2 Automobile system.

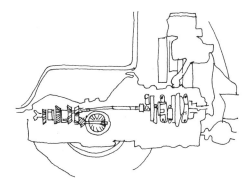

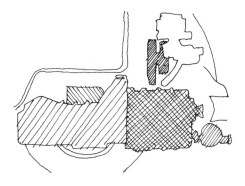

Figure 6-3a Abstraction by distillation.

Abstract sketches can express the structural articulation of a system. Here are some ways, using the automobile as an example:

1. *Distillation*—Removing from the drawing all those things that are not important to the analysis of the structure of the system's critical parts: highlighting the electrical system.

2. *Reduction*—Representing groups of parts with a smaller set of symbols makes it easier for most of us to understand the drawing and entertain changes; there can be several levels of reduction yielding increasing generalization. This diagram represents only the major automobile systems (electrical, mechanical, fuel, etc.).

3. *Extraction*—Through contrast or emphasis, a part can be given special attention while remaining within the context of its system: position of the distributor in the electrical system is stressed.

4. *Comparison*—Casting different systems in the same graphic language facilitates comparison of structural rather than superficial characteristics of different systems.

Figure 6-3b By reduction.

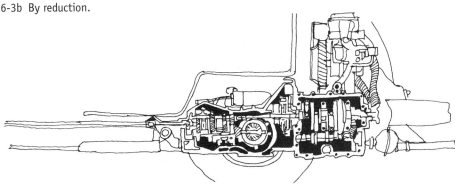

Figure 6-3c By extraction.

In design or problem solving, products, processes, beliefs, or other systems need to be represented in several ways, ranging from concrete to the most abstract. In McKim's words, "Operations often require imagery that is abstract and pattern-like. Which is not to say that abstract imagery is more important than concrete. Rather, abstract and concrete imagery are complementary. The flexible visual thinker moves readily back and forth between the two."[3] He suggested, "A way to obtain literacy and at the same time to acquire language flexibility, is to learn how to use graphic language to move thinking and expression from abstract to concrete meanings and back."[4]

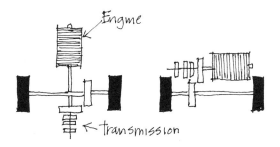

Figure 6-3d By comparison.

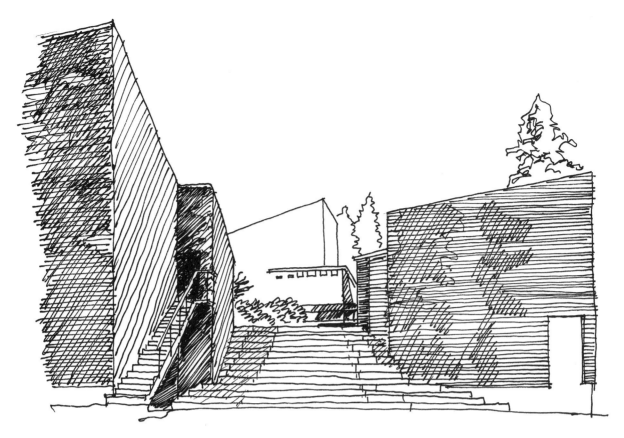

Figure 6-4 Perspective of entry to Sunyatsalo City Center, Alvar Aalto, architect.

ABSTRACTION AND EXPERIENCE

The power of abstract drawings in design is directly related to the depth of experience that the designer can associate with the abstraction. For the experienced designer, simple abstract symbols can represent highly complex concepts of form or space. Without the designer's background or associations, abstraction is of limited use. The diagram and plan of Aalto's community center take on several layers of meaning when accompanied by the perspective view of the building. Developing graphic thinking and design skills requires continuing experience of a variety of successful environments heightened by the use of representational and abstract sketches of those environments.

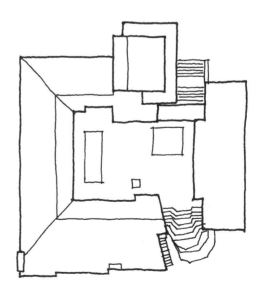

Figure 6-5 Concept diagram and plan of center.

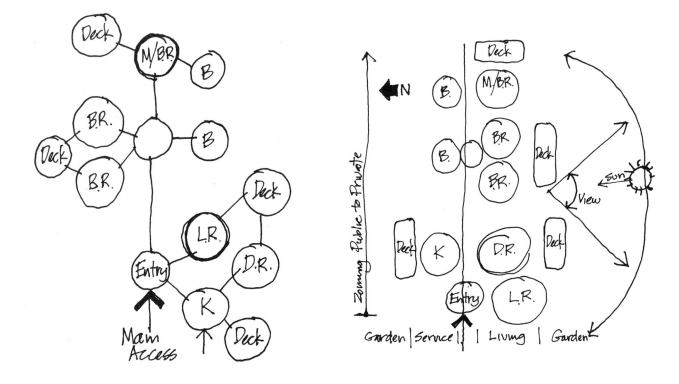

Figure 6-6a Basic relationship between functions.

Figure 6-6b Position and orientation.

TRANSFORMATION FROM PROGRAM TO SCHEMATIC DESIGN

Starting with the most simplistic model of design process, we can consider the challenge of handling information "exactly at the level of abstraction it has" throughout the design process. In the example shown here, the drawings evolve toward levels of lesser abstraction from the building program to a schematic design for a house. (The transformations after the schematic design that lead to the final building include preliminary design, design development, construction documents, and shop drawings. These are not shown because effective conventions already exist for representation of those stages. There are several sources for examples of those drawings, including books and the drawing files of architectural firms.)

The first diagram is an abstraction of the program of the house. The functions and the relationships between functions are indicated, as well as the hierarchy of these functions and relationships. The major access points are clearly visible. The "bubbles" have no positional significance because the program does not contain that sort of information. If the relationship links between functions are retained, the bubbles can be moved to several different positions without changing the basic information of the diagram. The second diagram responds to site and climate information, establishing both position and orientation of functions with respect to each other and the site. Natural light and heat, views, building access, and zoning of functions are also considered. The third diagram reflects decisions on scale and shape of the spaces required to accommodate the programmed functions. Here, consideration is given to functional needs and a planning grid. In the fourth diagram, spe-

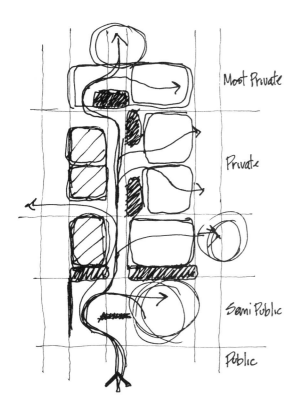

Figure 6-6c Scale and shape of space.

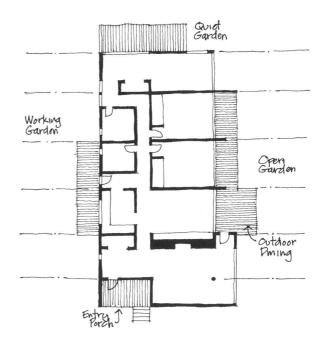

Figure 6-6d Enclosure and construction.

cific structural, construction, and enclosure decisions come into play. Sufficient formal definition has been indicated for the diagram to be called a schematic design.

This transformation from program to schematic design is only one of several paths that could have been taken. By understanding the intent of the diagrams at each stage, we ensure that options remain open, rather than locked into one form too early.

Most designers will agree that designing is not a "clean" process; in other words, it is not automatic, even-paced, directional, orderly, or totally rational. We would probably agree that it is highly personal, discrete while holistic, sometimes very clear and sometimes quite obscure, sometimes rapid and sometimes painfully slow, exciting and also tedious. In short, it is very human rather than mechanistic. And

that is why so many of us are so passionately hooked on designing.

Drawings, the visual language designers use, reflect all of the qualities I have attached to designing. In the following chapters I have tried to recognize the variability and individuality of design processes by not associating graphic thinking with one design process. Rather, I have presented the uses of drawings as discrete events to uncover the breadth of richness that exists and leave open to each of us all the ways and styles of graphic thinking or designing that we prefer, that we enjoy!

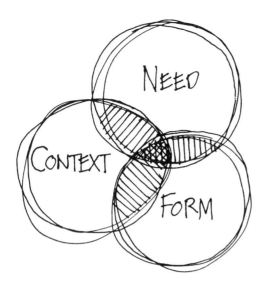

Figure 6-7a Structure of design problems.

ABSTRACTION APPLIED TO ARCHITECTURAL DESIGN

The rest of this chapter is based upon a more sophisticated model of the design process. The application of the tools of graphic abstraction to architectural design is aided by an understanding of the structure of architectural design problems. Horst Rittel has identified three variables of the typical design problem:

1. Performance variables which express desired characteristics of the object under design, and in terms of which the object will be evaluated ("construction cost," "aesthetic appeal," "overall quality," and the like).
2. Design variables, which describe the possibilities of the designer, his ranges of choice, his design variables ("height of ceiling," "shape of door knob," "type of heating," and the like).
3. Context variables, which are those factors affecting the object to be designed but not controlled by the designer ("land price," "likelihood of earthquakes," "type of eating habits," and so forth).[5]

A problem can be said to exist when there is some sort of misfit among these three variables in an environment. The design problem is solved when, as indicated in the diagram, there is a satisfactory relationship among need, context, and form. Consider a small printing company as an example. The original need was to accommodate a printing operation in the context of the downtown of a small city and the form provided was a small, one-story building. Over time, new problems could occur due to different types of misfits:

1. *Need/context*—Property values and the tax rate increase rapidly, even though the building still meets the printer's needs.
2. *Need/form*—The operation outgrows the building or the building deteriorates and is not adequate for the need.
3. *Form/context*—A change in the zoning restrictions makes a one-story building no longer a sound financial investment.

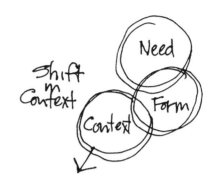

Figure 6-7b Misfit between need and context.

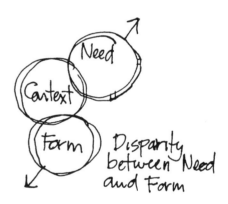

Figure 6-7c Misfit between need and form.

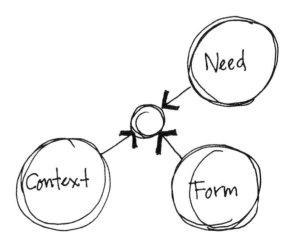

Figure 6-8 Sources of solutions to design problems.

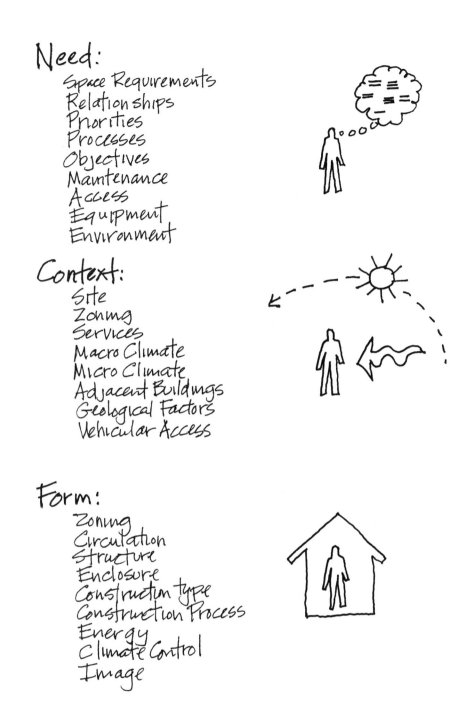

Need:
Space Requirements
Relationships
Priorities
Processes
Objectives
Maintenance
Access
Equipment
Environment

Context:
Site
Zoning
Services
Macro Climate
Micro Climate
Adjacent Buildings
Geological Factors
Vehicular Access

Form:
Zoning
Circulation
Structure
Enclosure
Construction type
Construction Process
Energy
Climate Control
Image

Figure 6-9 Design project information organized by major design variables.

The design problem can be caused by a change in any one or a combination of the variables. The solution to the problem may lie in changing any one of the variables or a combination of them. The design solution is not synonymous with the designed building; rather, the design drawings are the embodiment of a new balance between need, context, and form. The success of the design solution is measured by the way it responds to all three variables.

The categories of need, context, and form can also provide a convenient structure for organizing design project information. Design concerns, issues, priorities, or, as shown here, criteria can be gathered under these variable headings. This promotes a balanced view of the design problem and a more complete evaluation of design alternatives. (The application of evaluation criteria is discussed further in Chapter 9.) In this section, we deal with the graphic abstraction of the architect's design problem as described by need, context, and form.

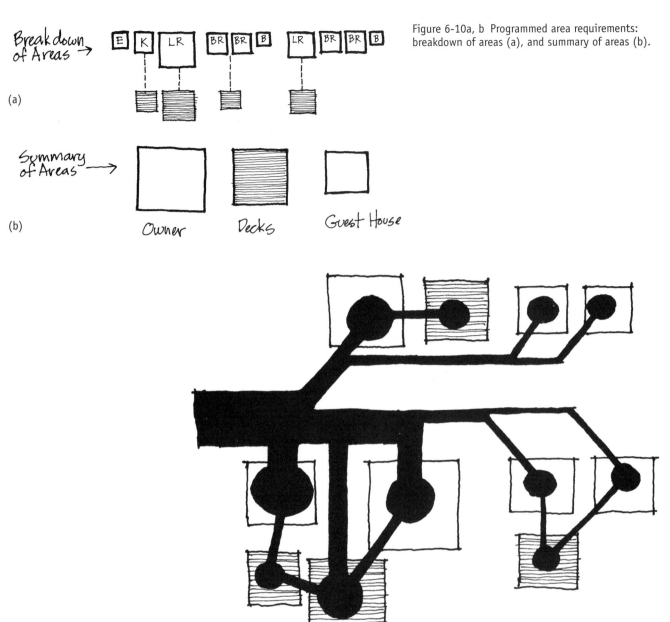

Figure 6-10a, b Programmed area requirements: breakdown of areas (a), and summary of areas (b).

Figure 6-11 Activity intensity.

NEED

The building program or brief usually contains most of the information about the client's needs. Programs for the average-size project, such as an educational or institutional building, can be quite complex. Although the program for our example, a four-bedroom recreational residence, is not very complex, it should serve to illustrate the basic types of diagrams that could be used to describe functional needs.

The first step is to get a good grasp of the quantifiable aspects of the program. Using squares to show the area requirements for different functions, the relationships of size are quickly apparent (Figure 6-10a). A summary of basic program areas (Figure 6-10b) aids consideration of some of the basic zoning alternatives and relationships to usable site area. Another quantitative diagram that can be quite useful shows intensity of activity or use. The intensity of functions is shown by the relative sizes of the circles, and the volume of circulation between functions by the width of the connecting bars. Detailed estimates of the intensity of activity are not usually made, but direct observation and informal analysis based on the designer's past experience should be sufficient to make the diagram useful.

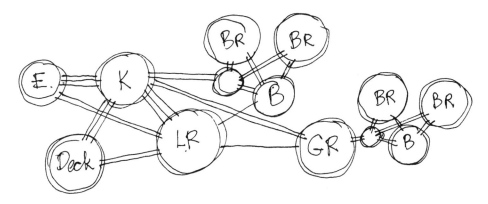

Figure 6-12 Bubble diagram of functional relationships.

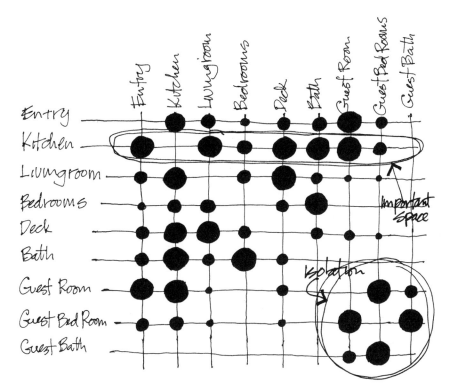

Figure 6-13 Matrix diagram of functional relationships.

Relationships

The bubble diagram has become a familiar tool to architectural designers. It can abstract the building program to conveniently summarize the activities to be housed and their required relationships. As we saw in Chapter 5, bubble diagrams are also easy to manipulate as the designer moves from building program to building design. As long as the basic rules of the graphic language are followed, these diagrams permit wide flexibility of thinking.

Another type of relationship diagram is the matrix. All the functions are listed along two perpendicular axes and then the relationship of each function to the other functions is categorized. The advan-

tage of such a matrix is in the ways it can be read by the designer. This example demonstrates that the kitchen is a critical point of relationship for the whole family and their guests, that the sleeping areas should be isolated from each other and from most of the rest of the house, and that the access to the guest areas should be controlled. Although it is true that most of these observations might be made intuitively for a house, the matrix promotes a restructuring of thinking that can stimulate new insights regarding needs such as separation or communication, particularly in more complex buildings. Finally, the matrix provides a simple graphic reinforcement of the designer's memory as he considers the building context and form.

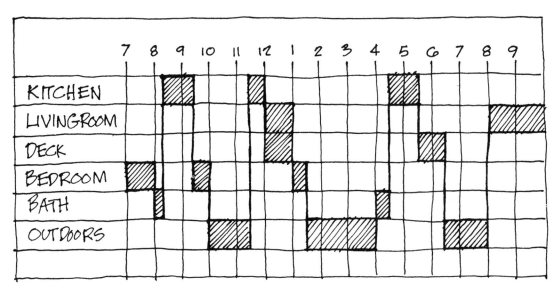

Figure 6-14a Log of space use.

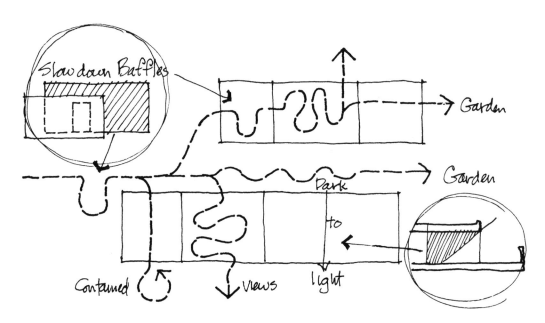

Figure 6-14b Kinesthetic map.

Physical Behavior

Although we might assume that most people use houses in pretty much the same way (judging from new housing development design), there are differences. These differences can have a lot to do with the comfort of a family in a particular house. One way to illustrate the use of a house is to make a log of spaces occupied by different family members during a typical day. The results may be surprising and may encourage the client to look at housing in a new way. There may also be implications for design priorities, orientation of spaces, and energy management.

Circulation is one of the most under-considered functions inherent in a building program. Many of the experiences of a house, its impact on people, take place as they move through and between spaces. These are referred to as *kinesthetic experiences;* they are dynamic experiences unlike sitting or standing in one space. Some architects have suggested that scenarios of desired kinesthetic experiences, in a graphic form, can be very useful to design. In its simple form, a kinesthetic map may use symbols for different experiences, but it is also possible to key perspective sketches to the map and help create a sense of what is desired. Again, such diagrams help the client and the designer discuss and think about the design problem.

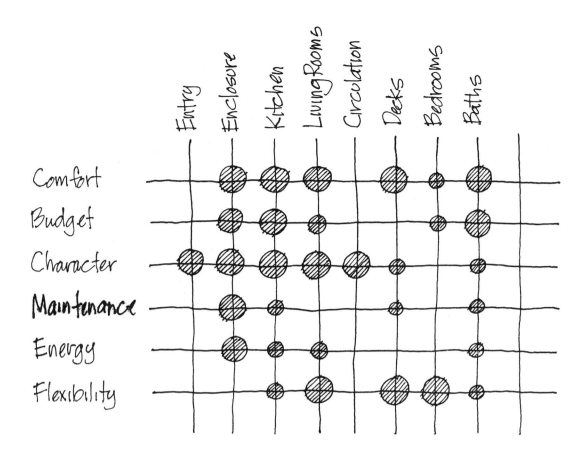

Figure 6-15a Matrix diagram of relationships between design issues and spaces.

Design Priorities

To make a successful house, an architect must help the client choose his priorities, as his desires often exceed what is financially possible. But priorities remain a vague notion for most people until they see a specific building design with a price tag. Then comes the pruning and pushing and pulling, ending with a design that looks as if it has been through a street fight. A matrix diagram clarifies priorities so the client can better understand them before proceeding to building-form alternatives. The matrix starts with a list of design issues and a list of functions. At each point of relationship in the matrix, we ask the importance of this issue to this function. The degree of importance is indicated by the size of the dot. When this process has been completed for each issue, the most important issues and functions (those with the highest cumulative degrees of importance) can be identified and a hierarchical list of issues and functions formed. When the matrix is reconstructed with issues and spaces arranged in their order of importance, it is possible to make some observations about critical areas of the design problem.

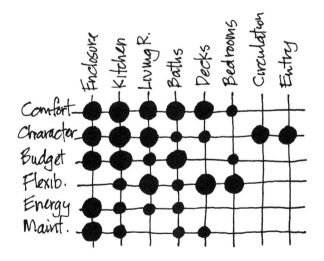

Figure 6-15b Revised matrix indicating priorities.

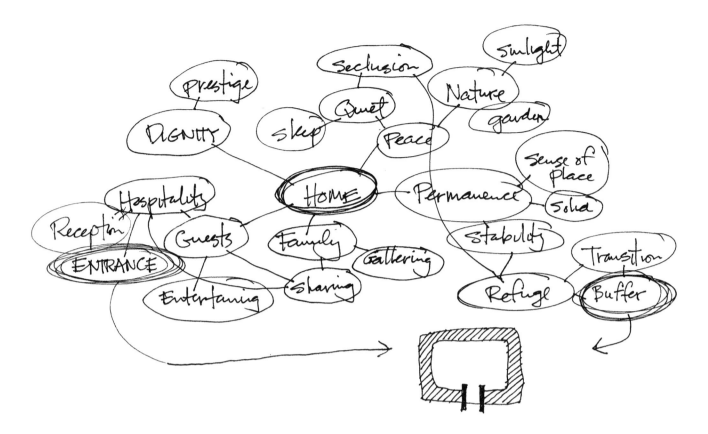

Figure 6-16 Verbal concepts map.

Design Objectives

Analysis of a design problem requires the exploration of the broad set of issues, contexts, and concerns. To initiate thinking about the problem, we can adapt a technique used in creative writing that builds a network of verbal associations. To bring the subconscious mind into action, the standard tabulated lists are replaced by a loose, open-ended method of notation that lets ideas develop in an organic pattern much like the roots of a tree. As a complex network of associations develops, we can begin to identify the most important issues and relationships.

As analysis of needs progresses, it is often helpful to speculate on optimum relationships among the activities that make up the building program. By illustrating alternative patterns of relationships, the designer can become more attuned to the issues of synthesis of a range of concerns. To avoid premature assumptions about physical forms that would be appropriate to solving the design problem, activities are purposely represented by nonspecific shapes. Some designers have referred to these shapes as "potatoes."

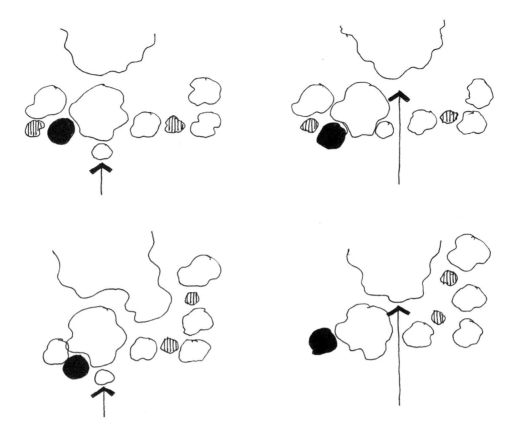

Figure 6-17 Comparative schematic layouts.

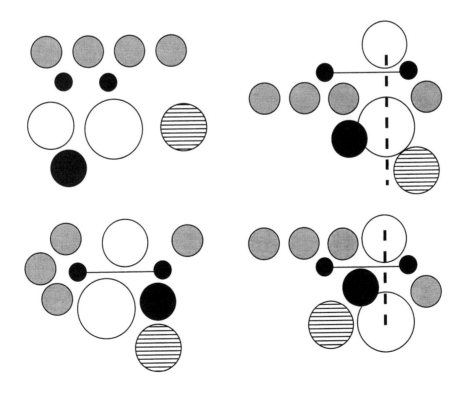

Figure 6-18 Comparative schematic layouts.

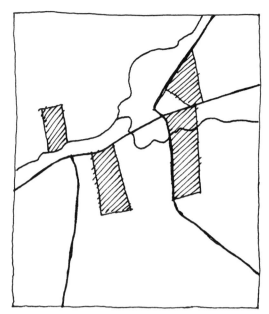

Figure 6-19a Available land.

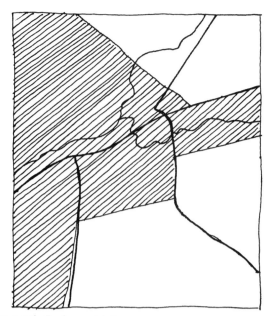

Figure 6-19b Zoning restrictions.

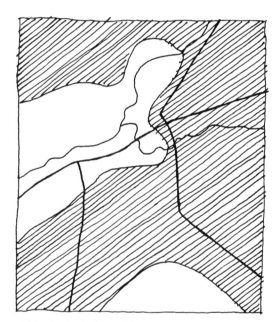

Figure 6-19c Geological conditions.

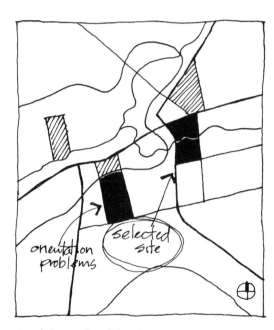

Figure 6-19d Composite of the three criteria.

CONTEXT

The identification of context variables helps the designer to set problem boundaries and places constraints on the number of design options available. The experienced architect welcomes these constraints because they help to focus his attention on the really viable alternatives. Context variables include site, climate, zoning or building ordinances, finances, time, and available construction technologies.

Site Selection

A composite graphic display of the effects of different criteria on site selection can assist both client and designer in choosing a site. The mapping starts by grouping several criteria under a few basic headings such as land availability (which might include the considerations of cost, opportunity, or services), geological characteristics, and zoning. Maps are made for each basic heading, showing the land that meets the criteria. The maps can then be overlaid to form one composite map. Now the most favorable sites can be easily identified and second-choice sites will also be evident.

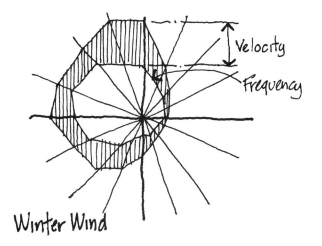

Figure 6-20a Direction and force of winter winds.

Figure 6-20b Direction and force of summer winds.

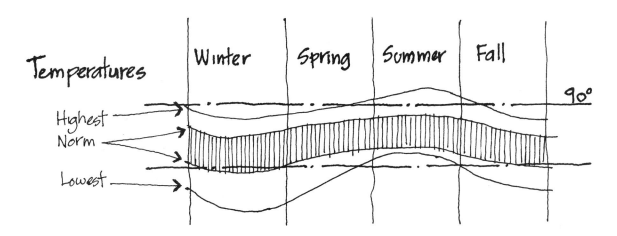

Figure 6-21 Annual temperature fluctuations.

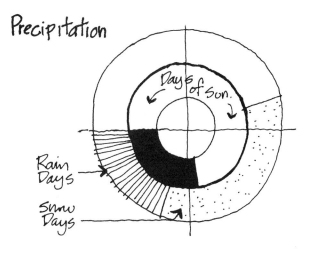

Figure 6-22 Sunlight and precipitation frequencies.

Other useful abstract sketches can present a more refined view of the action of climate over time. Because energy conservation is becoming a major consideration in housing design, we need more dynamic models of the action of climatic forces such as wind and sun. It is becoming easier to obtain reasonably accurate statistical data on weather, but the graphic presentation of this data is what makes it usable to the average designer.

Although climate is only one of several contextual elements that have an impact upon a design problem, climate considerations have traditionally been a dominant factor in architectural design. These diagrams can form the basis of a point of view about the problem that may be a source of basic design concepts.

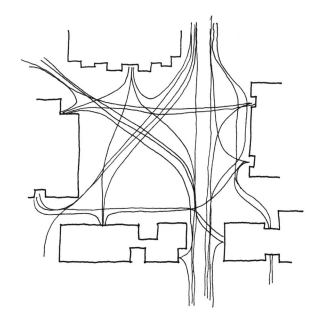

Figure 6-23a Circulation paths.

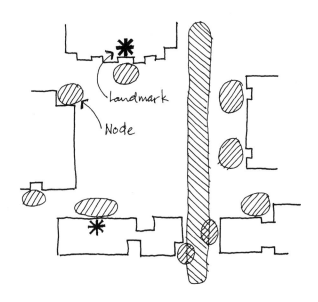

Figure 6-23b Social interaction zones.

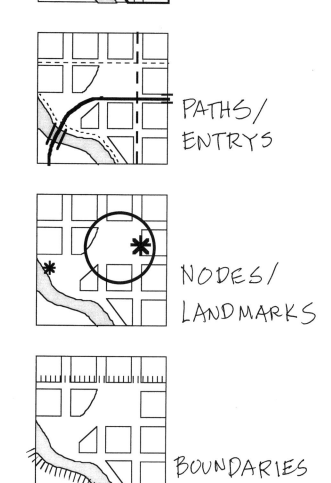

ZONES

PATHS/ ENTRYS

NODES/ LANDMARKS

BOUNDARIES

Figure 6-24 Urban image analysis.

Activity Patterns

When inserting a new structure within an existing environmental context, such as a college campus, current patterns of pedestrian activity should be an important consideration. The uppermost diagram above traces the dominant patterns of pedestrian movement and reflects to some extent their relative intensity. The lower diagram shows nodes or zones that are the most likely sites of social interaction. Landmarks are indicated because they often mark sites of arranged meetings between individuals. To the right is a series of site analysis diagrams based on analytical categories developed by Kevin Lynch.[6]

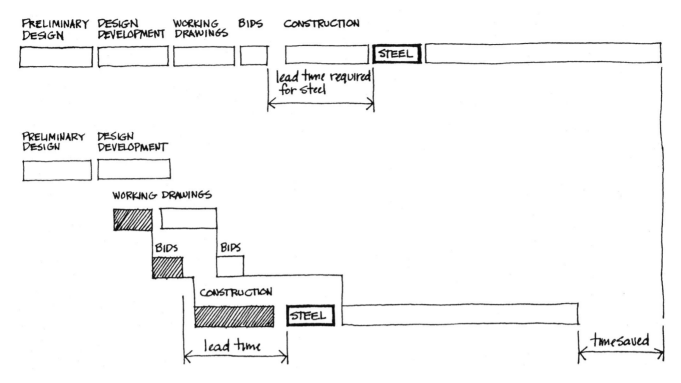

Figure 6-25 Comparative construction processes.

Construction Processes

Architects may overlook at times the impact of the construction process as a context for the design solution. Construction method is recognized as a strong determinant of form in vernacular architecture, and it is still influential in contemporary architectural design. With the pressures of financing and the variations in the cost of borrowing funds, innovations in construction processes are continually emerging. When these processes are included in the set of determinants of form, the designer enhances the probability of developing a successful design. Abstract representation of the alternative construction processes, as with other design determinants, promotes the designer's intuitive access to these considerations.

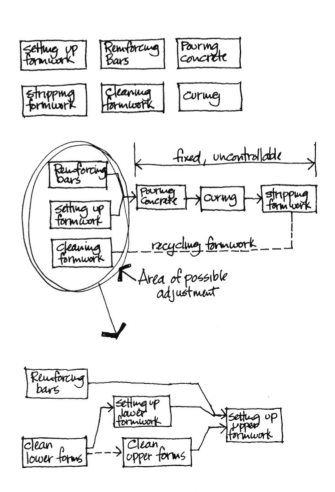

Figure 6-26 Construction sequence analysis.

Physical Site Analysis

Site features can include macro- and micro-climates, topography, natural circulation, views, and landscaping elements such as trees, bushes, rocks, or water. These site features must be considered in order to place and design a house. Abstract sketches can uncover problems and opportunities by showing the site features simultaneously. The illustration used here focuses on general site characteristics rather than on specific details. Focusing on generalities helps the designer to form a visual memory of the important site considerations. With the aid of these sketches, other perceptions can be derived, such as wind, privacy buffers, or the best site for building. For this recreational house, the sun pattern, the ridge of the land, and the summer breeze suggest the general orientation of the building. The existing site entry, disposition of the trees, and the small river to the south set up the prominent views and basic site circulation. This site analysis can be further extended, taking into account program area needs to explore some preliminary alternatives for building massing, as shown at the far right.

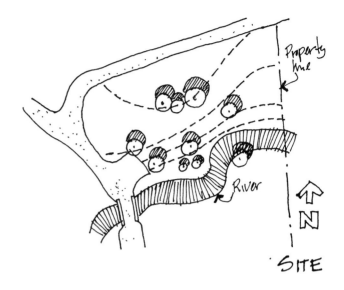

Figure 6-27a

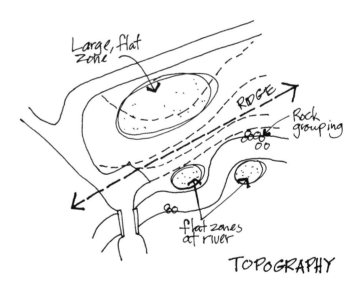

Figure 6-27b

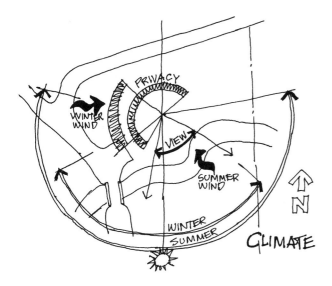

Figure 6-27c

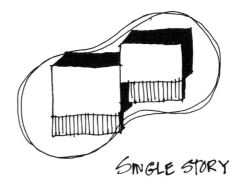

Figure 6-28a

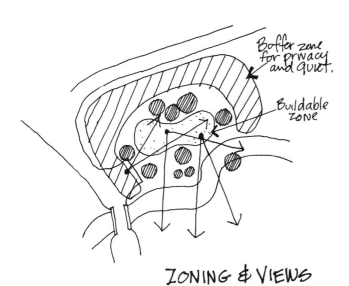

Figure 6-27d

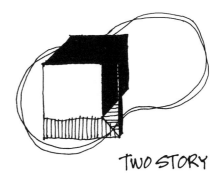

Figure 6-28b

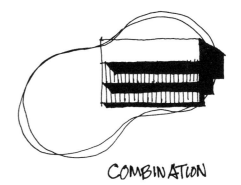

Figure 6-28c

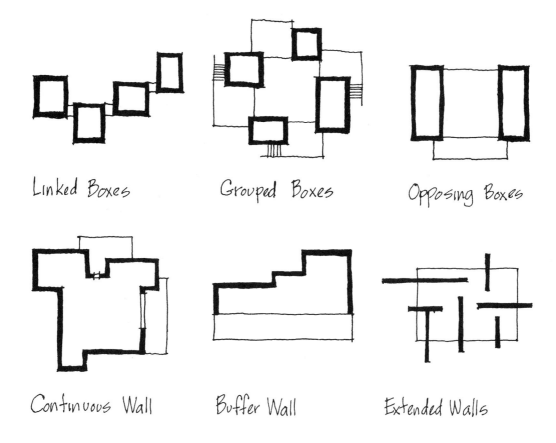

Linked Boxes   Grouped Boxes   Opposing Boxes

Continuous Wall   Buffer Wall   Extended Walls

FORM

The third set of variables, form, is under the control of the designer. In this area he can help the client make decisions after the need and context variables have been identified. But remember that the solution to the design problem is basically an agreement between need, context, and form. In a sense, all three sets of variables are flexible until a fit is achieved. Some designers expect the client's program and the context alone to dictate the solution, but form is equally important because there are a number of viable forms that meet specific needs. The architect must be as familiar with form variables as with those of need or context. The abstract sketches that follow are used to build a visual memory of form variables.

Space/Order

Variations of the spatial organization of a house are numerous. A few examples are shown here in plan diagrams using a similar drawing style to facilitate an easy comparison. The walls are drawn with heavy lines so the diagrams can emphasize space by clearly defining solid and void. Furthermore, titles are given to each organizational type as an important aid for easy recall.

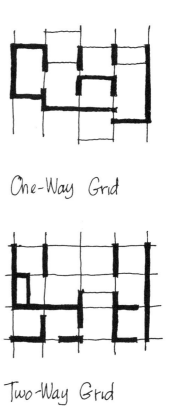

One-Way Grid

Two-Way Grid

Figure 6-29 Alternative spatial organizations shown in plan view.

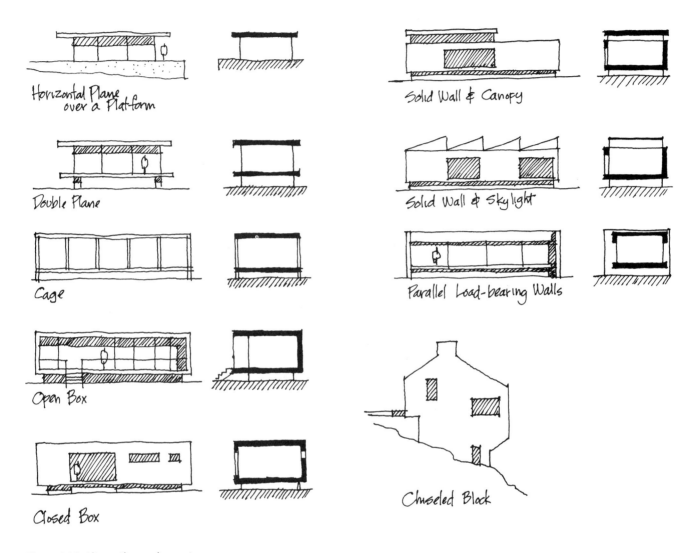

Figure 6-30 Alternative enclosure types.

Above, a range of organizational types shows three-dimensional options for spatial order and the implications for appearance. Structure and materials are also considered. Note how different approaches to enclosure can lead to variety in formal expression or aesthetic.

Figure 6-31 Important human-related sizes.

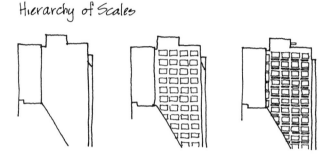

Figure 6-32 Dormitory building, New York University,
I. M. Pei and Associates, architects.

Scale/Proportion

Although they can enjoy the qualities of form, architects do not automatically perceive how the form variables are arranged to achieve a specific effect. In addition to their formal education, most architects spend a lifetime gathering insights or perceptions about such qualities.

One effective way of increasing perception is through visual analysis. The emphasis of a specific variable such as scale or rhythm in a sketch can be abstracted from the context of the building. Scale implies a relationship of sizes. The size of people is the handiest reference for other sizes; this is called *human scale.* Although it is obvious that all structures cannot be within our scale, we can feel more comfortable with a large building if certain of its features range in size from human scale to the overall building. Through graphic analysis, we can begin to understand how scale is handled in different buildings.

The effect of proportions on the design of a building can be represented for analysis in a similar way. Proportion is the relationship between dimensions (horizontal–vertical). Through abstraction, the impact of proportions on existing buildings can be better understood.

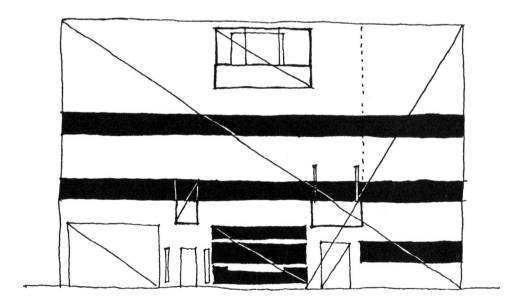

Figure 6-33 Entrance facade, villa at Garche, LeCorbusier.

Weight & Permanence

Figure 6-34 Traditional brick construction.

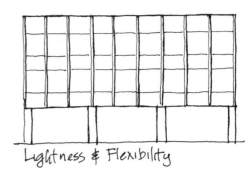

Lightness & Flexibility

Figure 6-35 Curtain wall construction.

Balance in asymmetrical facade composition

Figure 6-36 White Residence, Mitchel/Giurgola, architects.

Mass/Balance

Anyone who has taken up jogging is well aware of the importance of mass and balance in human experience. We all have a built-in sense of these qualities, causing us to respond to them in buildings. Furthermore, mass and balance are associated with many other feelings, such as security and flexibility. In a building, a sense of mass can convey security or permanence; a sense of airiness can convey flexibility or freedom. Throughout architectural history, many methods have been discovered for varying the apparent mass of buildings. By analyzing buildings that have clear sensations of mass, the use of such formal devices as horizontality, verticality, and emphasis can be uncovered.

Walking is a tremendous feat of balance. Much of the enjoyment of walking, riding a bike, skiing, and the like is derived from the tension between stability and instability. We have a finely tuned sense of balance that carries over into our visual perception. The different ways of articulating balance in building design can be also highlighted through abstract sketches. The sketches shown here deal with symmetrical and asymmetrical balance in composition and three-dimensional balance, an important part of architecture.

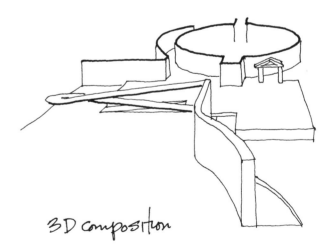

3D composition

Figure 6-37 Grabbeplatz at Dusselporf, James Stirling, architect.

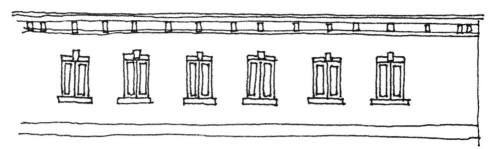

Figure 6-38 Evenly spaced windows.

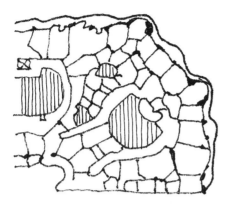

Figure 6-39 Casa Mila, Antonio Gaudi, architect.

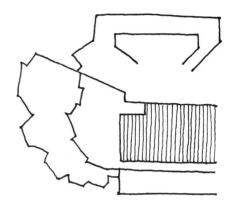

Figure 6-40 Wolfsberg Center, Alver Aalto, architect.

Repetition/Rhythm

One way of achieving unity in a building is through repetition of parts that are alike, such as windows or columns. Similarity of objects, even if only partially similar, is a way of emphasizing association. Members of the human race are recognized by a number of similar features in spite of the great diversity in their individual appearance.

The importance of rhythm in architecture is based upon its relationship to the human rhythms, walking or breathing, and the natural rhythms, the tide or the seasons. Just as music presents audio rhythms, architecture displays visual rhythms. In architecture, the principal means of achieving rhythm is spacing of parts; this is comparable to the intervals between beats or notes. The character of visual rhythms in a building depends on the size of both the intervals and the parts. Two basic types of rhythm can be identified. Staccato rhythm is formed by clear distinction between intervals and parts, such as mullions on a curtain wall. Legato rhythm is softer, formed by more subtle transitions between intervals and parts, as in the curvilinear architecture of Gaudi. There are also rhythms distinguishable by patterns of interval or part sizes, as in a facade by Palladio. And there are accelerating or decelerating rhythms, as in the Wolfsberg Center by Aalto.

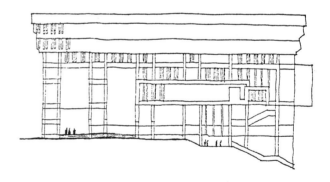

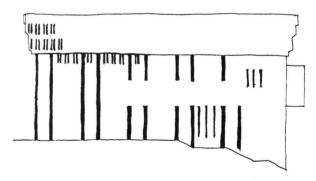

Figure 6-41 Boston City Hall.

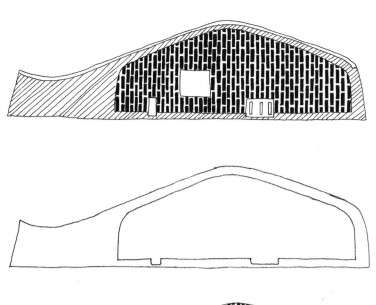

Unity/Diversity

The degree of unity or diversity expressed in a building constitutes another class of form variables. The other variables (scale, proportion, mass, balance, repetition, or rhythm) can be used to achieve unity or diversity. Some of the ways of increasing unity include framing or emphasizing a border; using a continuous pattern, modular grid, or a single shape, which is at the same scale as the building; and maintaining independence between the parts and the whole.

Diversity can be achieved by planned violation of the rules of unity: avoiding framing or consistent pattern; varying rhythms or modules; using multiple grids; and breaking up the dominating geometry.

Unity and diversity are not mutually exclusive; it is possible to overlay them and thereby increase the intensity of both attributes.

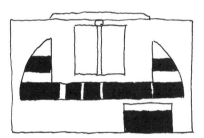

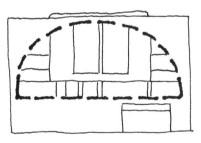

Figure 6-43 Ohio Town Hall project, Venturi and Rauch.

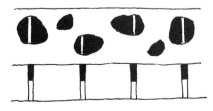

Figure 6-44 Assembly building at Chandigarh, LeCorbusier.

Form • **105**

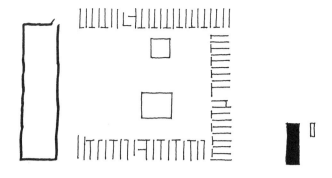

Figure 6-45 LaTourette monastery, LeCorbusier, architect.

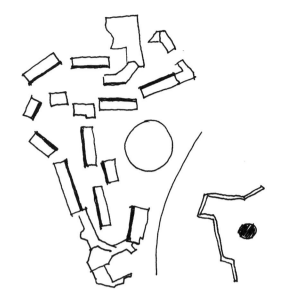

Figure 6-48 Kresge College, University of California, Santa Cruz, MTLW/Moore Turnbull, architects.

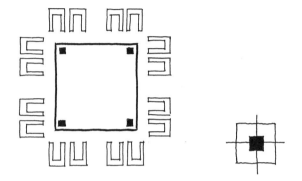

Figure 6-46 Hurva Synagogue project, Louis Kahn, architect.

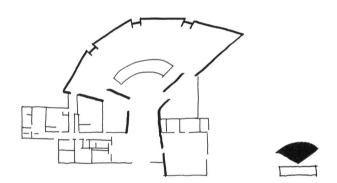

Figure 6-47 Mt. Angel Library, Alva Aalto, architect.

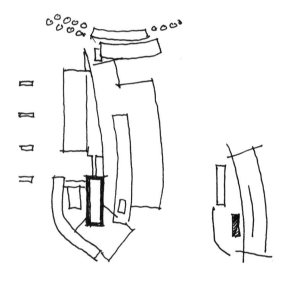

Figure 6-49 Amerika-Gedenkbibliothek, Berlin, Morphosis, architects.

Hierarchy

Conceptual strength and clarity often play an important role in the experience and use of a building. A sense of hierarchy can contribute much to the conceptual presence of architecture. Whether as analysis of existing buildings or as speculation about an emerging design, intentions can be highlighted by the use of abstract sketches such as those shown here. In corresponding sequence, starting at the top, the sketches in Figures 6-45, 6-46, and 6-47 present three approaches to hierarchy: dominant size, central location, and unique shape. As reflected in Figures 6-48, and 6-49, approaches to hierarchy are often combined to achieve greater impact.

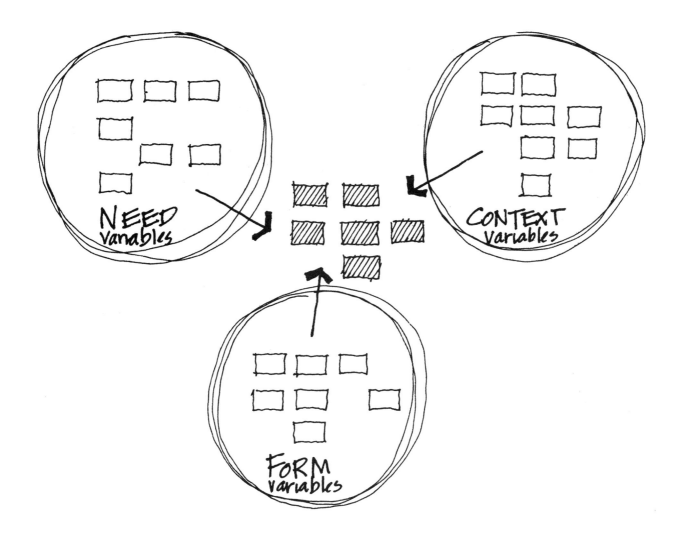

Figure 6-50

SOURCES OF SOLUTIONS

As was pointed out before, the origin of a design solution may be found in any one of the three types of variables: need, context, or form. On the following pages are case studies based on the recreational house example. In each study, an abstract diagram of one of the variables is used as the source of a basic organizing idea for the house; then constraints or considerations from the other types of variables are introduced to modify the concept. These studies should make clear some of the following advantages of abstract diagrams:

1. The variety of ideas visible at one time is very stimulating for thinking.
2. The differences in the three types of variables promote a variety of solution alternatives.
3. Attention is focused on general issues instead of details.

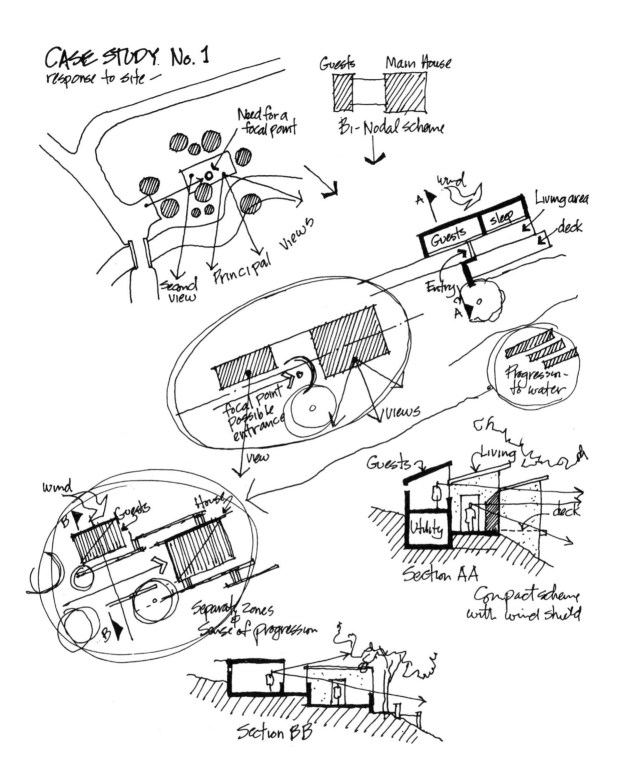

CASE STUDY. No. 1
response to site -

Need for a focal point

Guests   Main House

Bi-Nodal scheme

wind

Living area

Guests   sleep

deck

Entry

A

Principal   Views

Second view

focal point possible entrance

views

view

Progression to water

wind

B

Guests   House

B

Separate zones & sense of progression

Guests

Living

Utility

deck

Section AA

Compact scheme with wind shield

Section BB

Figure 6-51

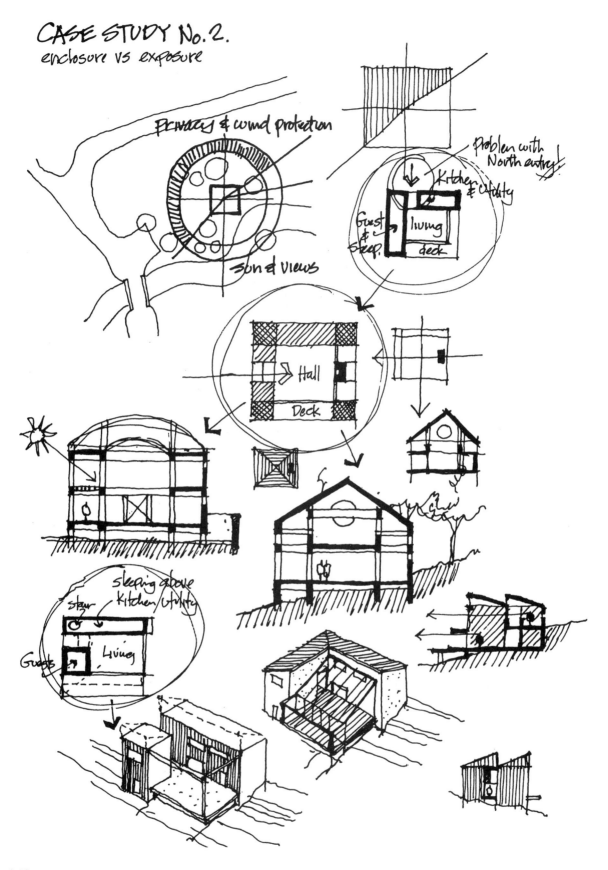

CASE STUDY No. 2.
enclosure vs exposure

Privacy & wind protection

sun & views

Problem with North entry!

Kitchen & utility

Guest & Sleep.

living

deck

Hall

Deck

sleeping above

kitchen/utility

stair

Guest

Living

Figure 6-52

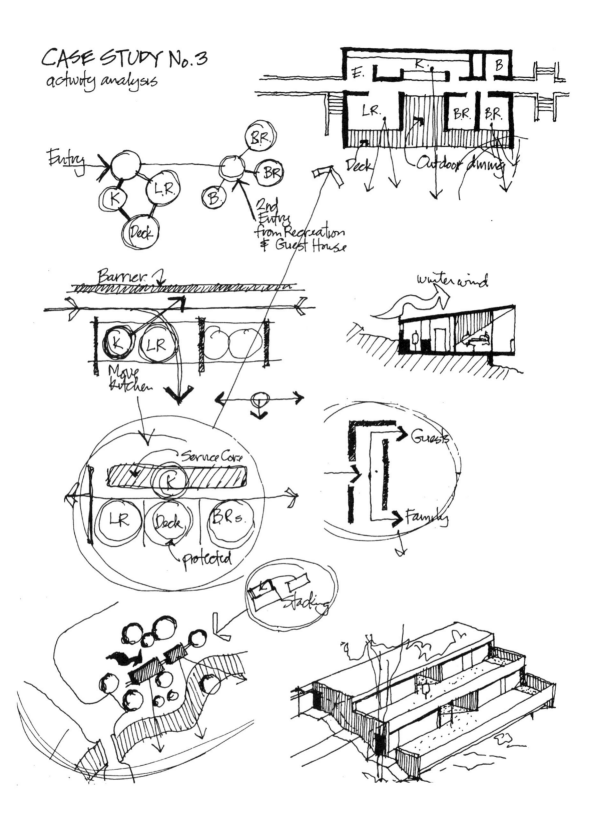

CASE STUDY No.3
activity analysis

Entry

K   L.R.
Deck

B   BR   BR.

2nd Entry from Recreation & Guest House

E.   K.   B

LR.   BR.   BR.

Deck   Outdoor dining

Barrier

K   LR

Move kitchen

winter wind

Service Core
R

LR   Deck   BRs.

protected

Guests

Family

stacking

Figure 6-53

110 • *Analysis*

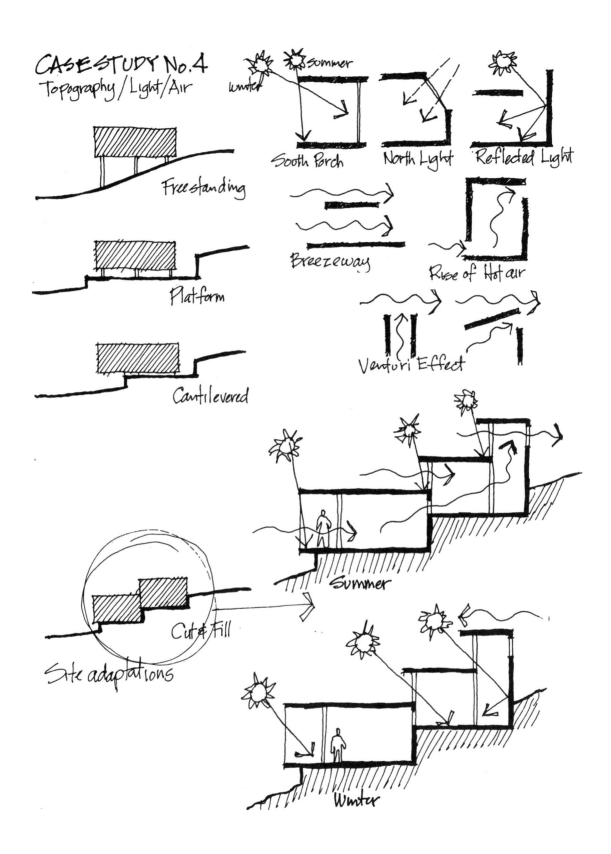

CASE STUDY No. 4
Topography / Light / Air

Freestanding

Platform

Cantilevered

South Porch

North Light

Reflected Light

Breezeway

Rise of Hot air

Venturi Effect

Site adaptations

Cut & Fill

Summer

Winter

Figure 6-54

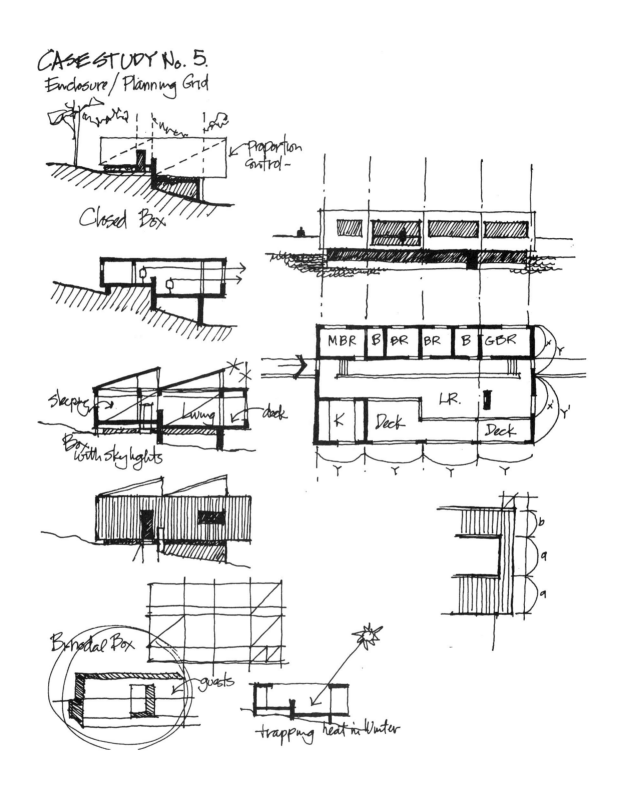

CASE STUDY No. 5.
Enclosure / Planning Grid

Closed Box

Proportion control—

MBR | B | BR | BR | B | GBR

LR.

K | Deck | Deck

sleeper

Living

deck

Box with Skylights

Bi-nodal Box

guests

trapping heat in Winter

Figure 6-55

112 • *Analysis*

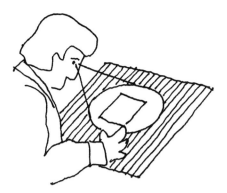

Figure 6-56 Viewing conditions.

ABSTRACTION AND PROBLEM SOLVING

The ultimate use of abstract diagrams is to help the designer commit to memory large amounts of project information. These diagrams can also be used directly as a record of design variables. The main advantage of diagrams as a graphic record is their immediately accessible information when all the diagrams are arranged in a large group. Creative designers fill sheets upon sheets of paper with diagrams and sketches of all types to record what they know and think about a design problem.

An abstract diagram must be simple and clear to be effective. If it contains more information than can be absorbed at a quick glance, it loses its effectiveness. Yet, it must provide enough information to form a distinct idea. Limiting the size of the diagram to a portion of our visual field is a method of partially controlling the amount of information given. A standard 8.5-by-11 sheet of paper fits within the visual field of a single individual, and the drawn diagrams can be as small as a half-dollar. When several designers work as a group, the visual field is expanded considerably. The firm of Caudill Rowlett Scott has developed the "analysis card" technique for group work. Diagrams, each about the size of a hand, are drawn on 5½-by-8¼ cards (I have personally tried 3-by-5 and 5-by-8 cards with success). During the problem analysis and design process, diagrams are drawn on the cards, which are then tacked on the wall for display to the group. This results in a continually updated display of the group's thinking. As an added benefit, the cards are easily moved to provide flexibility of ideas by association.

For legibility, ink or felt-tip pens are preferable to pencil or other media. Line weights should be geared to the viewing situation: a fine-line pen is good for the individual but a heavier marker is better for group display. Some architects make the translation from individual to group display by simple enlargement of the original diagrams or sketches.

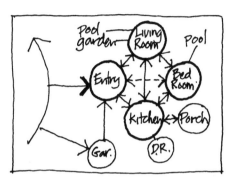

Too Complex

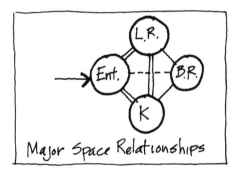

Major Space Relationships

Balance

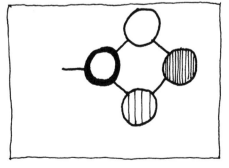

Too abstract

Figure 6-57 Analysis cards.

Figure 7-1

7 Exploration

While the architectural design process involves decision-making aimed at the reduction of alternatives in search of a final solution, it also involves elaboration aimed at expanding the range of possibilities. Most architects are not content to solve problems with existing knowledge; they want to expand their knowledge base at the same time. Architects are opportunity seekers as well as problem solvers. The drawings in this chapter are devoted to elaboration in the design process, deviation from the norm, expansion of thinking, and development of imagination.

We are just beginning to understand the untapped potential of our imaginations. Intuition, creativity, and imagination have traditionally been considered skills attributable to a limited group of people: inventors, artists, and geniuses. Many researchers of creativity share Koeberg and Bagnall's view that most people have the basic capacity for imagination but that it remains underdeveloped or unused:

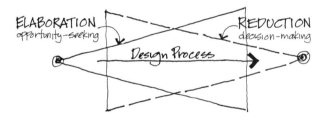

Figure 7-2

It is simple enough to list those "attributes of creativity" which are needed by the designer and to point out the reasons for their inclusion. But actual development and refinement of such behavioral characteristics is difficult since society makes it a relentless battle, an often thankless and rarely positively reinforced chore, to maintain such behavior. The same society which readily accepts the creative 'product' will chastise or deny the creative 'activity' required for such production because of its non-typical nature.[1]

Making creative behavior acceptable is the first step in promoting creativity in architectural design, and this chapter tries to provide more information about creative thinking with sketches to support it. If we can get through some of the mystery surrounding the personal approaches taken by architects, I believe specific techniques can be identified that make up a body of trainable skills.

Exploration can be defined as systematic investigation or traveling through an unfamiliar region in order to learn about it. The purpose of exploration in graphic thinking is the altering of graphic images so as to get a new look at them and thereby expand our thinking. We will be looking at three approaches to exploration:

1. Open-ended images that suggest a number of different perceptions or interpretations.
2. Transformation of images.
3. Structuring or ordering images.

These approaches are aimed at re-centering visual thinking. According to Robert McKim, "Re-centering vision is fundamentally an experience in unlearning. For most people, breaking lazy, category-hardened, fear-inducing habits of seeing is an educational task of considerable magnitude."[2] To make full use of these drawings for graphic thinking we must be comfortable with exploration that is not tightly focused, let the mind wander, and be open to unexpected results.

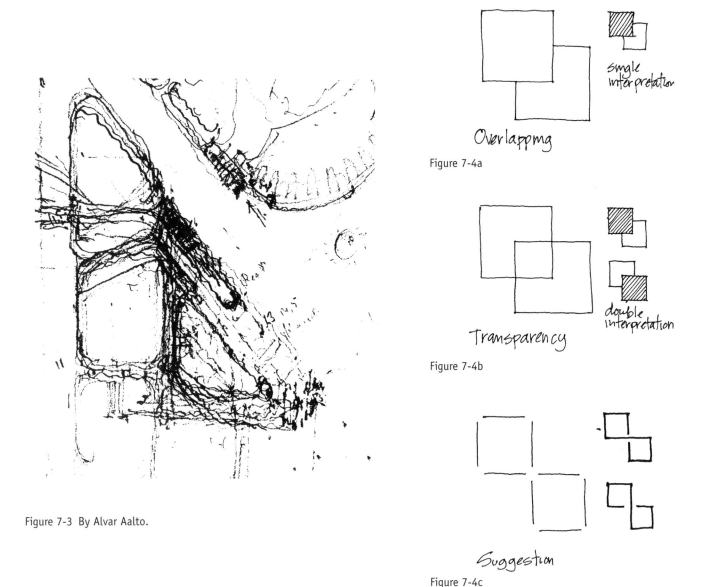

Figure 7-3 By Alvar Aalto.

Overlapping

single interpretation

Figure 7-4a

Transparency

double interpretation

Figure 7-4b

Suggestion

Figure 7-4c

OPEN-ENDED IMAGES

Terms like *ambiguous, collage,* and *multivalent* have been used to describe works of art and architecture that can be "read," interpreted, or appreciated simultaneously on several levels. These works are often said to have several meanings. Design sketches often have similar qualities of ambiguity, allowing the designer to think flexibly and in general terms. I refer to this as open-ended. Open-endedness can be achieved with transparency. This approach is based on the tradition of showing depth location by overlapping. Modern art introduced mutual overlapping: producing a transparent effect that allows two or more figures to occupy the same place. In concept, developing a transparency allows the designer to suspend decisions about the exact location of spaces or the boundaries between spaces.

Another approach to open-endedness is the incomplete, obscure sketch. By providing minimal information, the sketches focus on the most general issues while establishing the essential character of the architecture. The tentative feeling of the lines helps give some sketches an added sense of being temporary. To achieve a similar effect, some designers use a soft pencil to produce a wide, fuzzy line.

Open-ended sketches often convey a sense of immediacy and the confidence of the designer. Notice how a few lines provide impact. The white spaces help to pull the eye back to the key parts of the drawing. To produce effective sketches, the designer is required to work quickly and in a relaxed manner; the sketches should be an enjoyable process rather than an end in themselves.

Figure 7-5 By LeCorbusier. Strasbourg project.

Figure 7-6 By Louis Kahn. Concept study, University of Virginia
Chemistry Building.

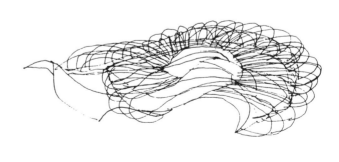

Figure 7-7 By Gerald Exline.

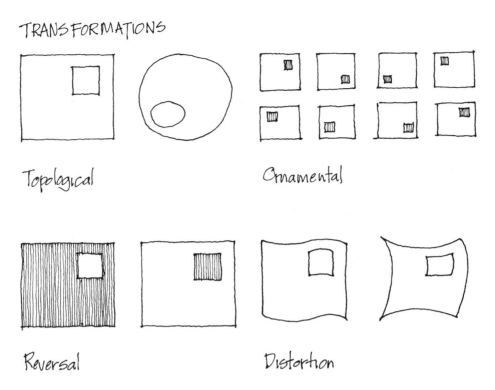

TRANSFORMATIONS

Topological

Ornamental

Reversal

Distortion

Figure 7-8 Four types of transformation.

TRANSFORMATIONS

The purpose of open-ended images is to invite changes in the images. Transformations, however, are specific changes made in the graphic images. The possibilities for change in graphic images are practically unlimited, but we will look at a few basic types of transformation. They are *topological continuity, ornamental grammar, reversals,* and *distortion.*

Graphic transformations can be very helpful to creativity in design. The stages of creativity have been described by Helen Rowan as "Preparation, Incubation, Illumination, and Verification.... the period of incubation frees the individual from previous fixations, he is then able to see the problem with new eyes when he returns to it."[3] Transformations are aimed at changing perspective or perceptions, making the familiar seem strange. It is important to remember that a period of preparation must precede incubation. The designer prepares by becoming immersed in the problem, trying to understand all the variables of need, context, and form. Once the problem becomes imbedded in his mind, he attempts to overcome preconceptions about the possible solutions by changing the existing graphic images.

Topological Continuity

In mathematics, the term *topology* is defined as "the study of those properties of geometric figures that remain unchanged even when under distortion, so long as no surfaces are torn."[4] A practical example of two objects topologically similar but different in appearance is the doughnut and the cup. The transformation from doughnut to cup shows how the same basic surface relationships are retained while the form is pushed and pulled.

A similar topological continuity is important to the exploration of design images. Many architectural students mistake a specific arrangement of parts for a topological or essential relationship of parts. If the true topological characteristics of a diagram are identified, many other arrangements of the parts can be explored.

March and Steadman pointed out the potential of topological continuity in comparing three houses by Frank Lloyd Wright:

In them he uses a range of "grammars," by which he meant, above all, the controlling geometric unit which ordered the plan and pervaded the details.... Whilst they may look different, they are in fact topologically equivalent. If each functional space is mapped on to a point and if, when two spaces interconnect, a line is drawn between their representative points...we find that they (the houses) are topologically equivalent in plan. Therefore, one topological structure was open to three very different expressions.[5]

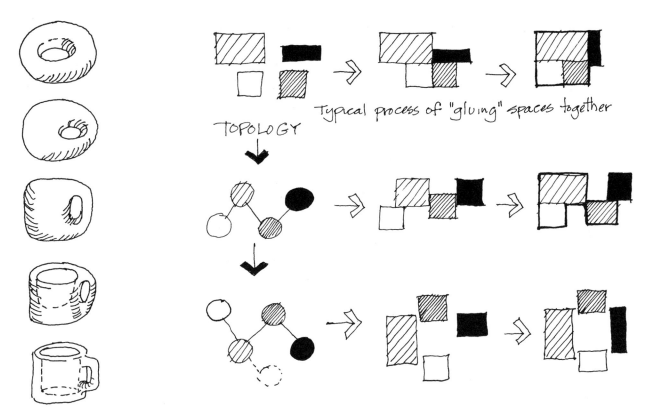

Figure 7-9a Topological similarity between a doughnut and a cup.

TOPOLOGY

Typical process of "gluing" spaces together

Figure 7-9b Evolution of topologically equivalent house plans.

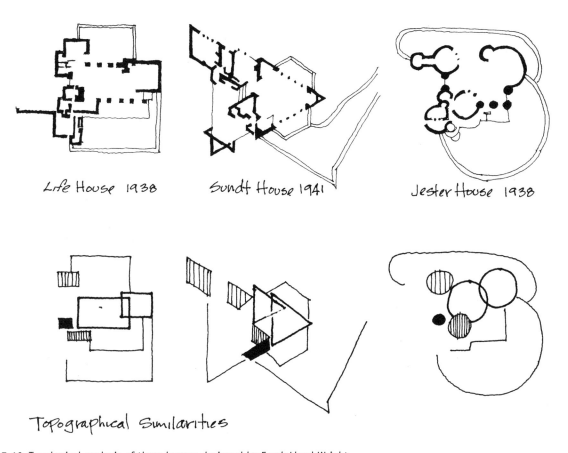

Life House 1938

Sundt House 1941

Jester House 1938

Topographical Similarities

Figure 7-10 Topological analysis of three houses designed by Frank Lloyd Wright.

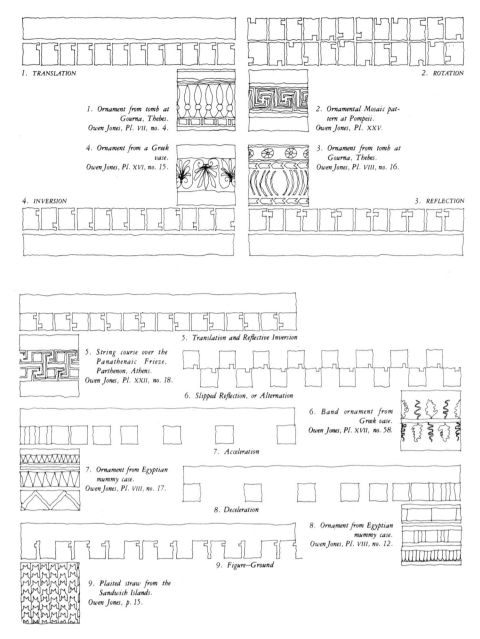

Figure 7-11 By Thomas Beeby. Basic manipulations of ornament.

Ornamental Grammar

Thomas Beeby, in his article "The Grammar of Ornament/Ornament as Grammar," clearly illustrates the application of ornamental grammar to building massing and design at many scales by the master architects of the modern movement. Specifically in the work of LeCorbusier, he shows the impact of the traditional training in ornamentation principles. A direct means of achieving a rich complexity in building forms is revealed. "LeCorbusier's early training in ornament placed a valuable method of working within his grasp. The principles found in Owen Jones and transmitted to LeCorbusier through L'Eplattenier remained with him throughout his career."[6]

As Beeby describes,

[There are] four basic manipulations of a unit to create ornament: translation, rotation, reflection, and inversion. The simplest type of band ornament, translation (illustration 1), is the repetition of the unit, always in the same orientation, along a horizontal axis. Rotation (illustration 2) is the repetition of the unit around the point of intersection of two adjacent sides. It accounts for pinwheels and other spiral configurations. With translation and rotation,

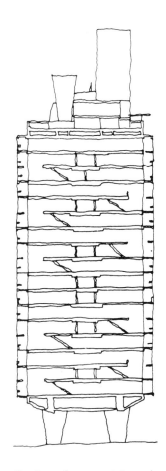

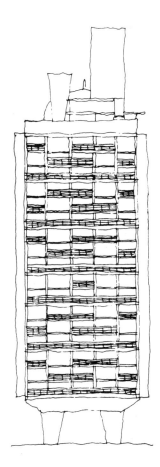

Figure 7-12 By Thomas Beeby. Applications of ornamental grammar.

the unit merely slides along the surface of the plane, in a straight line or a circle, but in both reflection and inversion the unit is flipped over in space to present its under side. With reflection (illustration 3), the unit is flipped over on one of its edges, producing bilateral, or mirror, symmetry. With inversion (illustration 4), the unit is flipped over its central horizontal axis. More complex configurations are derived from a combination of these four basic operations. Translation accompanied by reflection is probably the most familiar. Translation accompanied by reflective inversion is another typical operation (illustration 5). The complexity increases through devices such as shifts along the horizontal axis, or glide line, leaving gaps between units, to produce slipped reflection or alternation (illustration 6).... Also, by accelerating (illustration 7) or decelerating (illustration 8), the rhythm through decreasing or increasing either the size of the units or the distance between them, one can transform scale.[7]

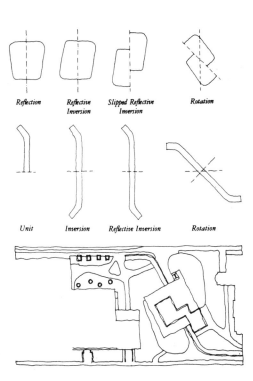

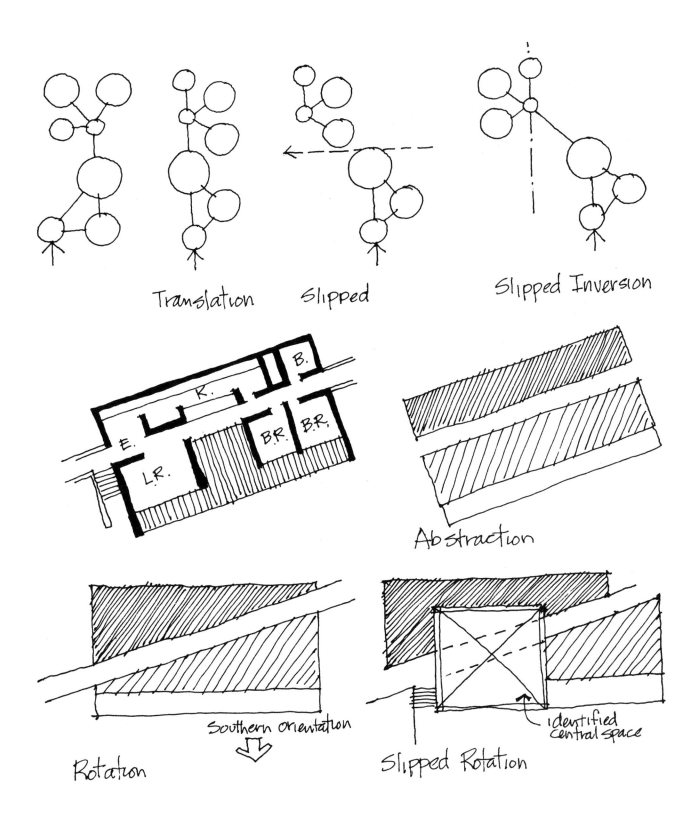

Translation   Slipped   Slipped Inversion

Abstraction

Southern orientation

Rotation

Slipped Rotation

identified central space

Figure 7-13 Applications of ornamental grammar.

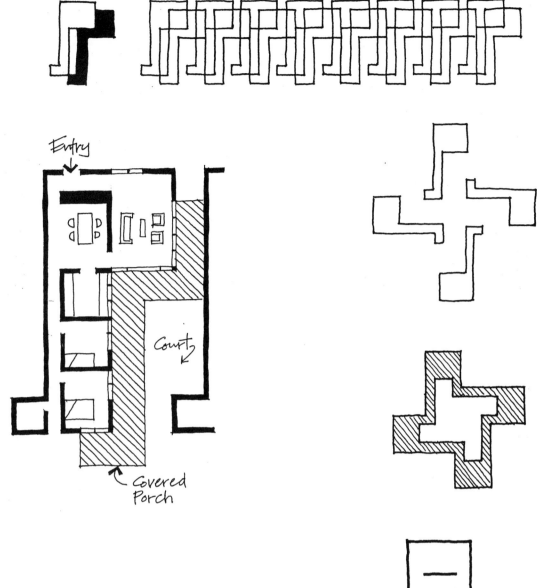

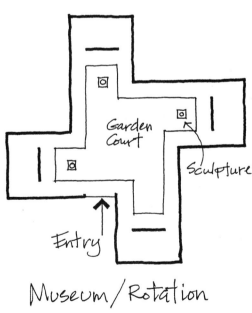

The implications of ornamental grammar for building design and planning are significant, but there are additional implications for the design process. Ornamental grammar can be used to transform more abstract graphic images, routinely uncovering new thinking. For example, we could take a program bubble diagram and through its rotation, reflection, or inversion change the starting point in problem solving. Another approach would start with a schematic plan; from this, an analysis drawing would be made to reduce the concept to basics, and the abstract drawing would be run through some ornamental transformations to uncover alternative concepts or insights into the structure of the original design.

We might also freely experiment with form, as shown above, and then seek a match between forms and known design programs.

Figure 7-14 Applications of ornamental grammar.

Figure 7-15

Reversals

Reversals are changes in an image from its first characteristics to opposite characteristics (light to dark, object to space, open to closed, etc.). Their usefulness derives from the qualities of the contrasting complement. The Chinese philosopher Lao-Tzu held that the essence of everything we could see lies in what we cannot see; the essence of man is not in his physical appearance, and the essence of architecture is not in the visible structure. The Taoist symbol yin and yang represents the absence of order, chaos, as a black background; the two revolving forms are yin and yang, the contrasting complements that make up order, night and day, a musical note and a pause, active and passive. The ideal condition, perfection, is symbolized as a dynamic balance between opposites: groups of people are defined by individuals and individuals are defined by groups; the color of an orange changes in intensity with the changing background.

Architectural examples of complements are walls and openings, materials and the joints between materials, vertical and horizontal, rectilinear and curvilinear. To change our perceptions, we change the emphasis of an image to its complement or contrast. The simplest form of reversal is called figure-ground drawing. Two sketches are made of a subject such as the Piazza San Marco (opposite). In one sketch, the buildings are shown in solid black and in the other sketch, the space between the buildings is shown in black. By looking at the two sketches at the same time, it is possible to get a better understanding of both space and buildings and the relationship between them. Figure-ground sketches can be used to study elevations of buildings, patterns, profiles, massing, and many other problems.

Figure 7-16 Figure/ground sketch, Piazza San Marco.

Figure 7-17 Reversals of architectural experience.

Another type of reversal is experience reversal. If the normal kinesthetic experience of a church progresses from small to large scaled spaces, a reversal of scale can evolve a new form. If it is normal for a beachfront house to be open and be oriented to the view, introduce enclosure and inward orientation. The design of a Japanese teahouse employs a wall to deny views in order to intensify the view seen through a small window. Designers sometimes have a problem trying to hide a building element; the solution could instead be to emphasize that very element.

Graphic images can also be used to reverse thinking processes. Instead of thinking of spaces as bubbles glued together, consider them as carved out of a solid block.

1. If a circulation sequence has been seen as a series of spaces, concentrate instead on the passages.
2. When a student gets hung up on one design solution or has trouble developing an idea, I suggest that the given building program be forced into a typical facility for a highly contrasting program or activity, for example, banking in a restaurant, a hospital function in a country club setting, or a home in a factory.

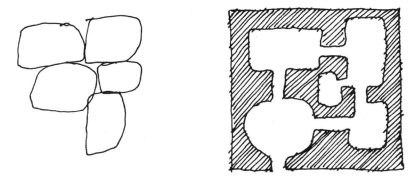

Figure 7-18a Reversal of perception, positive vs. negative space.

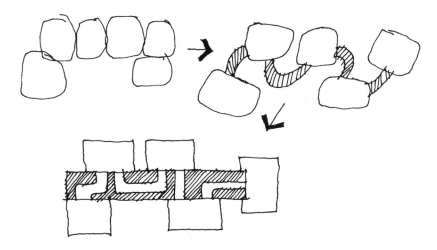

Figure 7-18b Links vs. nodes.

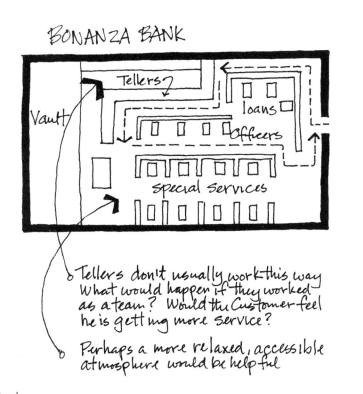

BONANZA BANK

Tellers

Vault

loans

Officers

special Services

○ Tellers don't usually work this way
What would happen if they worked
as a team? Would the Customer feel
he is getting more service?

○ Perhaps a more relaxed, accessible
atmosphere would be helpful

Figure 7-18c Restaurant vs. bank.

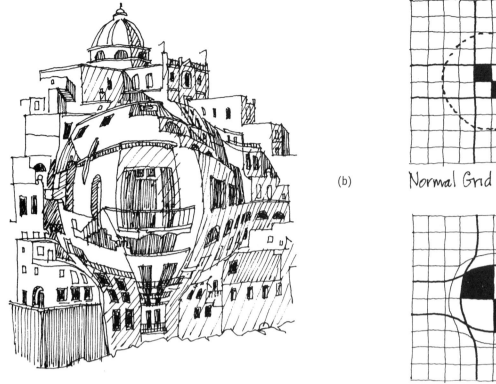

Figure 7-19a After M. C. Escher Lithograph, Balcony, 1945.

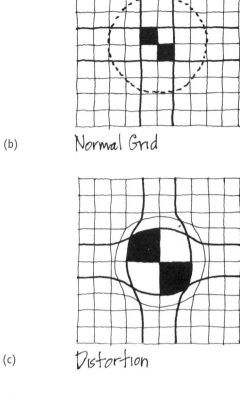

(b) Normal Grid

(c) Distortion

Figure 7-19b, c Analysis of lithograph.

Distortion

The Dutch artist M. C. Escher created a wonderful world of fantasy through optical illusions based on the representational systems of the Renaissance. He achieved distortions that dramatically alter our view of reality through simple manipulation of these representational systems, as in the lithograph *Balcony*. By way of an exaggeration of the projection method used for maps of the world, he imposes a simple grid over the conventional drawing and then doubles the size of the central section; thus the distorted grid is used as a reference system to complete the drawing.

The grid-manipulation method can be used as a simple way of distorting other types of images. For our purpose, the grids should be kept quite simple to remain in a sketch style. The examples of the bubble diagram on this page and the building plan on the facing page show just a few of the possibilities for grid distortion. Simple magnification or reduction of the scale of an image can produce a distorted effect. In addition, a number of special projection techniques, such as 360-degree views, are potential tools for distortion sketches.

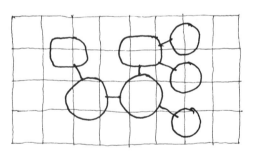

(a) Normal Grid

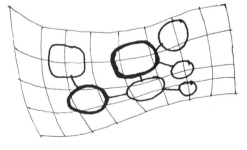

(b) Distortion

Figure 7-20a, b Distortion of a bubble diagram.

Figure 7-22 Variations on distortion.

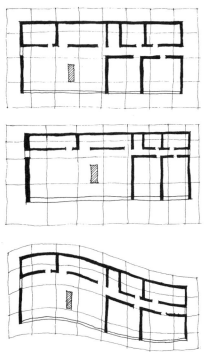

Figure 7-21 Distortions of a plan sketch.

Figure 7-23 Distorted projection.

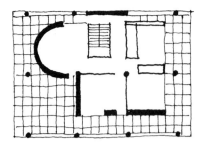

Villa at Carthage

Figure 7-24 Villa at Carthage, LeCorbusier.

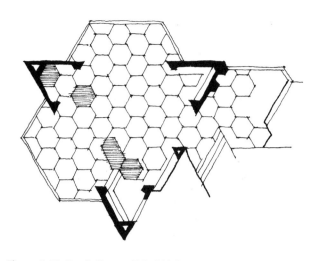

Figure 7-27 Sundt House, F. L. Wright.

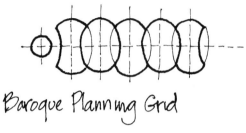

Baroque Planning Grid

Figure 7-25 Combinatory system of spatial elements, after C. Norberg-Schulz.

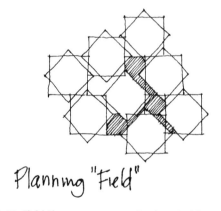

Planning "Field"

Figure 7-26 Field theory space organization, Architecture and Art Building, University of Illinois at Chicago, Walter Netsch of Skidmore Owings & Merrill, architects.

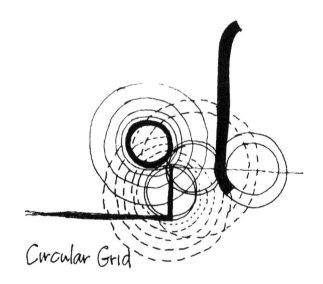

Circular Grid

Figure 7-28 Casa Papanice, P. Portoghesi, and V. Gigliotti, architects.

STRUCTURING OR ORDERING IMAGES

Peter Carl made an important observation about the *plan libre* developed by LeCorbusier, represented here by the plan for the villa at Carthage: "The importance of this invention is twofold: the use of gridded and layered space as a contextual device, and the nature of subsequent spatial gestures on those terms."[8] This is the basis for another method of transformation of images, namely, the use of ordering devices to create an artificial context within which new responses can be made.

Of course, generation of space and form by the use of geometrical patterns is not a new approach. In the eighteenth century, K. I. Dietzenhofer used a pattern of interlocking ovals to develop his baroque church plan. Frank Lloyd Wright used rectilinear, triangular, and circular grids as the basis for house designs. More recently, Walter Netsch designed buildings based on two square grids rotated to a 45-degree relationship, and Portoghesi and Gigliotti have developed houses within circular fields.[9]

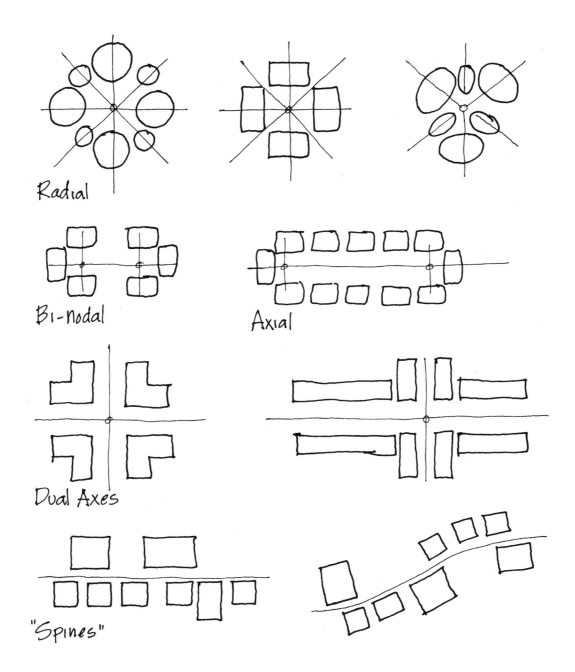

Radial

Bi-nodal   Axial

Dual Axes

"Spines"

Figure 7-29 Basic ordering devices.

Points and lines can be used in images for ordering functions or spaces, transforming the information into a new form. Points provide a focus for radial compositions of a wide variety. When two points are placed in close proximity, binodal configurations can be developed, but as the two points are pulled farther apart, a line is formed, opening up a number of axial arrangements. Axial orders include dual axes, major with minor axes, and parallel axes. Lines can also be used as "spines" for collecting and organizing a num-

ber of different spaces. These lines, referred to as *datums,* can be straight or curvilinear.

Above, the basic orders of point and line are extended or combined to form several ordering devices of varying degrees of complexity. They are not included as a kit of devices so much as they are meant to suggest possible manipulation alternatives by which each designer may explore his own tools.

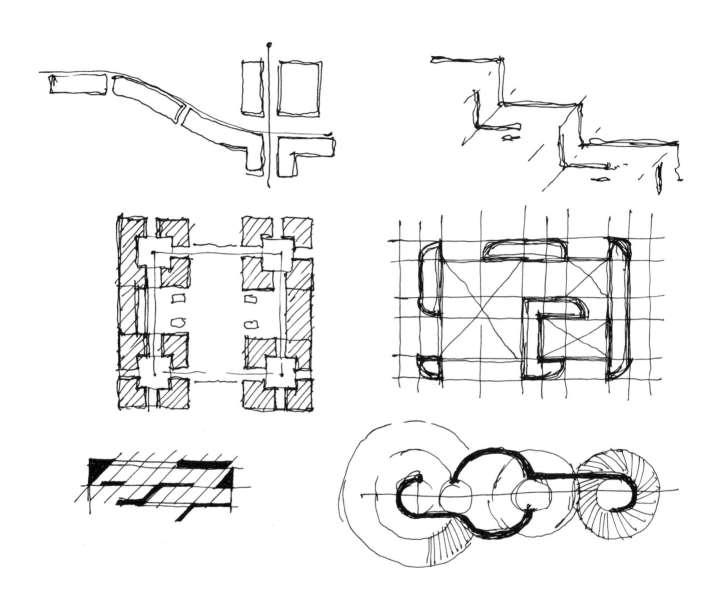

Figure 7-30 Extensions of ordering devices.

Matrix

The matrix provides still another way of applying order to the transformation of images. The example at right illustrates the basic application of a matrix. Different concepts of building placement on the site are shown across the top, and different degrees of articulation are indicated in the vertical direction. By showing the combinations of the two considerations, a number of forms evolve. The example below (from a student project) is a search for alternative configurations of an urban zone development. The basic orders are shown in the left vertical column and different combinations of city blocks in the right column. From these, different interpretations are formed.

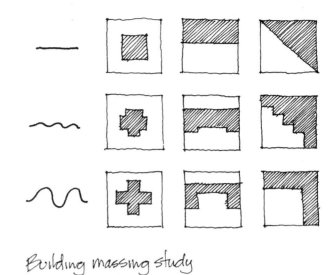

Building massing study

Figure 7-31 Matrix diagram of building massing alternatives.

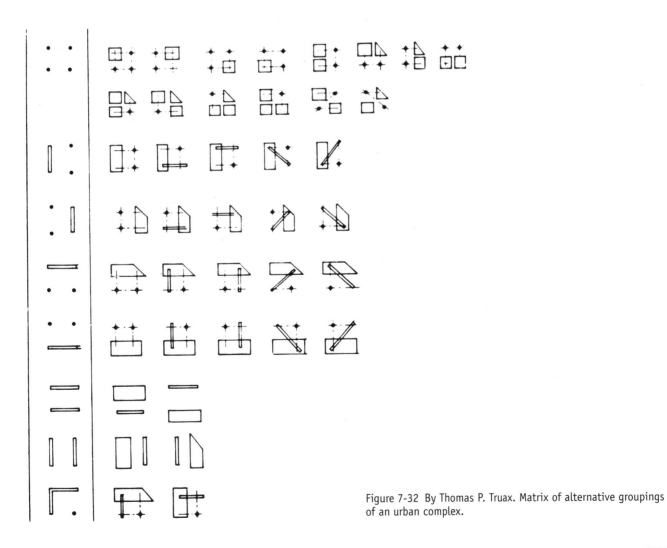

Figure 7-32 By Thomas P. Truax. Matrix of alternative groupings of an urban complex.

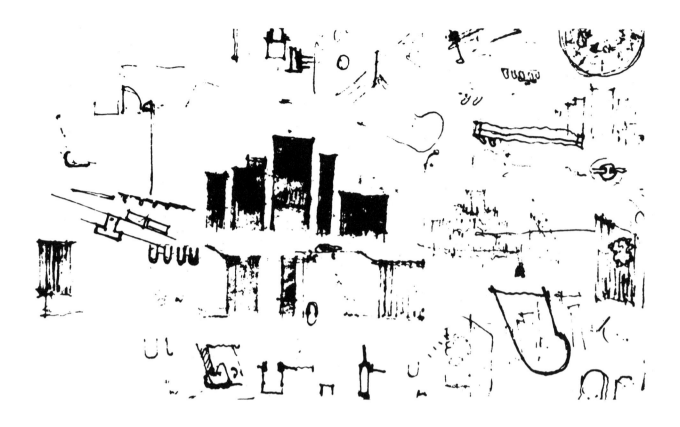

Figure 7-33 By Alvar Aalto.

A Pyramid of Possibilities

It is my hope that, as you begin to experiment with some of the sketch techniques in this chapter, the loosening up and freedom from rigid thinking will open up an exciting new perspective about designing. It can be an energizing experience that becomes addictive. Relax and enjoy it!

Part of the potential of exploration derives from the fact that ideas breed ideas. As the graphic thinking cycle gets moving with ease, the group of ideas rapidly expands in a very rough pyramidal progression. If only two new images are perceived for each one drawn, the growth in ideas can be amazing, but for many designers this is a big "if." They are afraid of wasting time by following their instincts or indulging in the fantasies of free association. Designers also have difficulty in suspending judg-

ment of ideas; they censor them before they ever get them on paper, and so they never get a chance to have a new look at their ideas, detached from themselves. The situation is comparable to an aspiring songwriter who never plays his music for other people. In isolation, he may be able to develop it to a point, but without testing it through the responses of other people, he will be handicapped.

If we look closely at the notes and sketches of some architects, the rapid growth of ideas becomes obvious. The growth is sporadic and multidirectional. Attention shifts from the scale of a plan or site plan to details of windows or handrails. There are also shifts in the types of sketches. Some architects rely heavily on plans as vehicles for concept development; others work exclusively in elevations, while still others are most comfortable with perspective sketches.

Figure 7-34 By Thomas Beeby.

In this short chapter, we have looked at the use of exploration in sketches as an aid to the processes of design incubation and creativity, but we have touched on only a portion of the material available that concerns the promotion of creativity. For a list of particularly good sources on this subject, check the bibliography in the back of the book under Creativity. In addition to the case studies on the following pages, a helpful list of manipulative verbs from *Design Yourself,* by Kurt Hanks, Larry Belliston, and Dave Edwards,[10] might stimulate some ideas of your own:

Multiply	Divide	Eliminate
Subdue	Invert	Separate
Transpose	Unify	Search
Delay	Distort	Rotate
Flatten	Squeeze	Complement
Submerge	Freeze	Soften
Weigh	Destroy	Concentrate
Fluff-up	Bypass	Add
Subtract	Lighten	Repeat
Thicken	Stretch	Adapt
Relate	Extrude	Repel
Protect	Segregate	Integrate
Symbolize	Abstract	Dissect

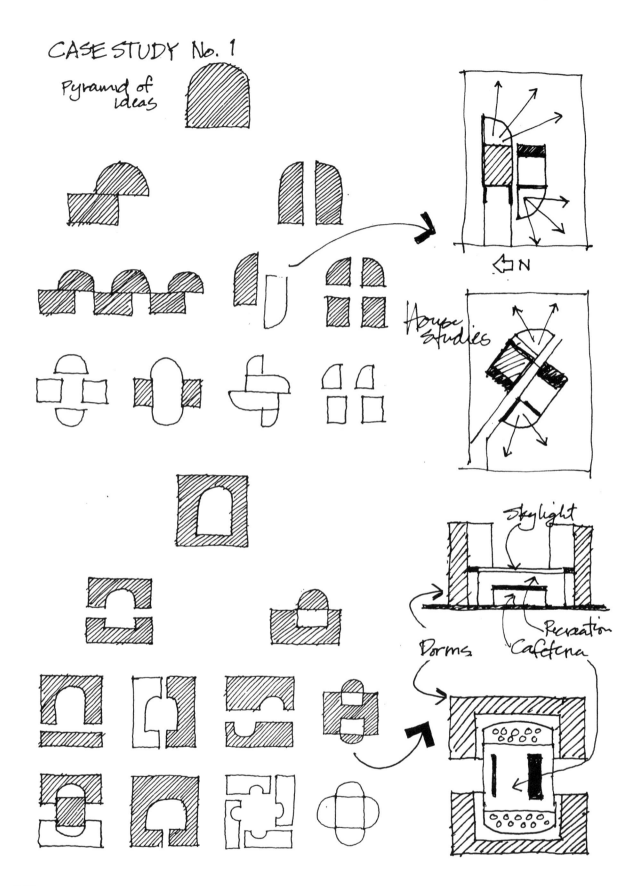

CASE STUDY No. 1

Pyramid of ideas

House Studies

N

Skylight

Dorms

Recreation

Cafeteria

Figure 7-35

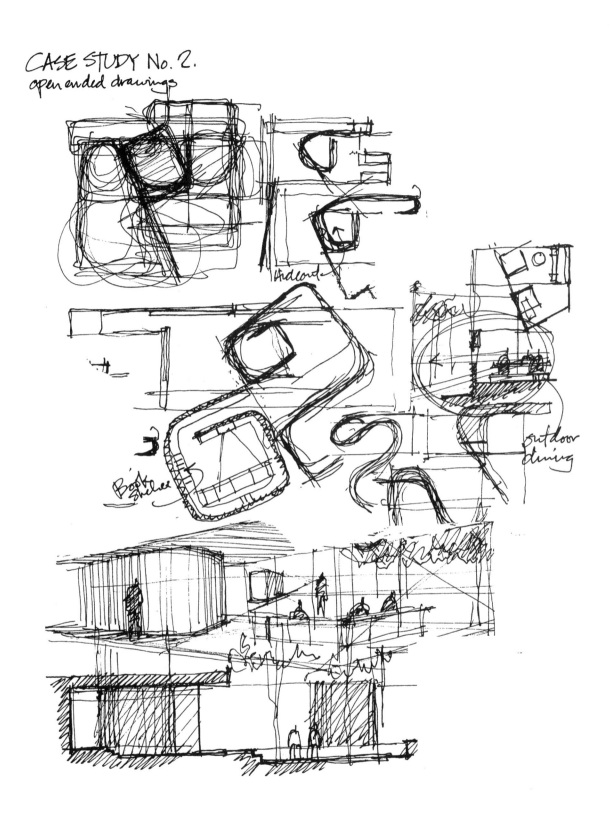

CASE STUDY No. 2.
open ended drawings

Figure 7-36

CASE STUDY No. 3
reversals/

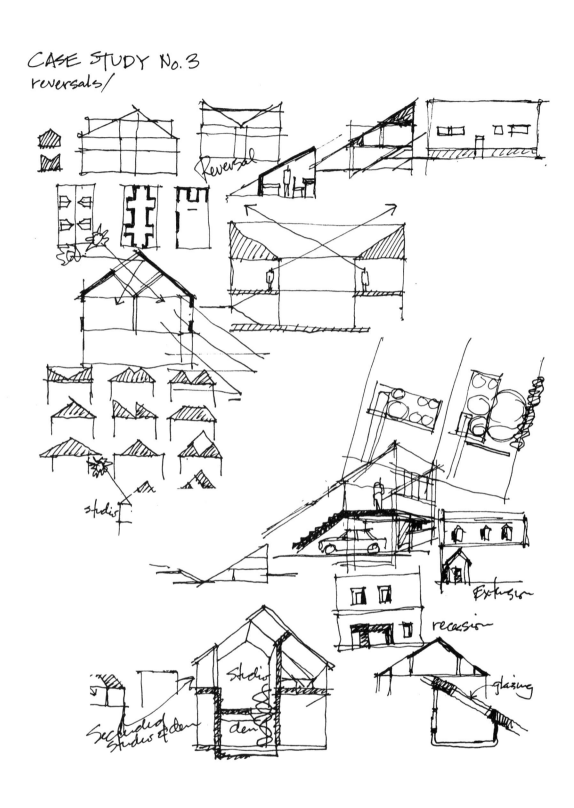

Figure 7-37

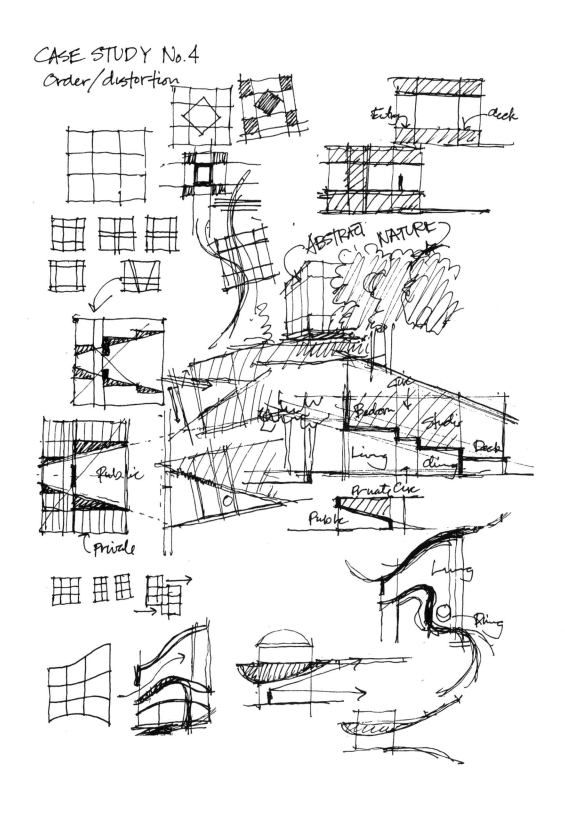

CASE STUDY No.4
Order/distortion

Figure 7-38

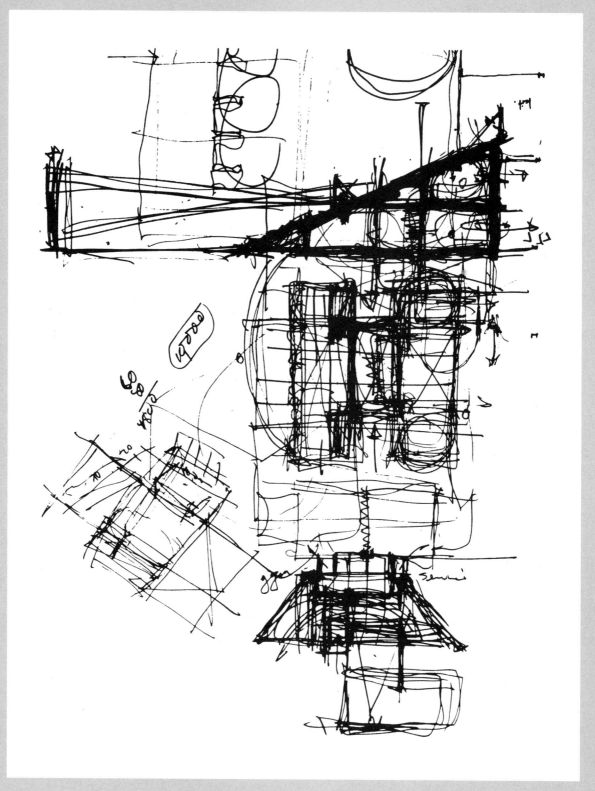

Figure 8-1 By David Stieglitz. Conceptual sketch.

8 Discovery

Most architects recognize discovery or invention as an important focus of their work. It is the satisfying payoff that beckons the creative mind. The intensity of concentration in thinking is very exciting. Look at the sketch by David Stieglitz on the facing page. It immediately shows us the energy, the action, the joy of discovery. It also reveals the skill and confidence with which the architect attacks his project.

Figure 8-2

The success of discovery in design is greatly dependent on the quality and quantity of the other types of graphic thinking. Discovery can be compared to picking and arranging a bouquet of flowers, which requires a sense of design and practice. Graphic representation, abstraction, exploration, verification, and stimulation are comparable to the preparation of the garden, the planting and tending of the flowers, without which there would be no bou-

quet. Discovery brings the power of the different types of graphic thinking to bear on a problem at a moment in time.

Before getting into the graphics that express discovery, I would like to digress for a moment and discuss creativity in the profession of architecture. The field of architecture is commonly viewed as being creative, and certainly some of the most creative individuals are architects. I believe that an architectural education is still one of the best curriculums for training creativity, although it is not a guarantee. Helen Rowan's report on studies of creative people identifies qualities they all seem to share. These include "a general openness to experience from both without and within; a toleration for ambiguity, confusion and disorder; the strong disposition to be independent rather than conforming; and the tendency to perceive through intuition focuses upon possibilities..."[1] Anyone who is or has been an architecture student will recognize these qualities; they permeate the traditions of architectural training from the wide variety of project types to critics and juries, to strong conflicts of opinion, to having to defend one's ideas, to being asked to go further than just solving the problem.

Still, there is a question in practice about the overall impact of creativity on the design process. Out of expediency or lack of support from clients or colleagues, we may neglect the development of our creative abilities. We can and should foster creativity in architecture for our own sake as well as that of the profession. As Helen Rowan put it, "...the experience of this century suggests that the quality of individual life, and perhaps the survival of human life as a whole, depends on the ability and disposition of human beings to think original thoughts, to reshuffle familiar facts into new patterns of meaning, to perceive reality behind illusion, and to engage in daring leaps of the imagination."[2]

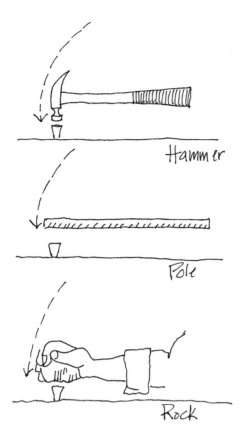

Figure 8-3 Leverage.

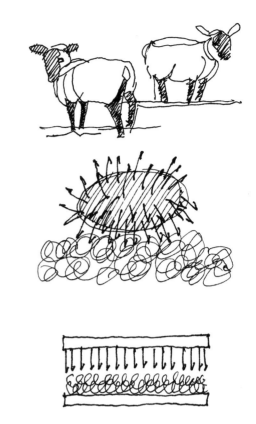

Figure 8-4 Fastening.

THE DISCOVERY PROCESS

For the architect or the designer, the process of discovery consists of two parts: *invention* and *concept formation*. Invention seeks the basic discovery, the original idea for the project; concept formation converts the discovery into a graphic and verbal statement that can give basic direction to the full development of the project.

Invention

David Pye wrote that invention "can only be done deliberately, if the inventor can discern similarities between the particular result which he is envisaging and some other actual result which he has seen and stored in his memory.... An inventor's power to invent depends on his ability to see analogies between results and, secondarily, on his ability to see them between devices."[3] The analogies are easily recognized in our everyday inventions. If we lack a hammer to drive tent stakes into the ground, we gain an insight to the solution by seeing a tent pole section or a rock at arm's length analogous to a hammer. Burrs caught in sheep wool were the inspiration for Velcro fasteners, and the cooling effect of the evaporation of perspiration from our skin is the basis of the idea of using semiporous containers to keep water cool.

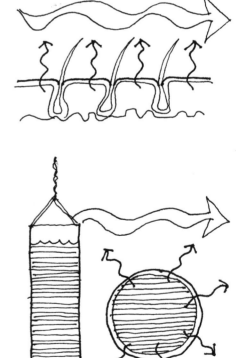

Figure 8-5 Evaporation.

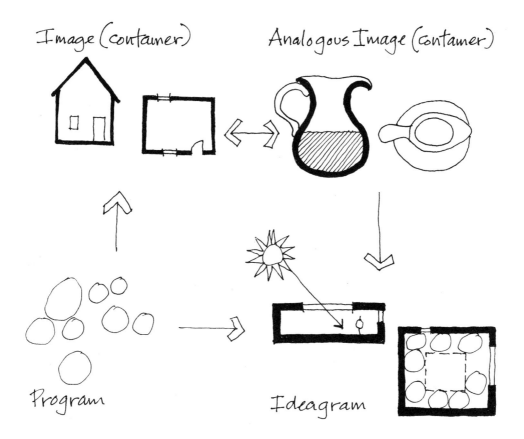

Again, using the example of the recreational house, we can sketch out a basic approach to invention in architecture. The starting point is the abstract diagram of the program for the house. This leads to a choice of one image of a house, namely a container that holds people. Almost simultaneous with the house image we have an analogous image, the pitcher, as a container of liquids. In the fourth sketch, the ideagram, the house program, and the image of the pitcher are combined to form a specific discovery of how the recreational house might take shape. In this example, the house is also seen as a container of energy, admitting solar energy through a hole in the top similar to the hole in the top of the pitcher. The concept for the house could be formed from this ideagram or the analogy could be extended further through observations such as: the only entry into the pitcher is through the top, so perhaps the major entry into the house could be via a stair dropping into the central court. Because the pitcher is supported as a cantilever from its handle when picked up, maybe the house could also be cantilevered from supports on one side.

Pursuing another analogy, house as campsite, might lead to the images of campfire, hearth, and gathering in a circle. Each of these images can be the inspiration for an alternative concept for the house form.

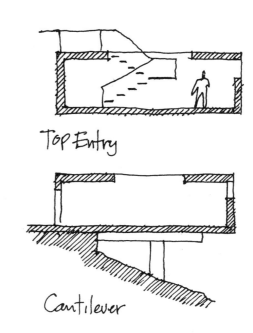

Figure 8-6 Analogy between a house and a pitcher of water.

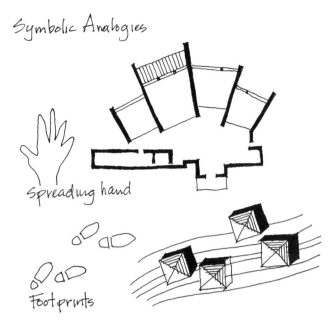

spreading hand

Footprints

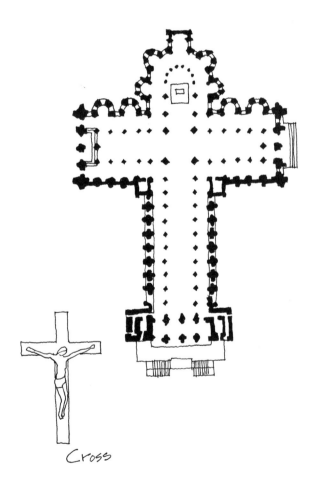

Cross

Analogies

In his book *Synectics: The Development of Creative Capacity,* William Gordon described four types of analogy: *symbolic, direct, personal,* and *fantasy.*

The example of the pitcher and the house as containers is a symbolic analogy, a comparison between general qualities of the two objects. Other symbolic analogies might be made between the spread of a hand and the extensions of a house or between footprints and canopied pavilions, which loosely constitute the house. One of the most prominent examples is the analogy between the Latin cross and the plans of many Gothic churches.

Direct analogy compares parallel facts or operations. In the examples opposite, the house is designed to have the same cooling characteristics as a tree: shade, evaporation, and air movement. And the roof supports for Nervi's exhibition hall emulate a hand balancing a tray.

In a personal analogy, far right, the designer identifies himself directly with the elements of the problem. Assuming that the prime consideration for this house is warmth and comfort on winter days without large uses of nonrenewable energy sources, the designer might imagine himself to be the house. To make himself comfortable, he might lie close to the ground below the ridge so the cold wind can pass over his head. This can be translated into a low-profile house below the ridge with trays of space covered by sloped glass skylights to admit the warm rays of the sun. When we want to be heard at a distance, we cup our hands to our mouth. The exterior chapel at LeCorbusier's pilgrimage church at Ronchamp adopts similar cupped shapes to project the priest's voice toward the congregation.

Figure 8-7 Symbolic analogies.

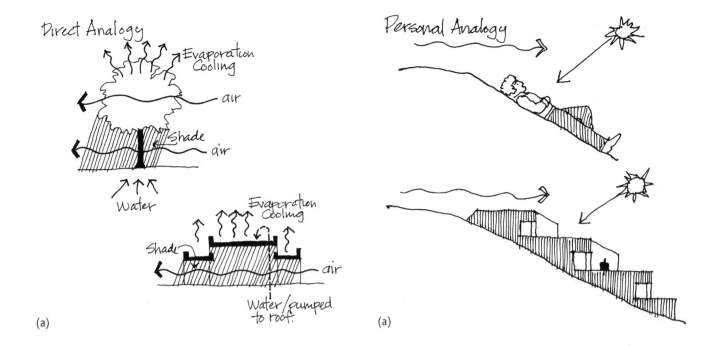

(a)

(a)

(b)

(b)

Figure 8-8a, b Direct analogies.

Figure 8-9a, b Personal analogies.

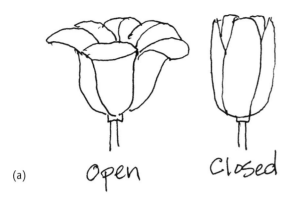

(a)

The fourth type, fantasy analogy, uses a description of an ideal condition desired as a source for ideas. In the case of our recreational house, the designer might fantasize about a house that opens itself up when the client arrives on the weekend and automatically closes up when the client leaves. It could be compared to a tulip that opens and closes with the action of sunlight, an automatic garage door, or a puppet that comes alive when you pick up the strings. The decks and the roofs over the decks could be like the leaves of the tulip. But how do they open and close? A motor is another energy consumer; is there another way? How can the puppet strings help? The final solution uses ropes and pulleys to raise and lower the flaps. The system is balanced so that the weight of a person on the decks can pull up the roofs, and the dropping of the roofs could pull the decks back up. The decks and roofs would be held in both open and closed positions by spring latches.

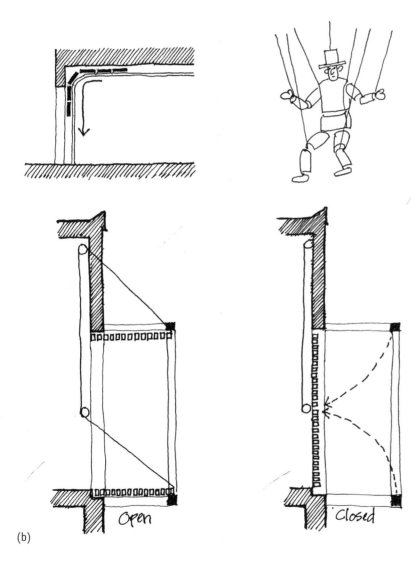

(b)

Figure 8-10a, b Fantasy analogies.

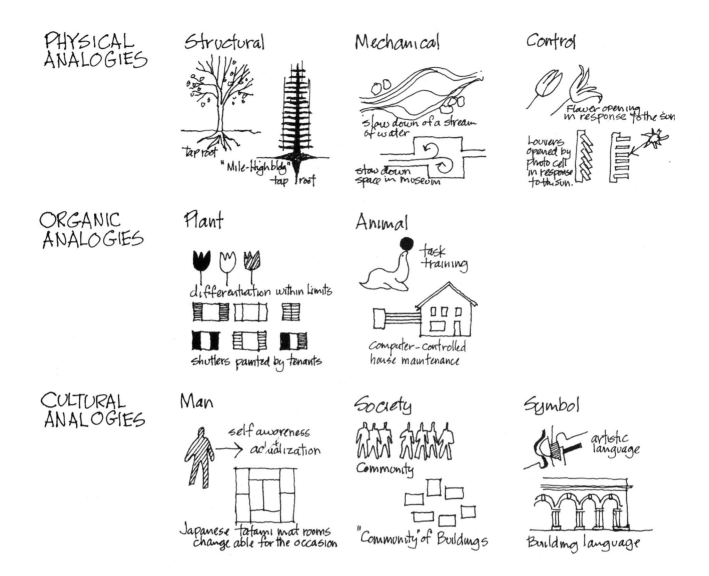

PHYSICAL ANALOGIES

Structural — tap root / "Mile-High bldg" tap root

Mechanical — slow down of a stream of water / slow down space in museum

Control — Flower opening in response to the sun / Louvers opened by photo cell in response to the sun.

ORGANIC ANALOGIES

Plant — differentiation within limits / shutters painted by tenants

Animal — task training / computer-controlled house maintenance

CULTURAL ANALOGIES

Man — self awareness actualization / Japanese tatami mat rooms changeable for the occasion

Society — Community / "Community" of Buildings

Symbol — artistic language / Building language

Figure 8-11 Eight different types of analogy based on a hierarchy of systems.

Sources of Analogy

The possible models from which to draw analogies can be classified by categories as physical, organic, or cultural, and the subcategories include:

1. *Structural*—Referring to shape or relationship.
2. *Mechanical*—The way something operates.
3. *Control*—Maintaining a condition.
4. *Plant*—Goal orientation and differentiation.
5. *Animal*—Behavior.
6. *Man*—Imagination and choice.
7. *Society*—Interaction, competition, organization.
8. *Symbolic*—Conventions, references, suggestion.

Often architects or designers limit their thinking to structural or mechanical analogies. The samples of the range of analogy types, shown above, should suggest some alternatives.

Increasing Effectiveness

We have all experienced times when our minds appeared frozen with a single thought that doesn't seem good enough or is unable to solve a critical problem. A few specific approaches that might help thinking get moving again are shown on the following pages.

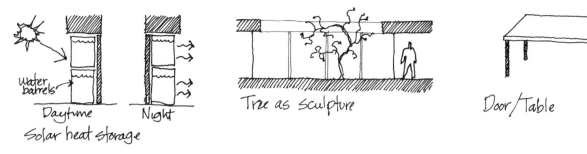

Figure 8-12 Examples of eolithic design.

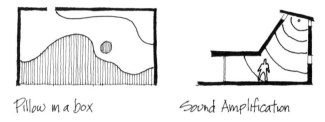

Figure 8-13 Concepts based on senses other than vision.

Eolithic Design Sometimes designers succumb to what Robert McKim calls "functional fixedness," the "tendency to sort objects into indelibly labeled containers."[4] As a result, they are unable to see their problem in any other light; kitchens or bedrooms, for example, are seen as having a single use. One cure for this difficulty is eolithic, or found-object design; the normal use of an object is disregarded in favor of a new use. Examples include barrels of water used for heat storage, trees used as sculpture inside a house, doors used as counters. The counter and storage setup of the kitchen could be used as a model for a studio or other workspace, and the bedroom might be converted into a dining or lounging space. The found-object approach can also be used with ideagrams; the binodal organization of a typical shopping center might be used in a house to generate more movement and interaction.

Escape Sometimes just getting away from the problem is enough to loosen the mind and open fresh views of the project. Escape can take the form of diversions such as entertainment, sports, or games; it can also be simply rest and relaxation, or "sleeping" on the problem.

Random Thoughts Even when not actually working on a problem, our subconscious minds are often still trying to solve the problem. Then suddenly we get an idea or an answer to the design problem. Some designers have these insights just as they are going to sleep or upon waking. It is important to write or sketch these ideas before they are lost. For this reason, many architects carry small notebooks with them or keep paper and pen handy near their beds or other places of relaxation.

Sense Awareness Working in a predominantly visual medium can sometimes lead to ignoring the other senses and may cut a designer off from a large number of sources for analogies. If we think of a house as being soft as a pillow in a box, it might lead to the use of curvilinear partitions. Comparing a house to a musical instrument could result in a metal roof to catch the sound of the rain or some way to amplify the sound of a breeze.

If this discussion of the use of analogies seems too simplistic, remember the great architects of this century. Wright, LeCorbusier, and Aalto used simple analogies as a source for many of their inventions. Geoffrey Broadbent comments:

> *Most architects—and artists—are extremely reluctant to admit the sources of their analogies. They think that such admissions would somehow diminish one's respect for their creativity; but far from it—they will merely confirm that they have brains and mental processes, which every other human being possesses. Our respect for them, in fact, might increase if they admitted that, given the same mental processes, they are able to make better use of them."[5]*

Broadbent goes on to describe a number of analogies that LeCorbusier used in his work, and observes that he spent

> *...a lifetime building up a store of analogies (his years of sketching being particularly fruitful). The analogies had become fundamental to his experience, absorbed, compared, contrasted, combined, overlaid by later experience, and changed by new perceptions; but they were there to be called on, and faced with a difficult design problem, LeCorbusier could draw on them. We too have our stores of analogies, not perhaps as rich as LeCorbusier's, but valuable nevertheless, because they are personal. Yet we fail to draw on them. It never occurs to us; they do not seem relevant and instead of that, we content ourselves by drawing analogies with other people's work."[6]*

Concept Formation

The basic concept, sometimes referred to as the *parti,* is an enduring mechanism used by architectural designers to establish the fundamental organization of a building and guide the entire process of design development. The parti, at its best, provides:

1. The first synthesis of the designer's response to the determinants of form (program, objectives, context, site, economy, etc.).
2. A boundary around the set of decisions that will be the focus of the designer's responsibility.
3. A map for future design activities in the form of a hierarchy of values and responding forms.
4. An image that arouses expectations and provides motivation for all persons involved in the design process. This is often done through the use of abstractions. ("My building is a spine" or "Our building bridges this gap.")

The typical parti sketch, like the one on the left by a fifth-year thesis student, shows both the determinants and the basic resolution of the form. In this example, the sketch of a floating research station in the Atlantic Ocean illustrates the vertical pontoons secured by cables, supporting a multilevel platform. The basic interaction with water, wind, and sun is also indicated.

The Ideagram

The sketches that have already been described as flowing from analogies, known as *ideagrams,* are the starting point for concept formation. Ideagrams are extensions of analysis diagrams that can be used as:

1. An aid to investigation and synthesis in the design process.
2. A framework in the design thinking process that leads to the final design product.
3. A literal model of the final product. In architecture this is referred to as conceptual clarity in the building.
4. An explanation of a design concept after the building design has been completed.

To show some of the potentials of the ideagram for developing design concepts, I have drawn three stages of evolution of an ideagram in the first column to the right. For each stage, there is a schematic design for a building in the next column. Shown in Ideagram 1 and Design 1 is a literal translation of the ideagram into a building form. This approach has a clear and forceful impact on the user; the effect is simple and dramatic. In Ideagram 3 and Design 3, a building form is being derived from a more complex ideagram. The resulting building may lack the simplicity or initial impact of the first building, but in turn it may offer a greater variety of experiences.

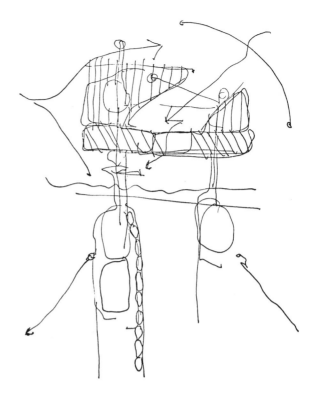

Figure 8-14 By Mark Sowatsky. Parti sketch, Atlantis 2.

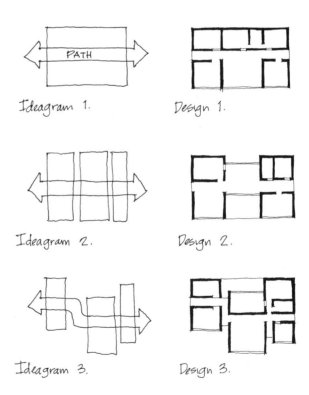

Figure 8-15 *(left)* Three levels of development of an ideagram.

Figure 8-16 *(right)* Corresponding schematic plans for the ideagrams.

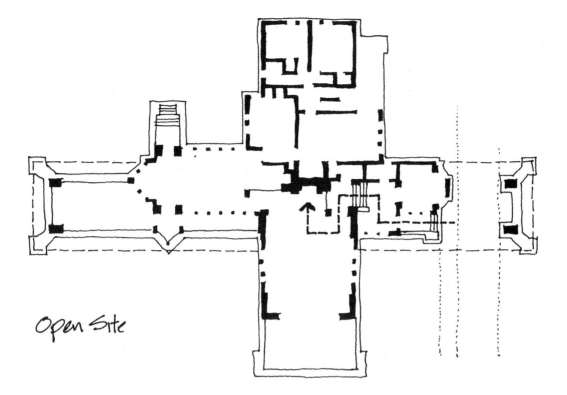

Open Site

Figure 8-17a Willitts House 1902, Wright, architect.

Prototypes

As with other design skills, concept formation need not be a mysterious process developed solely through trial and error. There is a lot to be learned from architects who are highly skilled at molding concepts, and here again sketches can be an important aid. On the next pages are examples of analytical sketches and abstract concept-getting techniques from the work of several architects.

The first examples are from the work of Frank Lloyd Wright. In the houses known as the Prairie Style, he used a basic plan of interlocking spaces dominated by a central hearth with an elaborate, indirect route of entry. Although the basic organizational parti remained constant, Wright's careful response to the unique constraints of each site produced a wide variety of building forms. As designers of houses, we can try to use Wright's basic parti or develop our own prototype plan and manipulate it in response to specific site conditions.

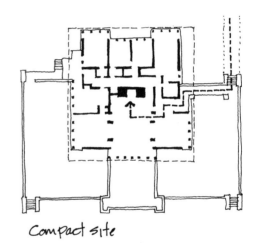

Compact site

Figure 8-17b Cheney House 1904, Wright, architect.

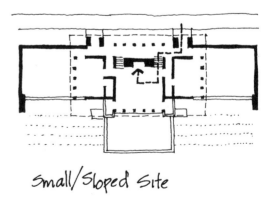

Small/Sloped Site

Figure 8-17c Hardy House 1905, Wright, architect.

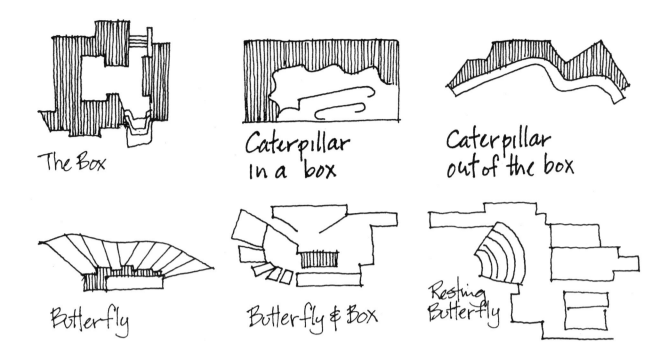

Figure 8-18a Prototype concepts developed by Alvar Aalto.

The Box

Caterpillar in a box

Caterpillar out of the box

Butterfly

Butterfly & Box

Resting Butterfly

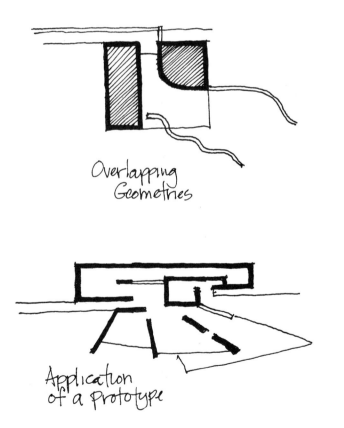

Overlapping Geometries

Application of a Prototype

Figure 8-18b Some applications of the prototypes.

In the course of his career, Alvar Aalto developed a number of archetypes for buildings noted for their incorporation of multiple grids or geometries. Some of these archetypes are shown here in abstract form. The titles are one way of simplifying and remembering the different partis. You can use your own method of categorization, but it does seem helpful to be able to attach a one- or two-word label. Many of Aalto's concepts seem to be derived from the acceptance of two contrasting contexts within one building, as in the combination of urban and rural settings in the town center at Saynatsalo.

One of these archetypes could provide a starting point for the design of the recreational house, or we could follow Aalto's approach to developing partis by looking for the double context in our project and evolving our own multiple geometries. Beyond this, a number of other variations should show up as more sketches are generated.

Additive

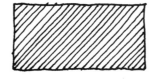

1. Maisons LaRoche et Jeanneret

Box

2. Villa à Garches

Frame

3. Villa à Carthage

Subtractive

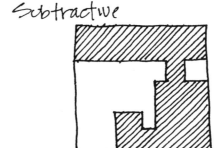

4. Villa Savoye

Figure 8-19a Four house concepts by LeCorbusier.

LeCorbusier was probably the most productive architectural inventor of the twentieth century. His inventions have filled many books, which I recommend you read. Roughly between 1922 and 1932, LeCorbusier designed four houses, each based on a different concept of a building. These were Maison La Roche (additive), Villa Savoye (subtractive), Villa at Garches (closed cube), and the Villa at Carthage (open skeleton). When LeCorbusier illustrated and wrote about these four approaches to a building, he had built houses as examples. But this way of generating a building parti extends beyond housing in its potential utility.

Also shown opposite are applications of these partis to our sample house so you can see how to increase the number of concepts formed within the limits of a single project.

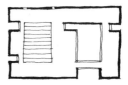

Small - Car Dealership

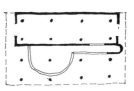

Library

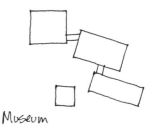

Museum

Figure 8-19b Applications of the concepts.

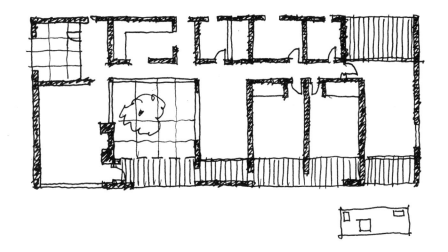

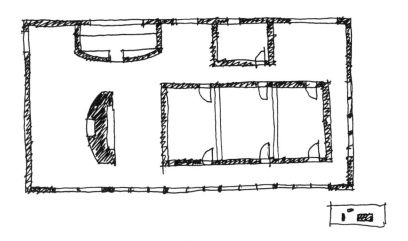

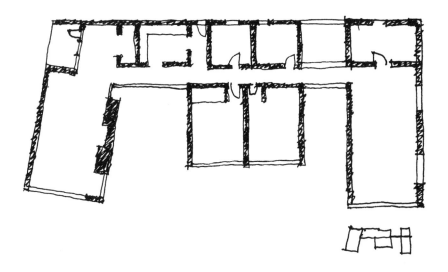

Figure 8-19c Applications of the concepts.

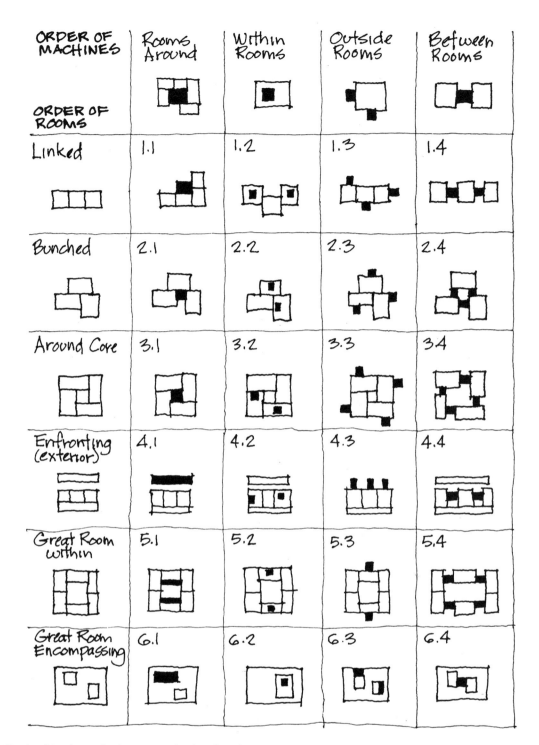

ORDER OF MACHINES → ORDER OF ROOMS ↓	Rooms Around	Within Rooms	Outside Rooms	Between Rooms
Linked	1.1	1.2	1.3	1.4
Bunched	2.1	2.2	2.3	2.4
Around Core	3.1	3.2	3.3	3.4
Enfronting (exterior)	4.1	4.2	4.3	4.4
Great Room within	5.1	5.2	5.3	5.4
Great Room Encompassing	6.1	6.2	6.3	6.4

Figure 8-20 Matrix of 24 alternative house organizations based on concepts developed by Moore, Allen, and Lyndon

In their book *The Place of Houses,* Charles Moore, Donlyn Lyndon, and Gerald Allen explain six different ways to organize rooms in a house and four different ways to incorporate machines (by which they mean wet and service cores) into houses. In the chart above, I have constructed a matrix relating their two lists of alternatives to produce 24 alternative prototypes. There are a number of other lists that categorize ways of organizing buildings; these could also be placed in a matrix to generate additional alternatives. On the facing page, some of the prototypes are developed into concepts for a house on our site, within the constraints of the specific building program.

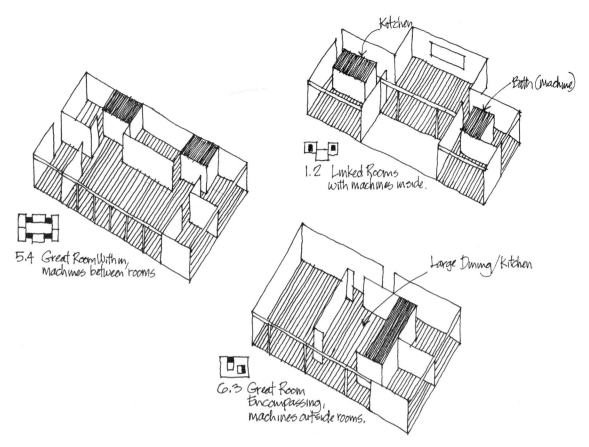

1.2 Linked Rooms with machines inside.

5.4 Great Room Within, machines between rooms

6.3 Great Room Encompassing, machines outside rooms.

Figure 8-21a Three organizations of the recreational house derived from the matrix.

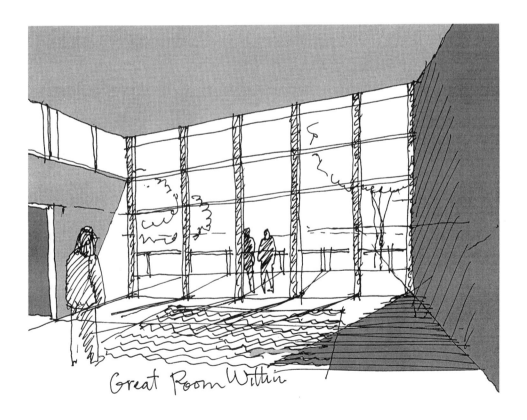

Great Room Within

Figure 8-21b Spatial implications of one of the house organizations.

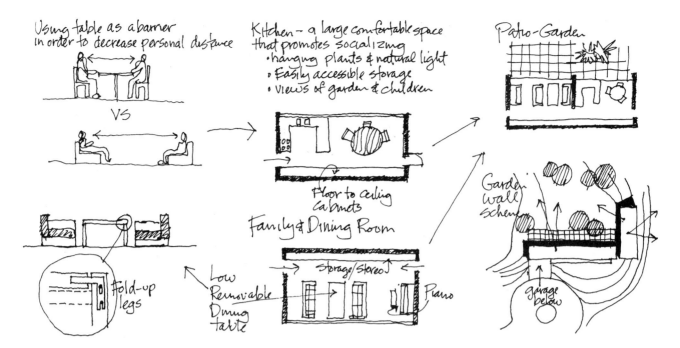

Figure 8-22

Pattern Language

For several years, a group at the University of California/Berkeley, headed by Christopher Alexander, has been working with a method of generating building designs, called pattern language. Basically, it is an approach that constructs concepts for a building by combining prototypes for smaller parts of the building. The working tool is a hierarchy of prototypes: areas that combine to make rooms, that combine to make buildings, that combine to make communities, that combine to make urban complexes, and so on. Pattern language appears to be less a prescription for the perfectly designed environment than a convenient format for formulating design concepts. Any designer is free to supply his own prototypes, although there is certainly merit in sharing workable prototypes.

Application of the pattern language approach, on the simplest level, to our house project might take the following form:

1. Based on past experience, we would start with an array of prototypes for different spaces from which would be selected those that seem most appropriate for this project. The prototype diagrams are quite simple, with short verbal identifications for ease of identification and manipulation.
2. The diagrams are combined into a pattern that represents a summary of the building elements and shows an overall idea of the building.

3. The pattern is now manipulated to respond to the specific site context and special needs of the client.

At a more sophisticated level of application, as illustrated on the facing page, space prototypes or patterns are more specific and oriented toward three-dimensional experience. The character of the space becomes a focal point for the identity of the prototype. Representational skills, discussed in Chapter 3, are obviously a help here.

I have found two useful ways of collecting patterns and using them in design:

The Building Type Notebook—An idea for a space is illustrated on an 8½-by-11 sheet of paper. These sheets are kept in a three-ring binder and used as a reference book for future projects.

Analysis Cards—Patterns are recorded on small cards similar to the ones described in Chapter 4. These can be filed by subject, ready to be pulled out for a specific design task.

Whether using cards or standard-size sheets, it is helpful to have a common format. The basic information includes a simple statement of the programmatic need and context ("dining space in a townhouse apartment"); a concise verbal and graphic statement of a prototypical response to the need; a more detailed description of the prototype or discussion of the pattern that is recorded on the back of the card or sheet.

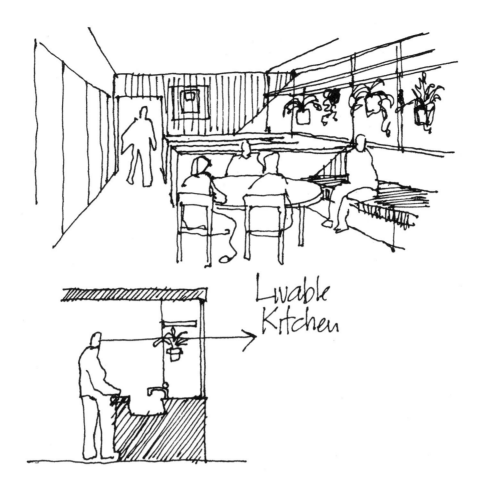

Livable Kitchen

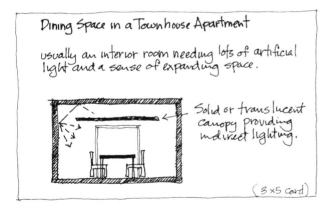

Dining Space in a Townhouse Apartment

usually an interior room needing lots of artificial light and a sense of expanding space.

Solid or translucent canopy providing indirect lighting.

(3×5 card)

Figure 8-23

When the designer is formulating concepts for the building design, he spreads the collection of relevant cards or sheets on a table or wall. Patterns or mini-concepts are then grouped as possible combinations and observed, but the designer must go beyond a simply additive process. In describing "pattern language," Christopher Alexander explained that "It is possible to put patterns together in such a way that many, many patterns overlap in the same physical space: the building is very dense; it has many meanings captured in a small space; and through this density, it becomes profound."[7] To achieve this sort of synthesis, or "compression," of patterns, the graphic thinking process can be applied, using cards or a clipboard to turn over ideas as one scans the display of patterns.

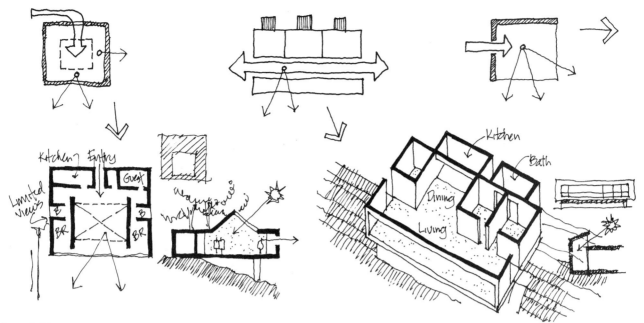

Figure 8-24

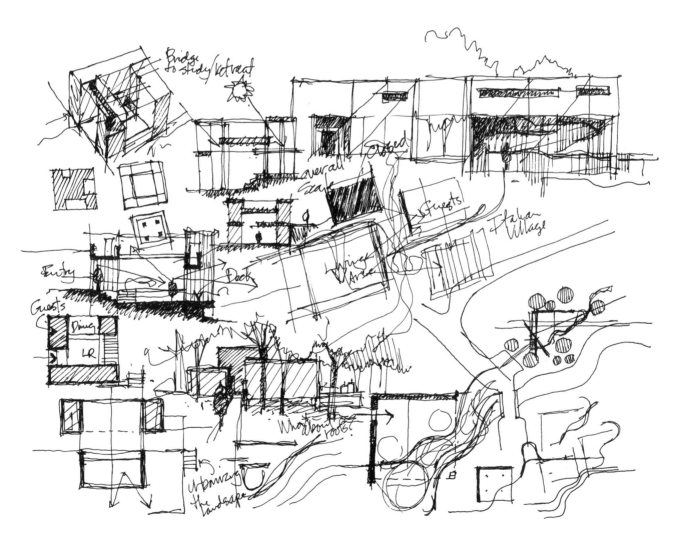

Figure 8-25

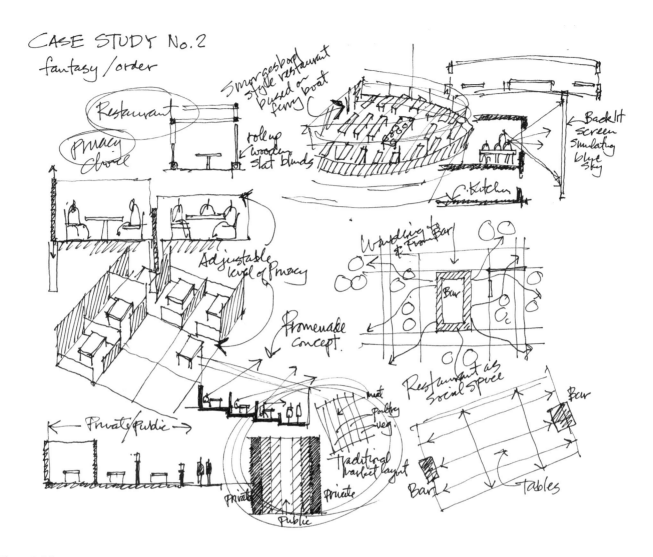

CASE STUDY No. 2
fantasy / order

Restaurant

Privacy Choice

Smorgesbord style restaurant based on ferry boat

roll up wooden slat blinds

Backlit screen simulating blue sky

Kitchen

Adjustable level of privacy

Promenade concept

Wandering to from Bar

Bar

Restaurant as social space

Private/Public

meat
poultry
veg.

Traditional market layout

private Private
Public

Bar

Bar

Tables

Figure 8-26

CASE STUDIES

Examples of ideagrams developed into concepts for the recreational house case study are shown here. The ideagrams, as you will recognize, are taken from the analyses of need, context, and form in Chapter 6 (analysis), from Chapter 7 (exploration), and from this chapter. In forming the concepts, ideas derived from one source are reworked to respond to other concerns. Prototypes, for example, are adjusted to fit the site, or site-generated ideas are made to respond to the building program. Variations on this approach are illustrated in additional case studies on the following pages.

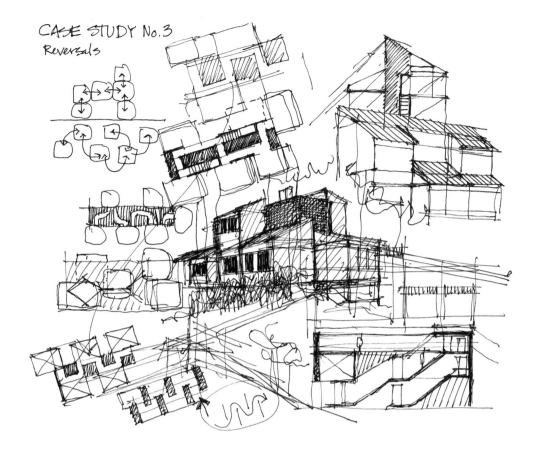

Figure 8-27

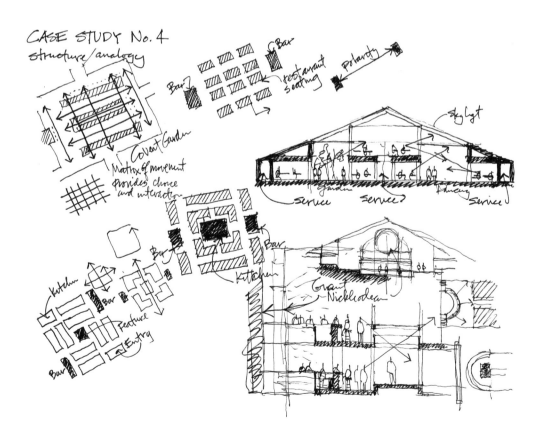

Figure 8-28

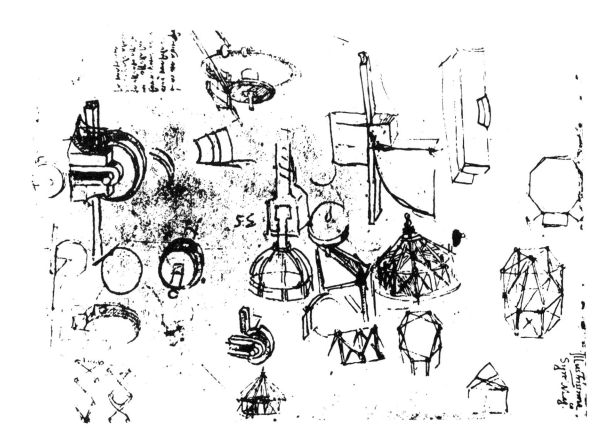

Figure 8-29 By Leonardo da Vinci. Studies of a temporaty structure for festivals.

The graphic thinking sketches that architects have used provide evidence of the application of analogy in their design process. Often these sketches are very small in order to pursue many different analogies on the same piece of paper. This permits the designer to work loosely and entertain all sorts of ideas; original trains of thought are recorded and can be returned to at will. Combining images derived from sketches can also generate further variations.

Figure 8-30 By LeCorbusier. Images for the Philips' Electronic Poem.

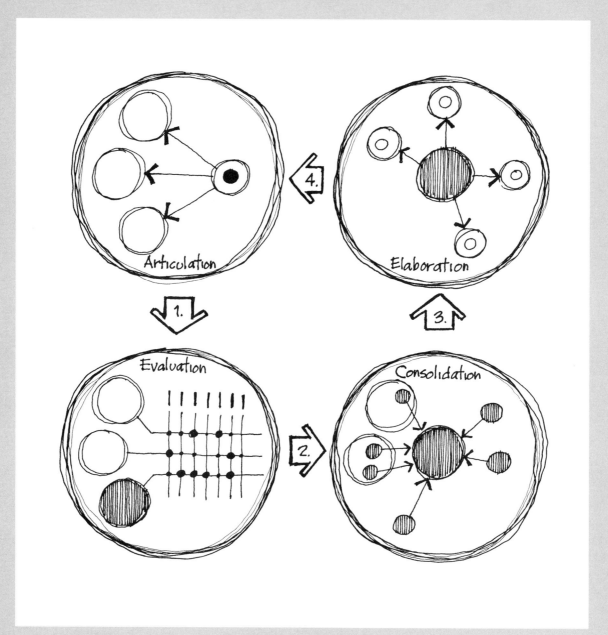

Figure 9-1 The verification cycle.

9 Verification

Within the realm of architectural design, *verification* refers to the usefulness of a design concept for a specific problem. The ultimate means of verifying the utility of a building design is a firsthand evaluation after the building has been constructed and occupied. However, postoccupancy evaluation would be of no help to the many decisions made in the process of designing and building. Therefore, architects usually go through a sort of preverification process. Within this context of pretesting design concepts, the utility of the verification mode of graphic thinking lies in moving from abstract images to the more complete, concrete images of the design concept.

Verification can be described as a cyclical process producing images that are increasingly specific or concrete. For example, the image of a sheltering roof is converted into a low, long-span hip roof, later having exposed wood trusses, and then to a specific color with wood shingles. The other progression of images is from larger to smaller parts of a building. One of the keys to quality design is the amount of attention given to the relationship of parts, from the building as a whole to the most detailed level. Eliel and Eero Saarinen were said to believe that the success of any part of a building design lay in the study of the next smaller and next larger building elements; design of a good room required the study of the furniture and of the building as a whole.

The model I use to explain the cyclical process of verification is shown on the facing page. There are four basic stages:

1. *Articulation*—The design image is extended through representational sketches of alternative expressions of the concept.
2. *Evaluation*—The alternative expressions of the design concept are tested against a set of criteria that represents a desirable performance. Evaluations of the alternatives are then compared.
3. *Consolidation*—The evaluation process usually generates a great amount of useful information in addition to the decision about alternatives. The purpose of consolidation is to try to incorporate as many good ideas as possible into the chosen scheme.
4. *Elaboration*—Having made a design decision at a new level of detail, the images now show the designer a whole new set of concerns from which he must form new design concepts. At this point, the recycling process is ready to start again with articulation of the new concepts.

Throughout the verification process, the choice of images must be deliberate if the designer is to maintain control over design development. Simply put, you can't judge the performance of something you can't see. As Kirby Lockard put it, "If the concept is to provide any particular kind of spatial or kinesthetic experience, then the representative drawings must be eye-level perspectives. Concepts that are based on some desired relationship to the physical context must be represented in perspectives of that context if their success or failure is to be evaluated. Concepts that are based on particular relationships to the human figure might be best represented in sections that show those relationships. Any design solution is best studied and evaluated with those drawings which best show the success or failure of its conceptual basis."[1] And, therefore, it is necessary for the designer to have a wide range of sketching skills, from abstract to concrete, from loose to meticulous, and to understand the special potentials of the different images those skills produce.

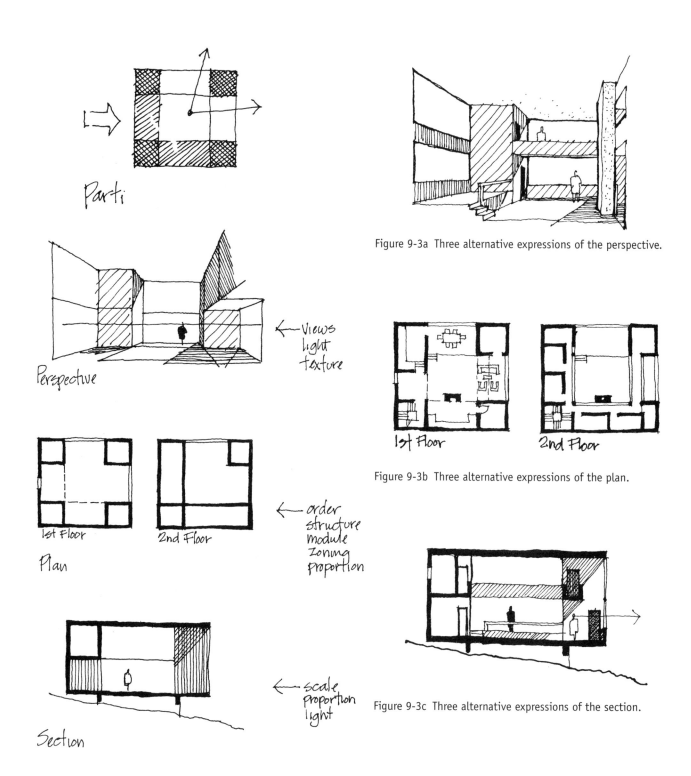

Parti

Perspective

← Views
light
texture

Plan

1st Floor   2nd Floor

← order
structure
module
zoning
proportion

Section

← scale
proportion
light

Figure 9-2 A parti and three different forms of its articulation.

Figure 9-3a Three alternative expressions of the perspective.

1st Floor   2nd Floor

Figure 9-3b Three alternative expressions of the plan.

Figure 9-3c Three alternative expressions of the section.

1st Floor   2nd Floor

1st Floor   2nd Floor

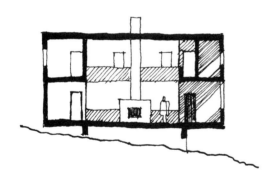

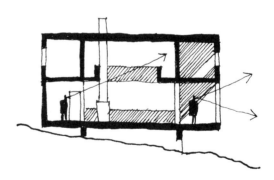

ARTICULATION

To get a feel for the range of images that are used to articulate a concept, the three sketches shown in Figure 9-2 address some feature of the design concept. The qualities or characteristics illustrated are noted for each sketch. In Figures 9-3a, b, and c, three alternative expressions are developed for each sketch.

A number of other implications of the design concept are articulated in Figure 9-4. They include such concerns as massing, scale, imagery, color, construction, flexibility, maintenance, territoriality, and comfort. Although the experienced designer may not need to look at all of these concerns within a given project, creative architects often use a specific project context to reexamine accepted design norms.

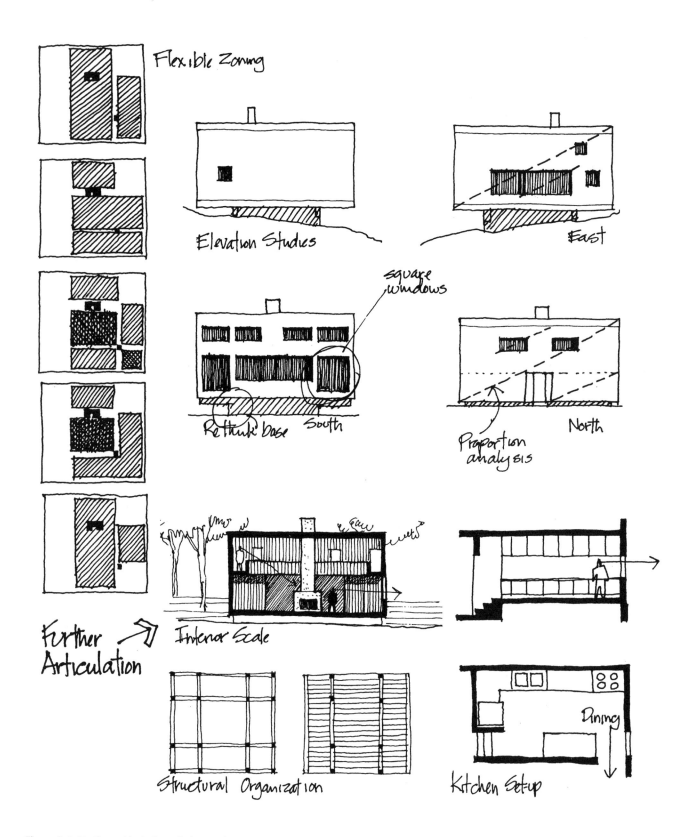

Figure 9-4 Further articulation of the parti.

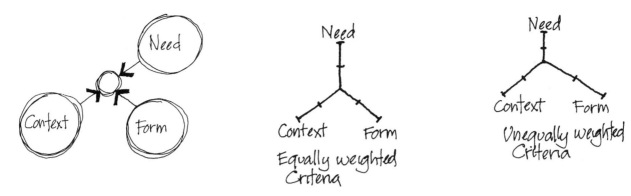

Figure 9-5a

Figure 9-5b

Figure 9-5c

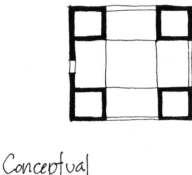

Conceptual

Figure 9-5d

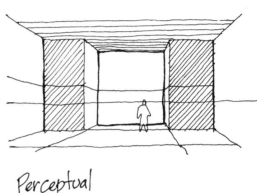

Perceptual

Figure 9-5e

EVALUATION

The definition of evaluation, placing a value on something, implies that there exists a set of values to which the evaluator refers. When evaluating a design, we use design criteria to represent these values. The first concern of design criteria should be comprehensive, covering all aspects of the design problem. For convenience, I have used as a model the house design problem described earlier. Criteria are deliberately developed under each of the three categories of need, context, and form, and a chart, such as the one in Figure 9-6, is constructed to assure that we look at the design concept from every angle.

The second concern of design criteria is how and whose values they represent. When designing a building, decisions are usually made on the basis of competing sets of values held by the client, the designer, the intended user, and even society (in the form of customs or regulations). In addition to showing an array of criteria, a balance of values can be recognized by the weighting of the criteria. Differences in values still have to be negotiated, but the designer can at least illustrate the relationship between values and the evaluation of a specific design.

The third concern of design criteria relates to the differences in the way we look at design ideas. Some architects can be said to be more conceptually oriented; that is, their evaluation is heavily influenced by such things as organization, consistency, and hierarchy as they are reflected in plans and axonometrics. Perceptually oriented architects are more interested in the direct experience of a person outside or inside the building. In my opinion, both conception and perception are important to the experience of a building and, therefore, important to the evaluation of design concepts. The designer must be aware of these two orientations of design and try to take a balanced approach to evaluation.

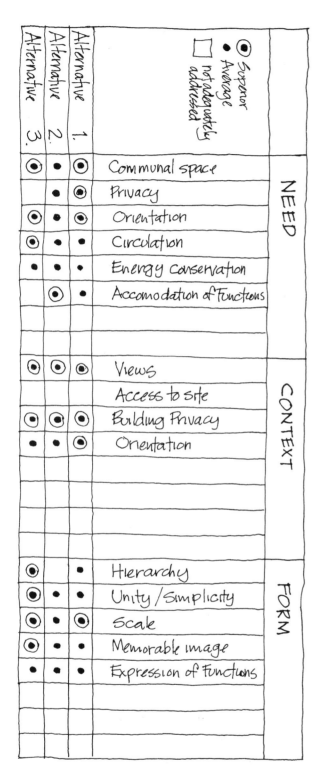

Figure 9-6 Evaluation matrix.

Legend:
- ◉ Superior
- ● Average
- ▢ not adequately addressed

	Alternative 3.	Alternative 2.	Alternative 1.	
NEED				
Communal space	◉	●	◉	
Privacy		●	◉	
Orientation	◉	●	◉	
Circulation	◉	●	●	
Energy conservation	●	●	●	
Accomodation of Functions		◉	●	
CONTEXT				
Views	◉	◉	◉	
Access to site				
Building Privacy	◉	◉	◉	
Orientation	●	●	◉	
FORM				
Hierarchy	◉		●	
Unity / Simplicity	◉	●	●	
Scale	◉	●	◉	
Memorable image	◉	●	●	
Expression of Functions	●	●	●	

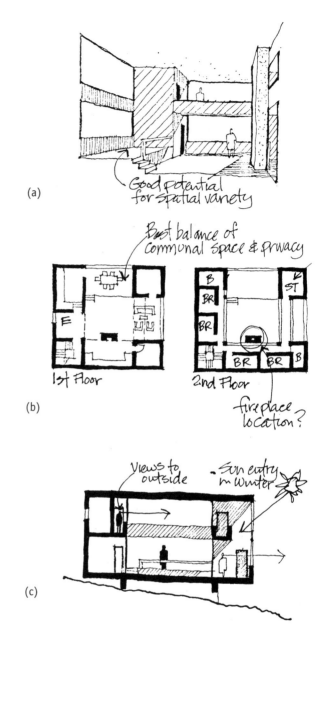

Figure 9-7a Evaluation of three perspective alternatives.

Figure 9-7b Evaluation of three plan alternatives.

Figure 9-7c Evaluation of three section alternatives.

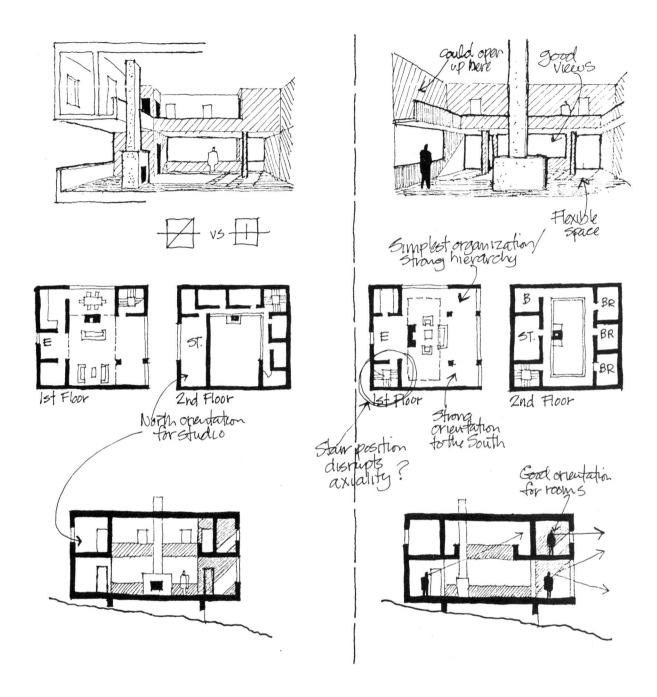

A chart, such as the one opposite, is used to compare evaluations of the alternatives (see the following page). It lists design evaluation criteria under the headings of need, context, and form. For each heading, the criteria are listed in order of importance, starting from the left, therefore accounting for priorities. Alternatives 1, 2, and 3 are rated as providing a superior or average response to each criterion; blank areas indicate no specific response. This chart allows an overall view of the success of each alternative.

Making notes during the processes of evaluating and comparing the alternatives is useful to further understand the strengths and weaknesses of these alternatives. In this manner, the designer can often identify the best ideas and expand on them with the information discovered through the display.

Cost Benefit

Other examples of graphic images used to assist evaluation appear on these two pages. The diagram shown to the right is an extension of analysis techniques developed by the architectural firm of Caudill Rowlett Scott.[2] The relative size of building areas and their approximate costs are shown side by side, providing an overview of the relationship between program needs and costs useful to both client and designer.

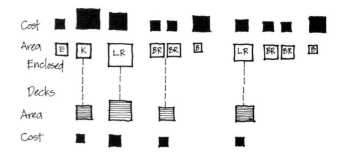

Figure 9-8 Display of cost-benefit analysis.

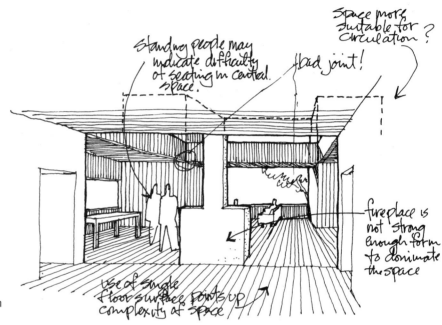

Figure 9-9 The perspective as an evaluation tool.

 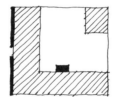 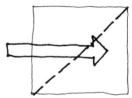

Figure 9-10 Conceptual sketches as evaluation tools.

Drawing Evaluation

Perspectives are so commonly used as selling tools that an examination of the perspective above might help to emphasize its potential as an evaluation tool. Here, the perspective is first rendered without conscious attention to the design of space. The drawing is now examined for clues to shortcomings. This approach is also applicable to finished drawings by professional renderers or even pictures of buildings by professional photographers. Conceptual drawings can also be evaluated by reducing them to ideagrams that point up the clarity or consistency of the design concept.

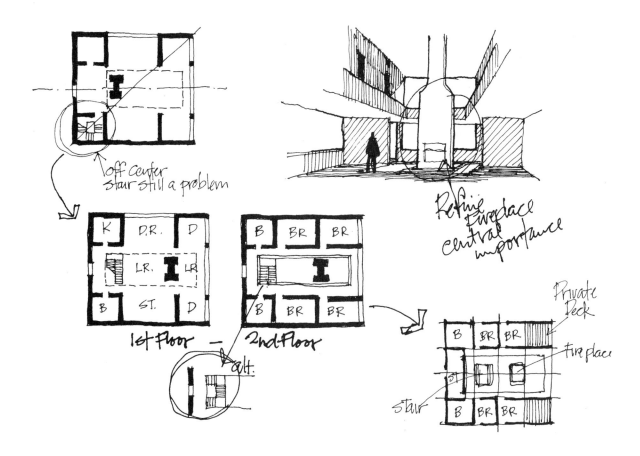

off center stair still a problem

Refine Fireplace central importance

K D.R. D
B LR. I LR
B ST. D

1st Floor

B BR BR
B BR BR

2nd Floor

alt.

Private Deck

B BR BR
St
B BR BR

Fire place

Stair

CONSOLIDATION

As the evaluation of alternatives helps us decide on the best route, a range of good ideas are uncovered, which the designer then attempts to incorporate in his final scheme. Many combinations are sketched as the design is pulled together, and even at the stage of the completed design, some refinements are still incorporated. The designer seeks consistency in all parts of the design. The end result is sketches that are more specific as to dimension, shape, and position.

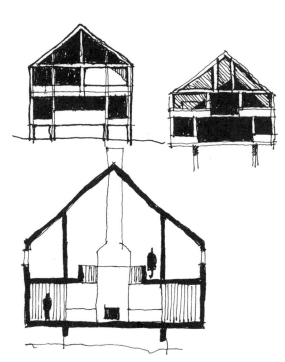

Figure 9-11 Selecting useful ideas and combining them.

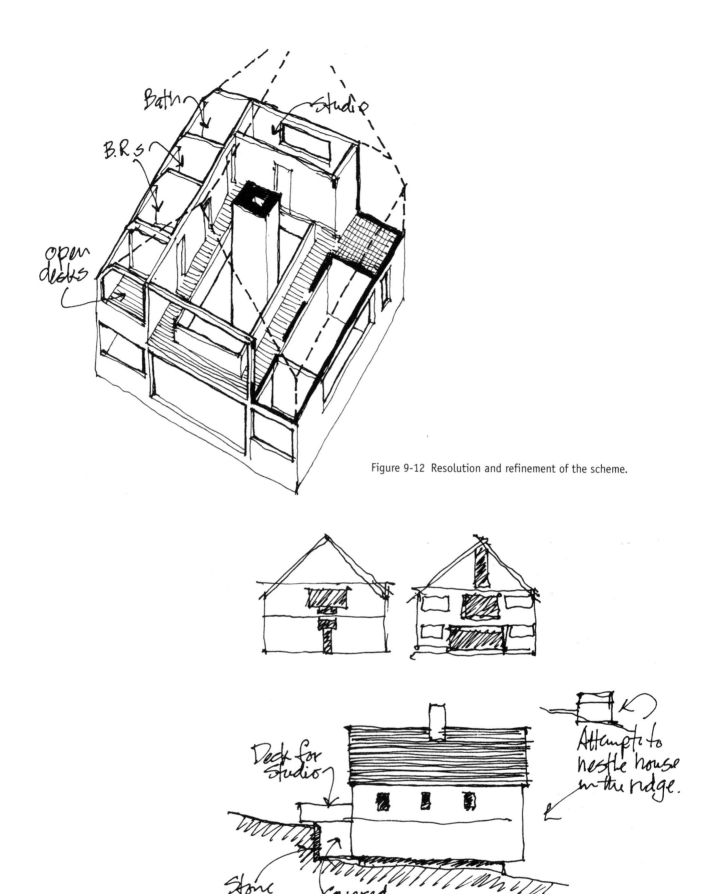

Bath

Studio

B.R s

open decks

Figure 9-12 Resolution and refinement of the scheme.

Deck for Studio

Attempt to nestle house in the ridge.

Stone Retaining Wall

Covered North Entry

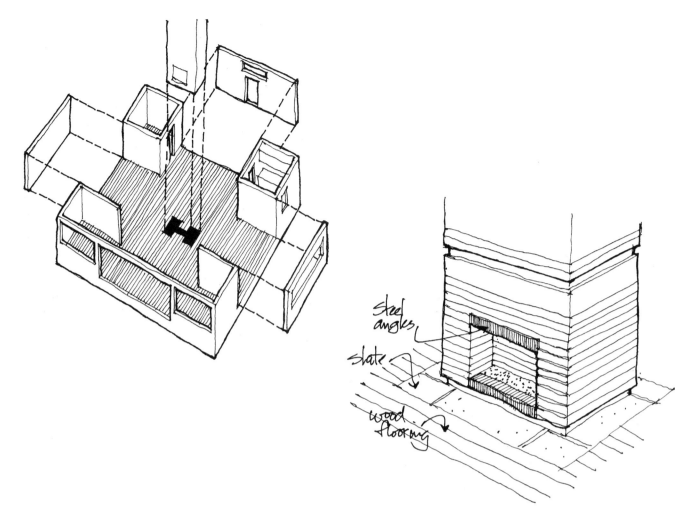

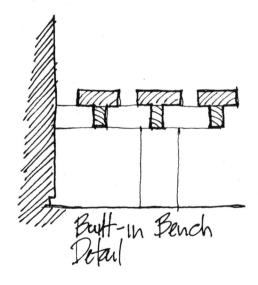

Figure 9-13 Identifying parts for further developemt.

ELABORATION

With the basic design decisions made and clarified, preparation is under way for the next cycles of verification. Decisions at one level of design open up many problems at other levels. For example, fixing the design of a room makes it possible to study windows, flooring, mechanical systems, storage units, and a number of special items such as fireplace or solarium. Concepts for each of the parts are developed within the context of the design of the whole room. But each concept in turn can be verified by repeating the methods described earlier in this chapter.

Figure 9-14 Developing details.

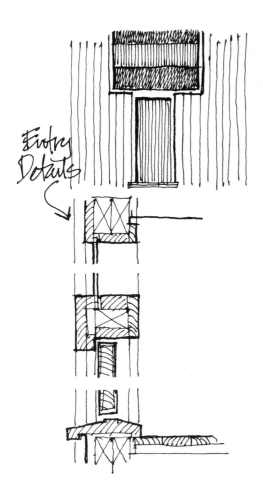

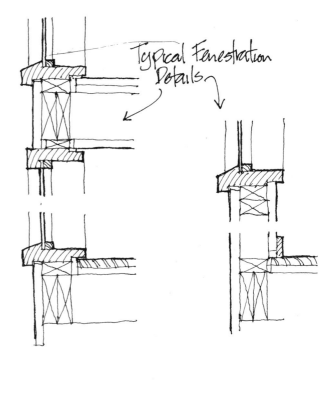

Details

At some point in designing, the architect must assure himself that the design concepts are realistic by asking whether the parts can be constructed. Will they fit together? Detail sketches place the design under a sort of microscope. The sample sketches on these two pages show, through the different views, the importance of how something is put together and how it should look. Additionally, the up-close drawings or sketches must show the context for the detail.

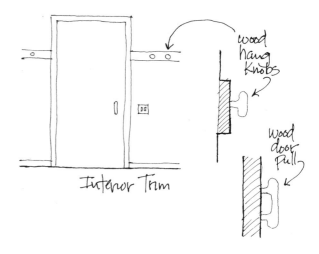

Figure 9-15 Developing details.

VERIFICATION AND EXPERIENCE

One of the advantages of experience in design is the opportunity to verify design concepts when the building is constructed. The designer accumulates a mental store of the concepts he has verified firsthand; he knows what works and what doesn't. In addition, with a certain amount of confidence, he can generalize new concepts from what he has learned and judged. As a result, many decisions can be made more quickly, facilitating the design process.

However, an ability to judge can sometimes deteriorate to the level of habit, and the designer makes decisions before looking at the design problem. The repeated use of specific concepts, technologies, or materials may lead to inappropriate preconceptions for the given problem. Many creative architects regularly retest accepted design concepts; they are constantly looking at their ideas, testing them, and evolving new concepts.

More serious is the use of concepts developed by others without a thorough understanding of their origin and derivation. This may often be a subconscious effect of a designer's exposure to existing prototypes and influences. The large overhanging eaves of Frank Lloyd Wright's Prairie schoolhouses have been imitated widely to the point of becoming a cliche. The typical application of these eaves to suburban houses

embodies little of the rationale of the original concept. Similar cliches can be found within both the Modern and Post-Modern movements. Typical commercial facade restorations seem the most susceptible to the use of these cliches.

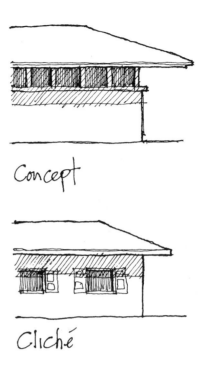

Figure 9-16

Figure 9-17a Modern movement cliches.

Figure 9-17b Post-Modern movement cliches.

COMMUNICATION

PROGRAM	**DESIGN**	**BUILD**
CLIENT	**ARCHITECT**	**CONTRACTOR**

USERS	**PLANNER**	**MANUFACTURERS**
MANAGEMENT	**LANDSCAPE ARCHITECT**	**SUPPLIERS**
FINANCE	**INDUSTRIAL DESIGNER**	**CONTRACTOR**
LEGAL AFFAIRS		**SUBCONTRACTORS**
PUBLIC AFFAIRS	**COST SURVEYOR**	**CONSTRUCTION MANAGER**
SALES	**ARCHITECT**	**CONSTRUCTION SUPERVISOR**
	MECHANICAL ENGINEER	
	ELECTRICAL ENGINEER	
	STRUCTURAL ENGINEER	
	CONSULTANT	

LAND DEVELOPER	**BUILDING SYSTEM DEVELOPER**	**CONSTRUCTION FINANCE**
REALTOR		**CODE ENFORCEMENT**
BUILDING MANAGER		
ANTHROPOLOGIST		
SOCIOLOGIST		

Figure 10-1 Participants in architectural design and building processes.

10 Process

In this section, we consider the current and future impact of communication on design activities. Our goal is a better understanding of the processes of design communication and the integral role of graphic thinking skills in individual, team, and public design contexts.

It is clear that our profession is undergoing a revolution involving fundamental change and fundamental continuity. Architecture has traditional methods that are important to environmental problem solving, but the scope of recognized environmental problems is expanding rapidly. There are two evident choices: expand the concept of the profession to encompass the full scope of emerging needs, or achieve a new unity of professional activity under another label like environmental design. Either way, these changes call for the reassessment of communication in design processes.

Changes in the processes of designing and building are immediately evident. More actors are involved at all stages and these actors are part of, and therefore influenced by, other professional or business contexts. The manufacturer must look beyond any single building or development for his ongoing concerns about marketing, production, and supplies. The zoning board must consider a building project within the context of an ongoing process of mediating public and private interests in the use of land.

Three important conditions for design are overlying this complex network of actors and activities.

1. Change in the concept of clients to include building users and/or the public.
2. Expansion of the design team to include clients, contractors, manufacturers, researchers, and others as the project requires.
3. Increase in the number and complexity of the concerns that shape the design and building processes.

This presents a new set of foreseeable challenges in three different design contexts.

1. *Individual*—The challenge of developing an ability to communicate rapidly with ourselves on increasingly complex problems in a way that accepts their complexity while trying to see them in comprehensive, systemic terms.
2. *Team*—The challenge of communicating to motivate, to share goals, and to bring the fullest impact of each team member's expertise and concerns on the problems.
3. *Public*—The challenge of developing communication methods that cross the boundaries of traditional professional language to allow the public equal access to the designing and building process. It is my belief that graphic thinking will be a major asset in meeting these communication challenges, if we are willing to develop the necessary skills.

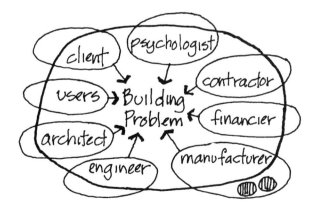

Figure 10-2 Interaction of the design team members.

179

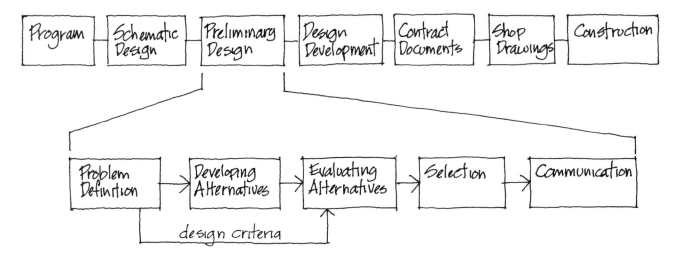

Figure 10-3 Design project and problem-solving processes.

A DESIGN PROCESS

Regardless of what is being designed or who is involved in designing it, there is a common objective: translating the client's program into a specific building or another response to his needs. In architectural practice this normally involves the following steps: building program, schematic design, preliminary design, design development, contract documents, shop drawings, construction. At each of these steps, the problems that must be solved require of the designer an effective problem-solving process. There are many good models for problem-solving processes. I prefer the following five-step model:

1. *Problem definition*—Identifying the specific limits of the problem to be solved. Then the various parts of the problem are analyzed to determine needs, constraints, and resources. Finally, the designer sets up specific design objectives.

2. *Developing alternatives*—The designer examines existing and new solutions and develops several viable alternatives.

3. *Evaluation*—Design evaluation criteria are adopted on the basis of the design objectives. Then the alternative solutions are rated using the design criteria.

4. *Selection*—Based on the results of the evaluation, one alternative is selected. If no one alternative is clearly superior, two or more solutions may be combined. In either case, the chosen alternative is usually further modified with some of the more successful parts of the other solutions.

5. *Communication*—The final solution to the problem must be described in such a way as to make it usable for the next stage of design.

This model is not as complex as it might seem initially. Take an example from the preliminary design stage:

1. The specific problem is the enclosure of a living space for a house. Needs include views, air circulation, sun control, and access to the exterior. Constraints include the overall plan and orientation of the house, the position of elements in the living space, and the climatic conditions impacting on the space. Among the resources are the construction technique, materials, and enclosure prototypes. The specific design objectives are: provide a panoramic view of the southwest while seated by the fireplace; shield the room from the intense summer sun, especially from the west, but allow the winter sun to penetrate and heat most of the area; provide for easy access to the exterior deck; assure security of the area at night.

2. The alternatives developed are a conventional arrangement of windows and a door; sliding doors with a roll-down protective door; a glazed wall with a sun screen.

3. Comparing the alternatives, the sun screen provides the best control of light but obscures the view; the conventional arrangement allows a view but does not control the sun or provide nighttime security. The roll-down door provides security but does not control the sun.

4. The roll-down door is selected but without floor-to-ceiling glazing, and a partial screen is used to control the sun.

5. To make a final decision before the design can proceed to the next stage, all the important sketches of the enclosure must be completed.

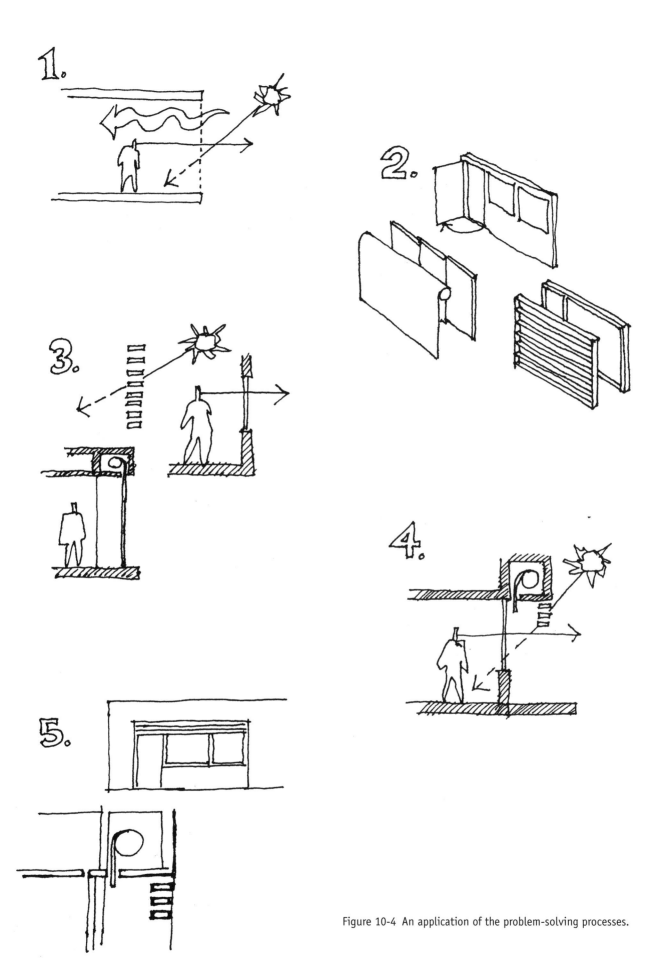

Figure 10-4 An application of the problem-solving processes.

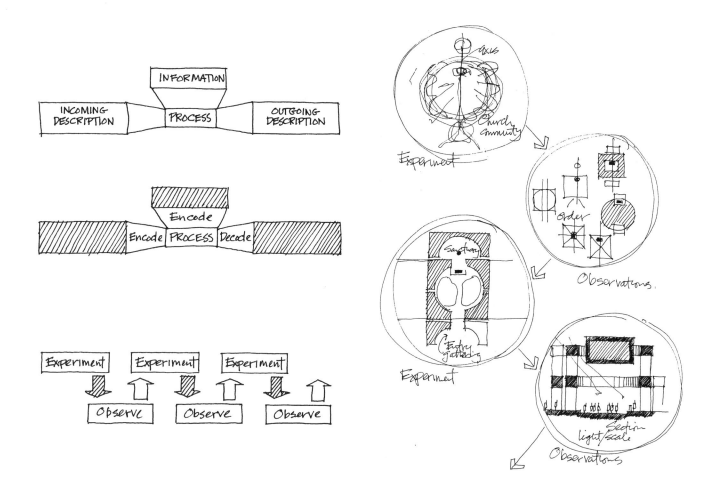

Figure 10-5 Design process models.

Figure 10-6 Process drawings.

Communication in the Design Process

Each step in a design process is essentially a communication task whereby one type of description is converted to another type appropriate to the next stage of the process. In schematic design, diagrams and text describing the design problem are converted to sketches that describe possible designs in a manner that promotes decision-making by the client; at another stage, contractors convert the architect's detail design drawings into shop drawings that describe building components and methods of assembly. In the process of converting descriptions, the designer handles considerable amounts of information that support thinking and decision-making.

In one view of these design processes, designers manage the multiple tasks of information management through the use of graphic communication. Incoming information is encoded in a shorthand graphic language that permits the designer to process a wide range of variables and develop a conceptual resolution of the various issues. After processing the information, it is decoded in a graphic and verbal language appropriate to communication to the next step in the design process.

Another way to view design communications is to consider design process as essentially a reiterative process of experimentation and observation. In the experimental mode, the designer uses graphic language that supports the opening of new areas for exploration. In the observational mode, the designer uses drawings or diagrams that support understanding and evaluating the results of experimentation.

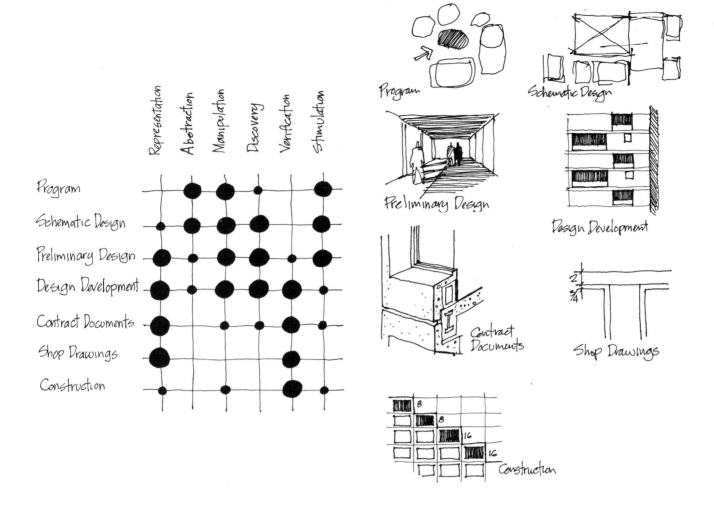

Figure 10-7 Matrix diagram of relationships between stages of the design project and different modes of graphic thinking.

Figure 10-8 Examples of sketches at different stages of a design project.

APPLYING GRAPHIC THINKING

Although the drawings that sum up each stage in the design process vary from abstract sketches at the beginning to the most specific hard-line drawings at the end, the thinking process can be supported throughout by the different types of sketches presented in the previous chapters. The matrix above shows where the modes of graphic thinking are primarily useful. To the right are some examples of sketches that could be used at each of the stages in the design process.

The following chapters consider some of the practical problems of creative thinking encountered by people within their design contexts. I try to show how some of the graphic thinking tools have been helpful to architects and designers, but the real test of the usefulness of these tools has to be made within the context of the special design processes each of us develops.

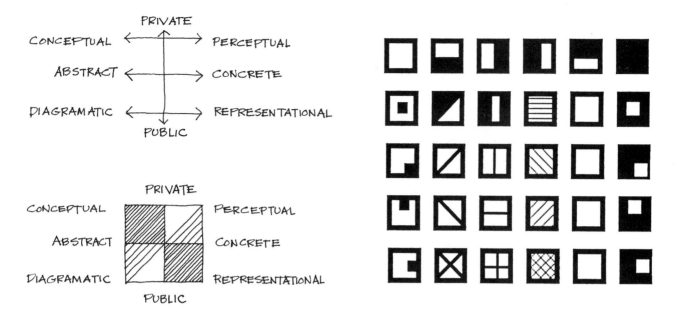

Figure 10-9 Functions of graphics.

Figure 10-10 Two-dimensional diagram.

Graphic Thinking Options

In this book we have discussed a variety of graphic thinking skills and tools. The world of visual communication offers these and other, yet to be discovered, diverse opportunities to support design processes. Paul Stevenson Oles has illustrated the scope of visual communication as a field whose boundaries are identified by the opposing extremes of four differentials: abstract–concrete, private–public, conceptual–representational, and diagrammatic–perceptual. A variation of Oles' diagram shows types of graphics that are most common, used to some extent, or underutilized. Conceptual and abstract graphics are found mostly in the private realm of the designer's thinking process; these form a graphic shorthand that supports the rapid pace of design speculation and enables the juggling of an extensive set of variables. Concrete and representational graphics are found mostly in the public realm, where the specific results of design decisions must be clearly illustrated. There has been some use of diagrammatic graphics in the abstract, conceptual processes and the application of perceptual graphics such as perspectives to concrete, representational tasks. But we are only beginning to explore the potential use of perceptual graphics in the more private design processes and the use of diagrammatic language for the more public tasks. The rapid growth of computer graphics should spread the use of both perceptual and diagrammatic graphics; on the one hand, concrete, perceptual drawings will be produced in a fraction of the time they now take; on the other hand, diagrammatic communication will be so accessible that it will be commonplace.

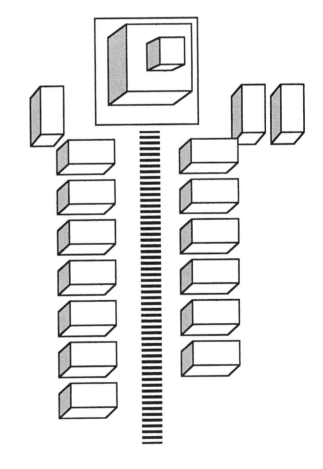

Figure 10-11 Three-dimensional diagram.

Figure 10-12 By Raymond Gaetan. Computer
model view.

Figure 10-13 By Raymond Gaetan. Computer
model view.

Figure 10-14 By Raymond Gaetan. Computer
model view.

Figure 10-15 By Tim Treman. Interior view, library project, Muncie, Indiana.

Figure 10-16 By Tim Treman. Exterior view, library project, Muncie, Indiana.

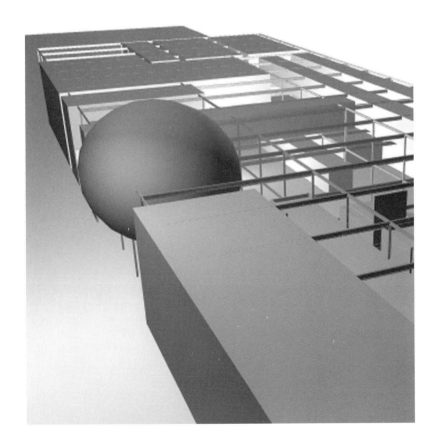

Figure 10-17 By Raymond Gaetan. Computer model view.

Figure 11-1 *(top)* By Alvar Aalto.

Figure 11-2 *(bottom)* By David Stieglitz. Buffalo Waterfront Redevelopment Project.

11 Individual Design

The development and support of individual design thinking is best promoted by the individual designer. Some architects prefer to work in a manner similar to Alvar Aalto, using a loose, multiple-line drawing that gives them an almost tactile experience of their process. The specific characteristics of the chosen media of expression play an important role. Choices of drawing instrument or surface are deliberate, usually providing a level of comfort that supports the flow of ideas. The discovery of a similar degree of comfort with the medium of computer graphics is one of the challenges of achieving its effective use.

Other architects may use a more systematic, deliberate, or economical approach to their work. They apply ordering devices based on theoretical constructs discussed in earlier chapters. These might include modular grids, variations on a theme, or formal manipulations of component-based systems.

To be effective, designers must be comfortable with their own method of thinking. This means that they must carefully select the methods, tools, and environment best suited to their style of thinking. This chapter looks at alternative styles and some of the means for supporting effective thinking within individual design processes.

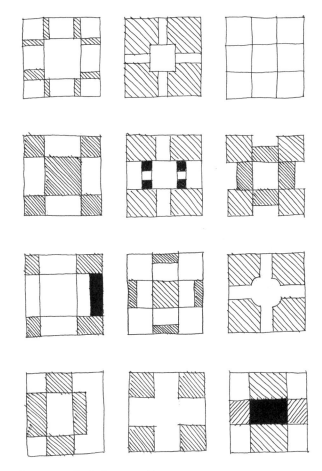

Figure 11-3 Variations on a theme.

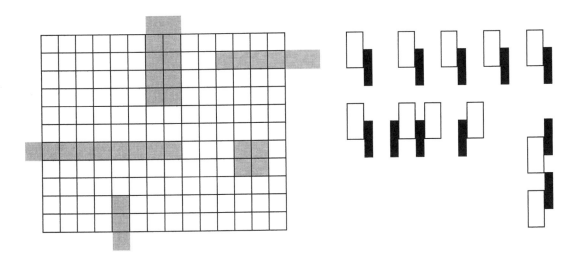

Figure 11-4 Ordering devices.

Figure 11-5 Drawing instruments.

PREPARATION FOR DESIGNING

Although thoughts can be represented graphically by using a great number of media (and there are whole books devoted to these different media), each designer must find materials and instruments with which he will be most comfortable. It is worthwhile to experiment with these different tools. They should be easy to use and maintain, and they should be portable. Personally, I prefer pens to pencils because they produce a high-contrast image, making consistent line quality easy. They are permanent, which discourages the time-consuming habits of erasing or redrawing. I have found four types of pen that meet my needs:

Liquid-ink cartridge pen—Using permanent, jet black ink; it produces a smooth, quick line. Most points wear out eventually, so I use cheap pens with fine rounded points and keep several handy in case one wears out.

Pointed felt-tip pen—This used to be the most common type of felt-tip. It has the advantage of providing a second line weight by using the side of the point, but the ink often thins out, resulting in less sharp images.

Fine-point felt-tip pen—Many of these pens have a thin metal tube that greatly reduces the wear and

deforming of the point. Look for the pens with the darkest black ink.

Extra-fine-point rollerball—These used to produce an uneven or unreliable line, but have been greatly improved and have a longer-lasting supply of ink.

For good results, the drawing instrument must be matched with the right paper. Although the liquid cartridge pen works on most papers, nonporous, smooth-finish paper is the most adaptable for all pens. I buy cheap, white 8½-by-11 photocopy paper in 500-sheet packages. My test for an acceptable match of pen and paper is whether the pen can be moved quickly in any direction without catching or skipping.

Many architects get good results with soft pencils or colored pencils, and some combine media. Everyone's interests and thinking differ, so each person should try to find a simple but effective medium for their personal graphic thinking.

ENVIRONMENT

It is curious that architects, whose profession is concerned with suiting environments to needs, spend little time studying the environment in which they

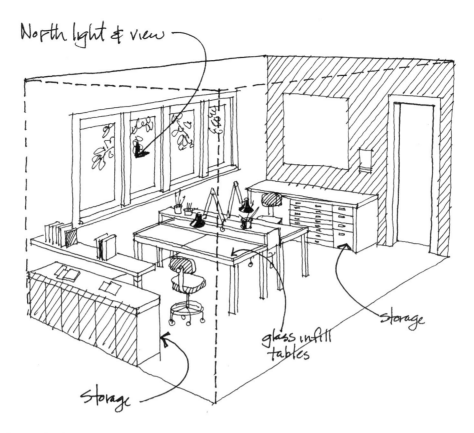

Figure 11-6 Studio environment setup.

work. Robert McKim provides us with a good description:

> *A visual-thinking environment for one person should be as well-designed as a contemporary kitchen. Work areas should be well illuminated, preferably with natural north light and without shadow or glare. The drawing surface should be large and adjustable in height and angle. An additional stand-up table should be available for three-dimensional work; spilled glue and knife marks soon spoil a drawing surface. Organized storage should be provided close to each work area to diminish distracting clutter. Chairs and stools should provide back support in a working position. To alleviate back tension and also to provide for the important element of change, a stand-up, vertical drawing surface should be available: a blackboard, easel, or wall-mounted roll of paper. A large tack-space is needed for displaying current idea sketches. Although admittedly an affront to those who associate productive work with open eyes and erect position, the visual thinker should also have access to a quiet place where he can relax and turn his thoughts inward—or stop thinking entirely: a reclining chair, a couch—even a relaxing bath![1]*

Architects and designers should consciously select the visual environment in which they work to com-plement their own style of thinking. I find that my own development makes me responsive to everything visible. I support concentration by using a clear desk with a blank white vertical surface directly in front of me. Other designers may need a very stimulating environment for thinking.

MENTAL/PHYSICAL CONDITION

The right materials and environment must be accompanied by a good mental and physical state for the individual to think or solve problems effectively. Everyone is subject to tension and stress in their work, and this is especially true of practicing architects. Experienced architects try to pace themselves because they know that mistakes are made under excessive pressure. Frequent exercise and recreation are a basis for a good mental state, but designers can also take specific measures to improve their preparation for work. Relax eyes by closing, then rotating them; ease neck tension by sitting upright with back supported and slowly bend the head forward, backward, and to each side in a circular motion; relax the whole body by stretching and deep breathing.

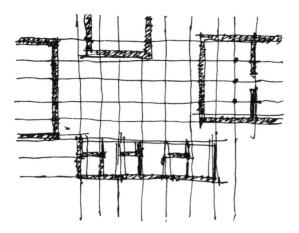

Figure 11-7a Abstract sketch.

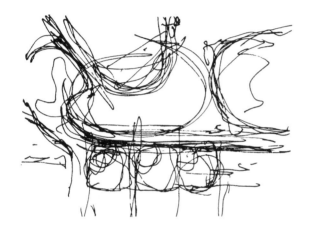

Figure 11-7b Concrete sketch.

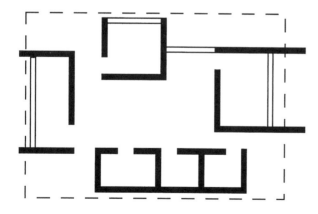

Figure 11-7c Hardline drawing.

ABSTRACT TO CONCRETE THINKING

Graphic thinking is most effective when it respects basic thinking processes. Lawrence Kubie asserts that "Thinking processes actually are automatic, swift and spontaneous when allowed to proceed undisturbed by other influences. Therefore what we need is to be educated in how not to interfere with the inherent capacity of the human mind to think."[2] For this reason, the media and type of drawings used by architects for graphic thinking differ significantly from the drafted, "hard-line" drawings usually associated with architectural design. Graphic thinking sketches must be rapid, flexible, and unrestricting to thinking processes.

Within the range of these sketches, there are two basic tendencies: exploratory abstract sketches and definitive concrete sketches. According to McKim, these respond to two types of thinking. "The first is fast, crude, holistic, and parallel, while the second is deliberate, attentive, detailed and sequential."[3] Designers generally lean toward one or the other of these types of thinking and probably use a little of both. To increase effectiveness, each designer should be aware of his basic type of thinking and be able to recognize when the other type is appropriate.

CONCEPTUAL TO PERCEPTUAL THINKING

Conceptual thinking seeks out the underlying structure, order, or meaning of experience; it attempts taking possession of the experience, comparing it with other experiences, and interpreting it in the light of our knowledge of reality. Perceptual thinking tries to take in the direct experience of an environment, noting the elements from which it is composed and the personal reactions the environment evokes. Often these two modes of thinking are thought of as separate or even in opposition. Creative, dynamic thinking depends upon full integration of conception and perception because they inform and give meaning to each other. Knowing that there are about four hundred varieties of goat's-milk cheeses produced in France adds something to the experience of eating one of them; nevertheless, knowledge of these varieties does not have much meaning until you have tasted one of them. The history of Gothic church construction, including principles and variations, when combined with the overwhelming sensations of moving through the darkness and light of a Gothic church nave, provides a complete, integrated awareness that could not be achieved should either the conceptual or perceptual element be missing.

The designer must be able to move freely between conceptual and perceptual thinking and should avail himself of a variety of graphic means to achieve their integration.

Distortion
referencing
the ideal
form.

Figure 11-8   Leicester Square, London.

Private

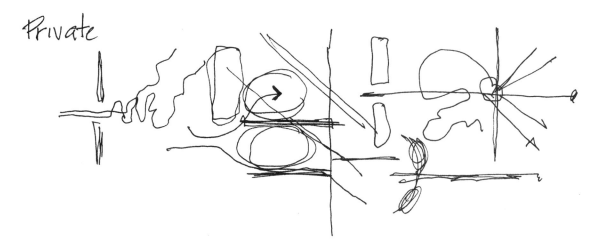

Figure 11-9a Private sketches.

Semi Private

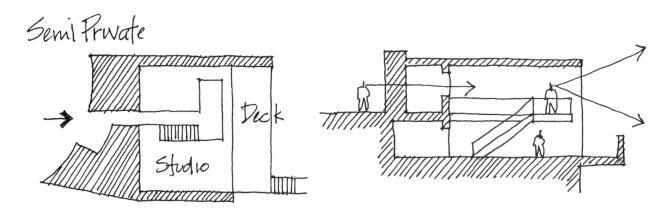

Figure 11-9b Semipublic sketches.

Public

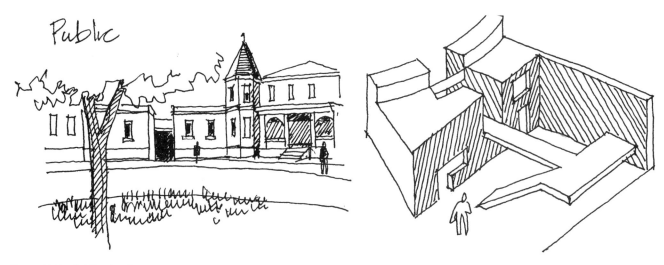

Figure 11-9c Public sketches.

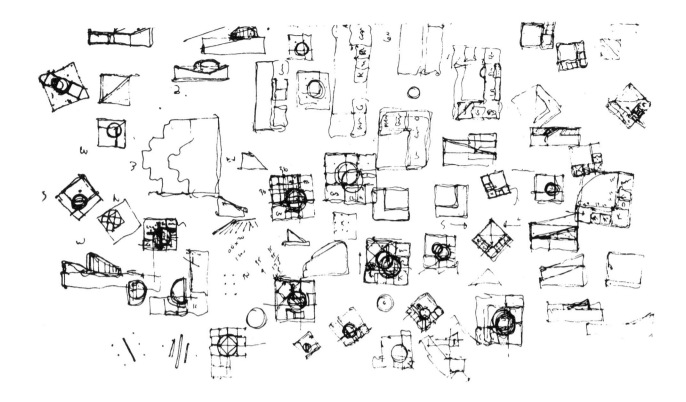

Figure 11-10 By Thomas Beeby. Studies for the Seyfarth House.

PRIVATE TO PUBLIC THINKING

Thinking and the communication it may require have two modes. In the public mode, the individual develops his ideas by communicating with other people. Colin Cherry points out that "Communication is essentially a social affair.... The very word *communicate* means *share,* and inasmuch as you and I are communicating at this moment, we are one.... What we share, we cannot each have as our own possession...."[4] In this sense, there is a public aspect to all ideas because none of us lives in a vacuum. What we hold in our minds comes from interactions with the people and environment that surrounds us.

In the private mode of thinking, the individual develops ideas in isolation from others; communication in this form is directed back toward oneself. Many architects are reluctant to show the sketches they use to develop ideas, and some even have difficulty discussing them. These sketches are tentative and crude compared to presentation drawings, and they often represent incomplete thoughts. But these sketches also reveal the struggle of a mind that doesn't have all the answers. For some designers, this might be embarrassing because of an illusion that the great design concepts flow instantly and completely from the creative mind. But perhaps there is more to it. Conceptual sketches are very personal statements, almost a diary. We are intuitively aware that they can reveal very private feelings, concerns, or fantasies. They are no one else's business.

Although individual design activity requires both public and private communications, the choice of mode is personal. Each designer develops his own style of sketching as an aid to thinking. Some may choose to develop a clarity that can communicate to other people, while others may develop a private graphic language. Either way, you have to be comfortable with it. If you can enjoy sketching, chances are thinking will also be more enjoyable.

OVERCOMING OBSTACLES

Even the best preparation does not assure success in design. Architecture students and sometimes even practitioners run into thinking and problem-solving obstacles. The following list describes some of the more common obstacles and some possible responses.

1. *Can't get started*—If you try to tackle problems that are too big, you become overwhelmed. Try to break down the problem into different parts. Instead of designing the whole school, analyze its parts: classrooms, recreation, administration, etc. When these problems are under control, look at how the parts can fit together to form a school.

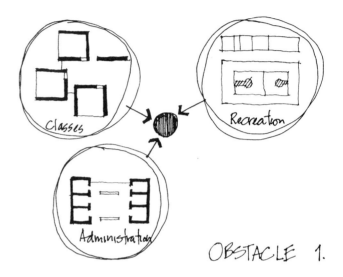

Figure 11-11a

2. *Can't get any good ideas*—Sometimes we have a fear of failure; we are afraid that our solution will be judged to be very poor by others and that they will lose confidence in us. This requires separating one's self from the design problem. If failures in life meant that one's life was a failure, we would all be in deep trouble. Fortunately, life goes on, and this problem will soon be forgotten. The future holds difficult problems as well as easier ones. It may help to treat the problem as a challenge in a game. Try your best and use all of the resources available. Use some of the techniques of manipulation already discussed and take a new look at the problem. If you cannot move ahead on the basis of your assumptions, then arbitrarily change them. If there doesn't seem to be a suitable solution for the kitchen, consider a house without a formal kitchen. It may not be a solution, but it might lead to a solution.

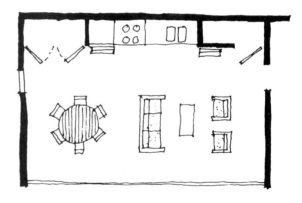

Figure 11-11b

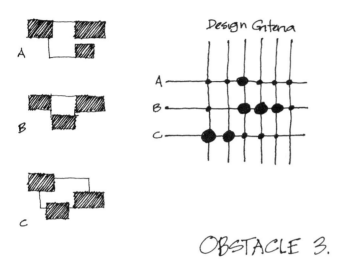

OBSTACLE 3.

Figure 11-11c

3. *Can't make a decision*—Sometimes designers cannot progress on a project because they find it difficult to come to conclusions or decide on a course of action. Spelling out the available alternatives and then comparing them in light of a few basic criteria can facilitate choices. Representing criteria and the ratings of alternatives in graphic images makes it possible to have a picture of the information needed to decide.

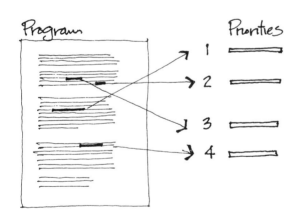

OBSTACLE 4.

Figure 11-11d

4. *Can't finish*—Once a design instructor advised that if we were working under pressure and heard a tapping sound, we should stop and see if it was we who were dotting in the grass on our drawing. He said this was a sure sign that we were avoiding a critical problem in the design. If you find that you are filling up time or just going through the motions, it may help to go back to the original program or problem statement and ask what the basic design objectives are and what the design must achieve minimally not to be a failure. The chances are you will find the deficiency and save yourself a lot of trouble later on.

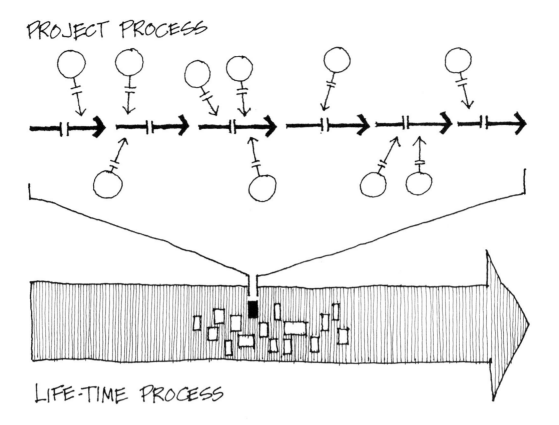

PROJECT PROCESS

LIFE·TIME PROCESS

Figure 11-12 The lifetime context of the individual design project process.

DESIGN AS A LIFETIME PROCESS

Design methodology has some difficulties, such as its focus on the single project and presenting a rather mechanical model of design work. It gives the impression that the information is poured in at the beginning and at strategic points along the way; then the machine, called logical thought, grinds and chews the information, expelling an appropriate product at the end. The actual complexity of the design process might be better understood if we imagine the machine as having several switches to make the individual parts stop and go, speed up, or slow down. Furthermore, each switch has a control that flips the switch back and forth at random. These controls represent the action of the human mind within a design process, for our minds are constantly active and reacting to a whole environment surrounding a specific project. In many cases, the design process of a successful architect becomes understandable when seen as one small part of the architect's life. His design process is governed by patterns of thought, interests, and values that are constantly evolving.

Graphic thinking can be a significant aid to such development. Charles Jencks noted of LeCorbusier, "He started keeping a sketchbook, a pocket-sized writing pad, to jot down ideas, visual impressions and anecdotes. These sketchbooks, of which there are more than seventy covering the whole of LeCorbusier's life, were in themselves a significant addition to Jeanneret's development, for they became a new medium of expression and a source-book for later ideas." Jencks goes on to quote LeCorbusier: "When one travels and works with visual things—architecture, painting, sculpture—one uses one's eyes and draws, so as to fix deep down in one's experience what is seen. Once the impression has been recorded by the pencil, it stays for good, entered, registered, inscribed."[5]

Creative architects often become fascinated with a particular problem or form that they mull over for many years, drawn toward what they feel are fundamental ideas or concerns. For example, Wright pursued many notions in his lifetime regarding such things as plan organization, structure, and materials, which he could pull together in a single design such as the Kaufman House at Falling Water. In effect, the success of this house is the result of very thorough research over a good portion of his career.

Figure 11-13 The accumulation of design concepts in buildings by Frank Lloyd Wright.

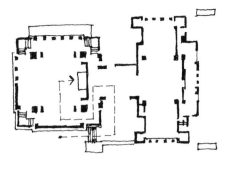

Unity Temple

Figure 11-13b Binodal organization with indirect path entry.

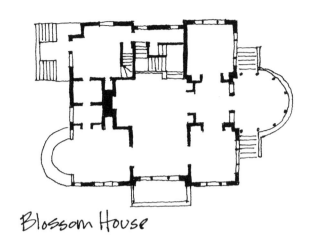

Blossom House

Figure 11-13a Cross plan with interlocking spaces.

Winslow House

Figure 11-13c Three-part horizontal organization of the facade.

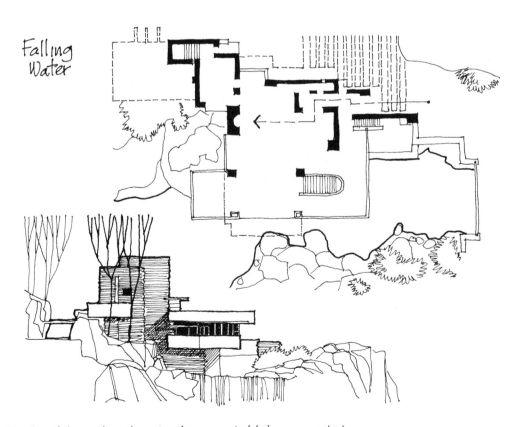

Falling Water

Figure 11-14 Combination of the previous elements using new materials in a new context.

Figure 11-15 Elevation sketch. Guggenheim Museum.

The careers of current and future designers will be significantly influenced by digital media. If we keep in mind the implications of design as a lifetime process—the persistence of ideas and the stimulation of a knowledge base—digital media promise a tremendous opportunity. Significant new tools include:

1. An impressive array of illustration tools in object- and pixel-based computer graphic applications.

2. An expanding variety of documentation choices in print, video, and projection formats.

3. Unprecedented resources for achieving and retrieval of a full range of visual images.

The impact of these new capabilities is directly proportional to our ability to connect graphic images with thought processes.

Figure 11-16 Elevation sketch. Guggenheim Museum.

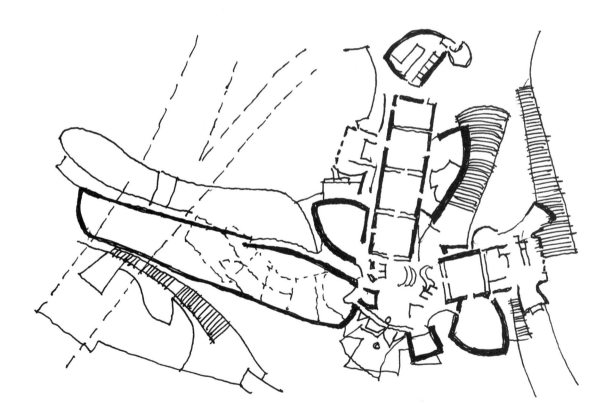

Figure 11-17 Plan sketch. Guggenheim Museum.

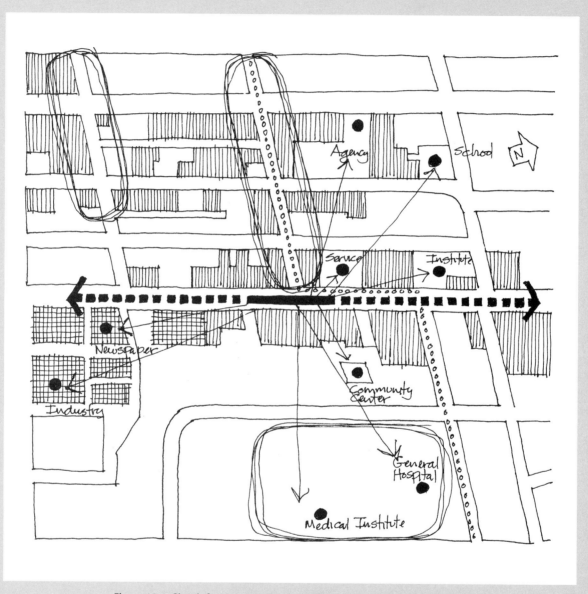

Figure 12-1 Sketch for a transportation analysis team: transit station area.

12 Team Design

Although a great portion of this book deals with individual design thinking, in our world, design rarely takes place in isolation. Geoffrey Broadbent stresses the point: "In the nature of architectural design, it is not possible for any architect to wield power without the full collaboration of others. With very few exceptions, the architect inevitably works as a member of a group; however strong his personality, he still needs a great many other people—architects, technicians, consultants, contractors, and so on—to translate his ideas into reality."[1]

The project-based design team has been one of the major features of the modern American architectural firm. Offices such as Skidmore, Owings & Merrill, The Architects Collaborative, and Caudill Rowlett Scott contributed significantly to the development of the team concept. They demonstrated that problem-oriented teams have several advantages:

1. Much more expertise than that possessed by an individual architect can be brought to bear on the project.
2. A wider range of building types can be tackled.
3. More creative thinking can be stimulated through teamwork.
4. A firm has a better chance of survival when it is based upon a principle of organization rather than the personality of a single architect.

The team concept has expanded well beyond the limits of the traditional architectural design team. Teams now include clients, users of the intended building, contractors, financiers, social scientists, manufacturers, and specialists. We have learned that the success of a design often depends on all of their inputs. Teamwork has also overcome the constraints of time and space. Through the use of the Internet, teams may be composed of architects, consultants, and clients dispersed around the globe in different time zones.

TEAM COMMUNICATION

Graphic communication can play a very important part in the success of teamwork. To be effective, team members must constantly share information and ideas. With the use of graphic thinking skills, these contributions can be quickly presented to the group and remain always available for retrieval and manipulation. In addition, drawings help knock down the barriers built by professional jargon, thereby allowing persons from different disciplines to communicate, as exemplified on the facing page with a project team that includes an architect, a planner, a systems engineer, and a transportation specialist.

Scientific research has recognized the importance of a research community sharing thoughts as the scientists pursue the same problem. Chemistry, for example, has evolved a graphic language that shares a broad range of ideas about complex problems. The graphic description of the DNA molecule is a dramatic example of the importance of the integration of graphics and thinking. The discovery of the double-helix structure of the DNA molecule was hailed as a major breakthrough, opening up a whole new era of research in organic chemistry. Graphic thinking has aided the DNA research in several ways:

1. A model of the central object of research that is useful and acceptable to all of the research community.
2. A model that presents new challenges and problems to be solved.
3. A model that provides a direction for individual researchers to continue work in their different areas of specialization.

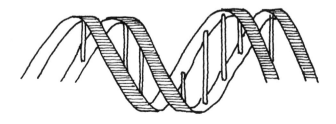

Figure 12-2 Diagram of double helix model of the DNA molecule.

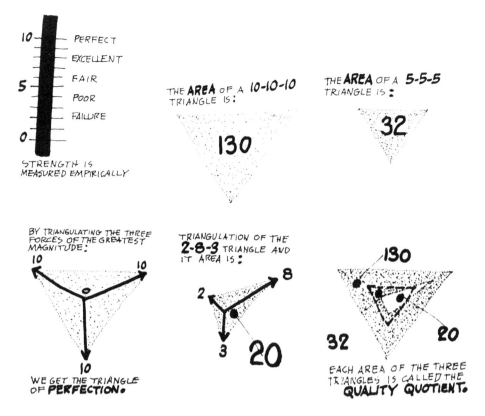

Figure 12-3 By William Caudill. Evaluation diagrams for projects.

Currently, several architectural firms are developing graphic techniques to assist design teams. The firm of Caudill Rowlett Scott (CRS) was a leader in team communication. In *Architecture by Team,* William Caudill explained the graphic techniques used by CRS teams to analyze problems, generate solutions, and evaluate results. He stressed: "Once there are empathy and communication among members, the team will move and every member will benefit. Without the two, people cannot work together. Without the two, there is no team."[2]

Sharing design objectives is an important part of successful teamwork. In the early stages of a project objectives may not be entirely clear. However, the team can often identify those influences or "design determinants" that they agree should have impact on the final resolution of the design. Diagrams like those shown opposite serve as visual reminders of those determinants throughout the design process.

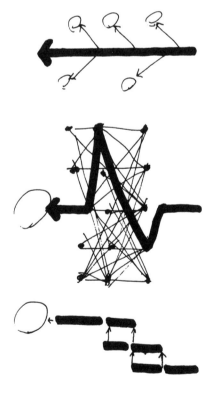

Figure 12-4 By William Caudill. Project process diagrams.

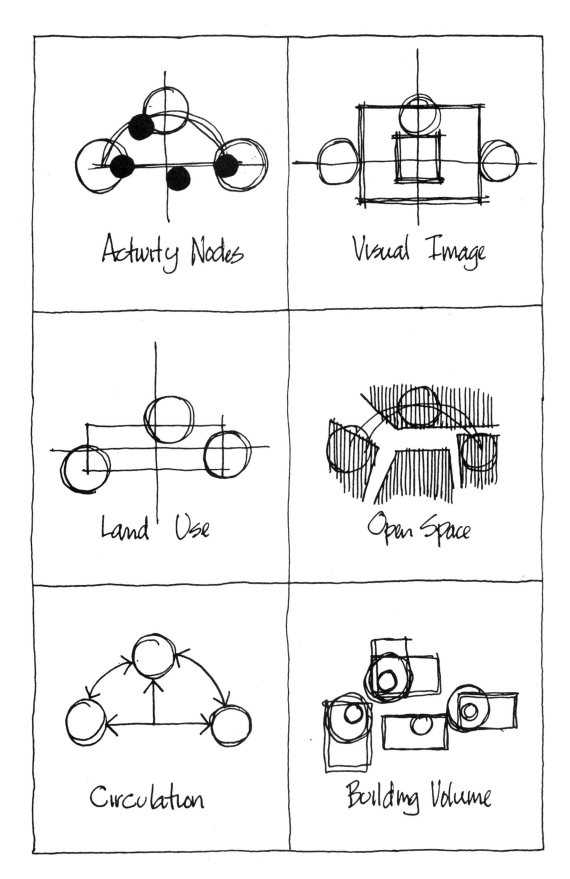

Figure 12-5 Analysis diagrams.

APPLYING GRAPHICS

Graphic notation can contribute to team design by illustrating two important needs: information and processes of working toward a solution of the design problem. The design brief (distinguishable from the building program, which normally refers to the program of building functions) contains most of the information needed to complete a building design. The design brief includes:

The program of functions
Description of users
Client's objectives
Financial constraints
Time constraints
Zoning restrictions
Site analysis
Site access
Macro climate
Micro climate
Building prototypes
Special planning considerations
Construction system

The diagrams and sketches on these two pages illustrate some of the ways information from the design brief can be presented to the whole team.

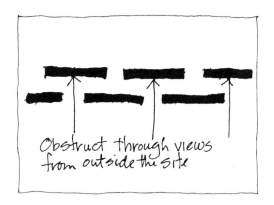

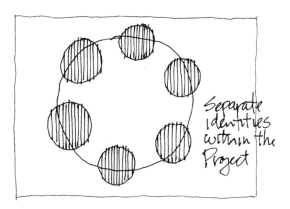

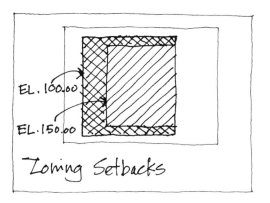

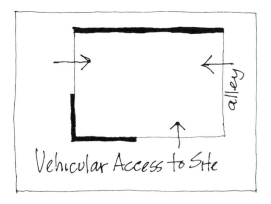

Figure 12-6 Analysis card examples.

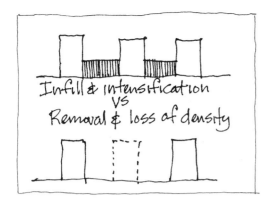

Infill & intensification
vs
Removal & loss of density

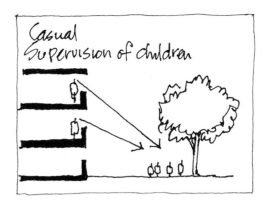

Casual
Supervision of children

Shifts in apartment sizes

1 br.

2 br.

3 br.

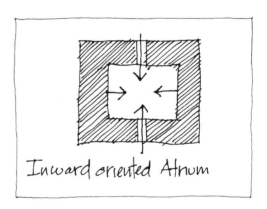

Family Groupings

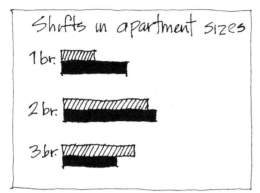

Hierarchy of Dwelling Units

Inward oriented Atrium

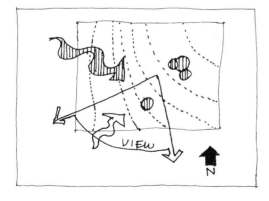

VIEW

N

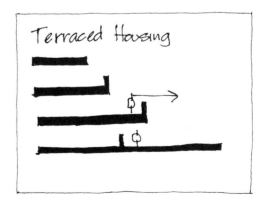

Terraced Housing

Figure 12-7 Analysis card examples.

Figure 12-8 Evolution of the process network diagram.

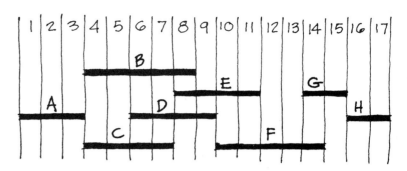

BARCHART

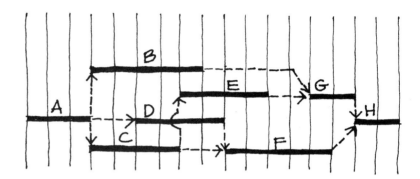

BARCHART SHOWING PRECEDENCE

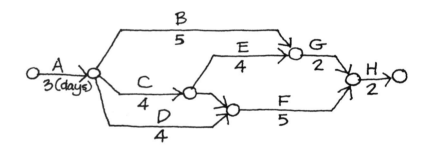

NETWORK

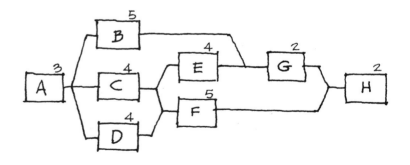

TASK-ORIENTED NETWORK

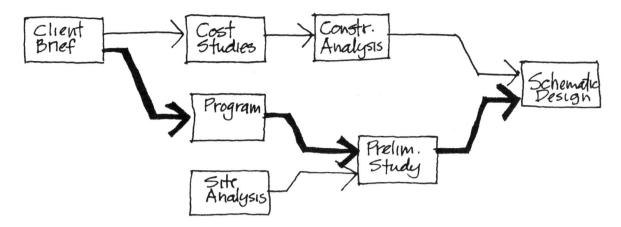

Figure 12-9a A simplified network.

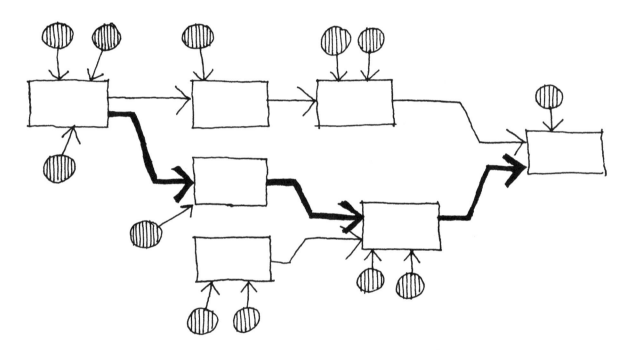

Figure 12-9b Attachment of information to the network.

TEAM DESIGN PROCESS—MAKING A NETWORK

When many people must work together, it is often helpful to make a flowchart of all the tasks and where they fit in the context of the entire project. These networks evolved from simple bar charts, which show a simple schedule of tasks. By showing the necessary sequence of tasks, the basis is laid for an elementary network.

Networks can become quite elaborate if they include the most minute tasks, but I prefer to keep them simple in order to concentrate on the most basic activities. This simple network becomes a sort of rack on which to hang descriptions of information needed for different tasks. Since complex buildings or complex design processes require changes in team composition at different project stages, a network is also a handy way to identify points at which special expertise is needed.

Figure 12-10 Notes from a concept generation meeting.

TEAM CREATIVITY

Because graphic thinking increases the output of ideas for the individual, the possibilities for a group are geometrically increased, assuming that the way is opened for everyone to communicate. Alex Osborn[3] developed a method called brainstorming that helps to keep the channels of thinking open. He identified four rules that must be followed to generate ideas within a group during brainstorming:

1. Suspend judgment on anyone's idea.
2. Freewheel; let your imagination roam.
3. Strive for quantity of ideas.
4. Build on each other's ideas.

If one member of the brainstorming group concentrates on producing sketches of the ideas generated, the already fertile situation is even more intensified as he feeds back information to all members of the group. The number of possible new associations is at least doubled. The sketches should be as quick and loose as the ones shown here. Remember that only a simple recognizable symbol for the idea is required; in some instances, this might be a word or phrase.

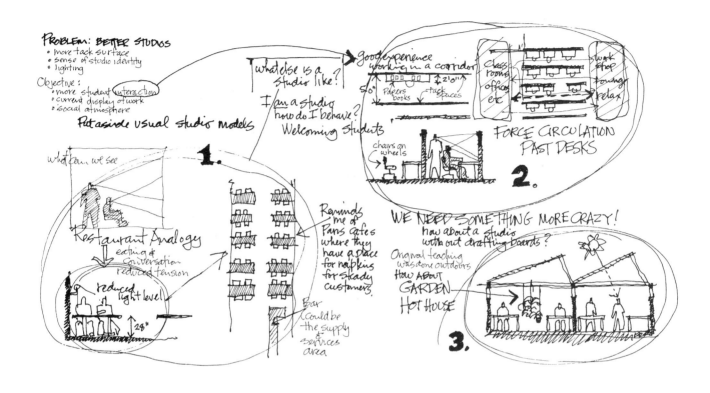

Figure 12-11 Notes from a brainstorming session.

EVOLVING TEAM TECHNIQUES

Team thinking is an evolving area of research and creativity. New approaches are continually tested, and visual communication could play an important role in realizing the potential of teams. As technological advances (graphic simulation and reproduction) are made, the speed of graphic manipulation and feedback is greatly increased. Real-time, large-screen video projection, practical three-dimensional computer graphic modeling, and laser-disk visual libraries will provide unprecedented visual tools. The possibilities are indeed exciting.

Making useful and practical advances in team thinking depends on the quality of relationships among the team members. A few suggestions may help:

1. Accept each other's contribution to the situation as having equal potential.
2. Place personal goals below team goals.
3. Help each other by concentrating on each member's input.
4. Have your sense of humor ready and use it.

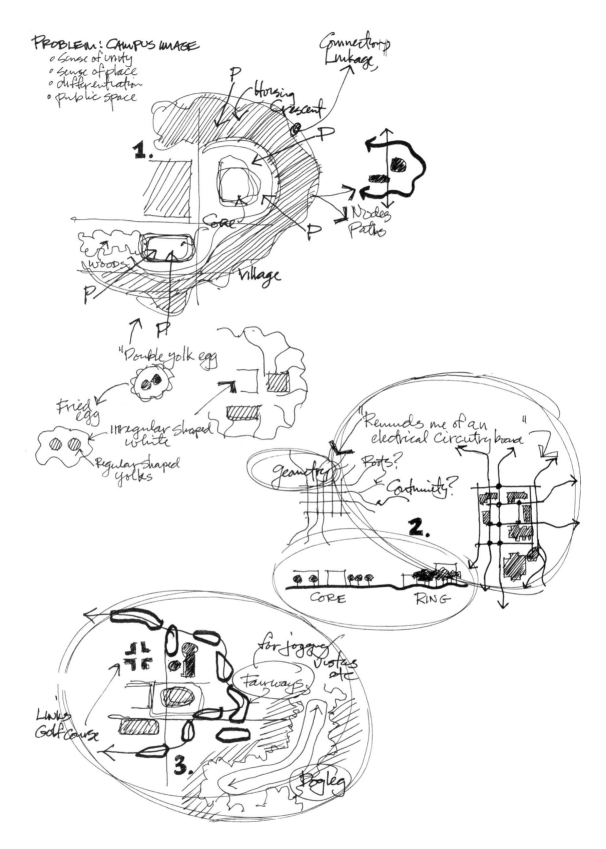

Figure 12-12 Campus study.

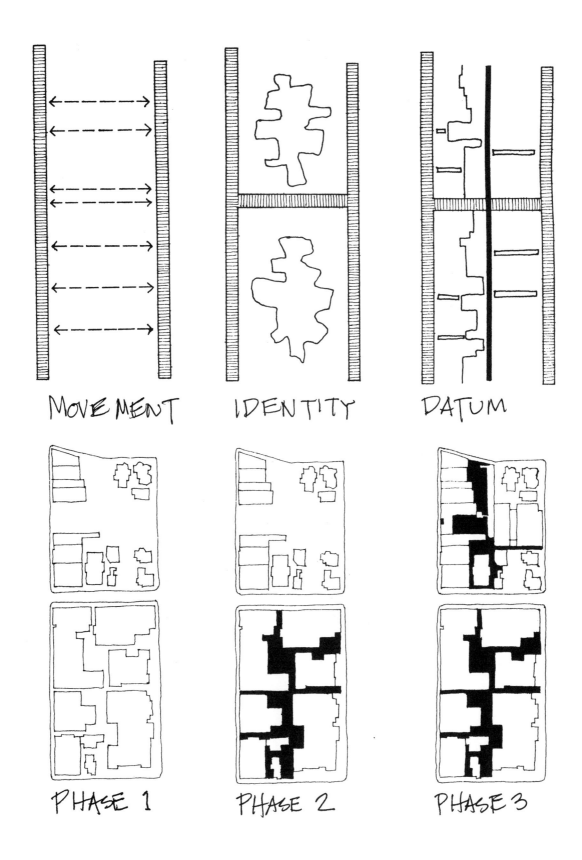

Figure 12-13 Urban core studies.

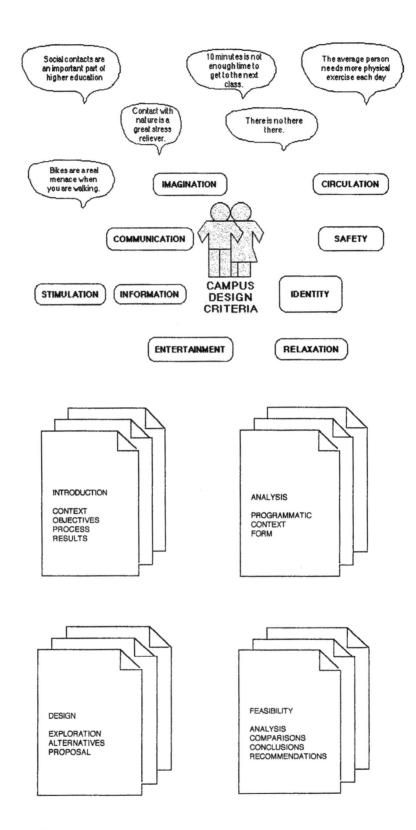

Figure 12-14 Computer-generated team notes.

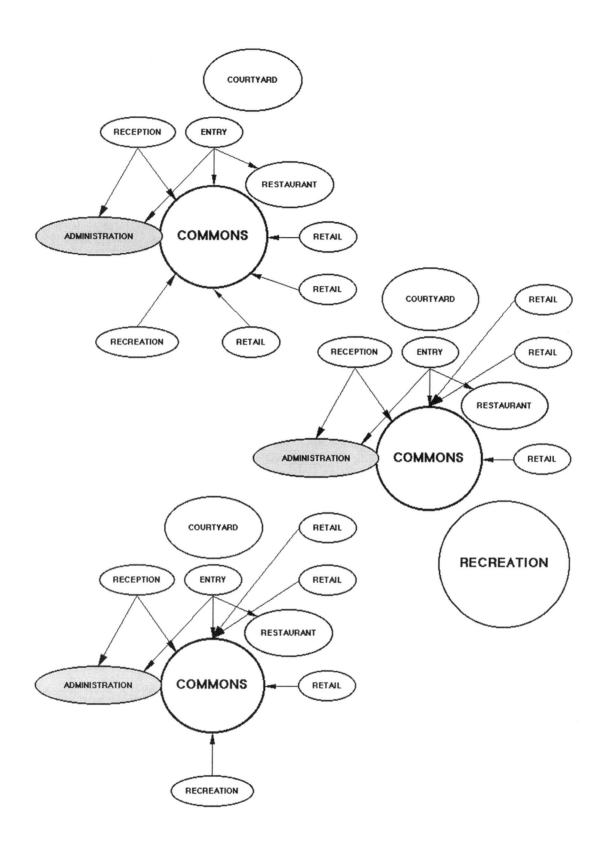

Figure 12-15 Computer-generated team notes.

Figure 13-1 Public-oriented graphics from the Athens, Ohio, Urban Design Study, P. Laseau and G. K. Nishi.

13 Public Design

The general public is taking a more active role in the planning and design of communities, and people are working more closely with design professionals. Graphic thinking has changed to accommodate this new development. This chapter discusses the fundamental shifts in the public's attitude and shows how these shifts support design and problem-solving processes.

Explorers of the fifteenth and sixteenth centuries verified the newly introduced concept about the shape of the earth, and this changed forever man's sense of relationship to his world. In our century, explorers of the universe added another dimension with the concept of the earth as a "spaceship," a wondrously brilliant island floating in the vast blackness of space. Once again, the impact of our concept of relationship to our environment, the earth, has and will have fundamental consequences. Other dramatic changes have altered our view of the world: horse and buggy to spaceships; musket to atomic annihilation; telecommunications; minicomputers; energy crisis; large-scale pollution of air and water; electric power failures; and so on.

Books such as *The Age of Discontinuity, Future Shock,* and *The Temporary Society*[1] have attempted to describe these shifts in values. In the area of architecture and environmental design, the shift in values is most dramatically expressed in the historic preservation movement. Now that change has become a central feature in our lives, people are beginning to exercise their judgment over which changes are desirable and which are not. They are developing new perceptions about historical buildings as sources of continuity in communities. They seem to seek stability in an atmosphere of overwhelming change.

I believe that we are seeking a new sense of identity for ourselves and our communities. The increased value placed on the environment is already having important effects on our economic system; companies are searching for locations with a great influx of people rather than moving people to where the jobs are. Early successful design responses to the preservation movement as in Ghirardelli Square and the Cannery[2] in San Francisco have been followed by a wave of rediscovery and preservation movements in the main streets of towns across the country. Community development associations are springing up everywhere as consumer movements convince an increasing number of people that they can personally do something to improve their lives and their environment.

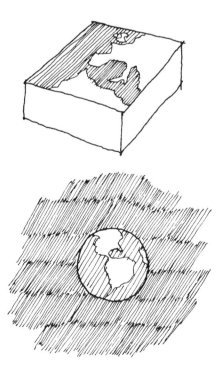

Figure 13-2

One-Way Communication   vs   Two-Way Communication

(a)   (b)

Figure 13-3a, b Contrast in approaches to design communication.

Figure 13-4 Freehand drawing done over a drafted version.

Figure 13-6 By Harry Eggink. East Cambridge residential neighborhood.

Figure 13-5 By Harry Eggink. Local retail street, East Cambridge study.

COMMUNITY DESIGN

Jim Burns claimed that architects must work more directly with the public to avoid the mistakes of the past.

"Some of the environmental changes...have had negative impacts that were not easily discernible at first. They seemed to be good things to do—to relocate a museum or provide new housing or put a sports arena in a park. What happened eventually was that the museum lost participants, the housing was disliked, the park patrons shunned the sports facilities. The reason for these kinds of failures is usually that the changes broke connections between people and the opportunities their community offered."[3]

The best way to assure that people are not cut off from community opportunities is to involve them in the design of their communities.

If the architects are to promote the involvement of the public in the design process, they must take a look at the way ideas are communicated. Some architects are accustomed to making highly polished presentations to clients or boards of directors. Their drawings are slick, with an air of finality and certainty. When such drawings are used in a public participation design project, the communities have the feeling they are being talked at and not talked with; they are intimidated and discouraged from contributing their ideas, no matter how much to the contrary the designer pleads.

Inviting communication starts with the character of the sketches.

1. Sketches should always have a loose, freehand quality, a sort of incompleteness suggesting that they can be changed and will be improved with additional thinking. Even if a perspective has been mechanically constructed, it can be traced over freehand to achieve a more tentative feeling.

2. Keep sketches simple and avoid abstractions that require interpretation. The examples above from a Cambridge urban design study[4] are quite effective. Many people find it easier to relate to aerial views.

3. Use many labels to easily identify the parts of the drawings. The cartoon caption bubble is a useful device for labeling or conveying the possibilities of an environment.

Figure 13-7 By Steve Levine.

Figure 13-8 By Steve Levine.

TAKE-PART WORKSHOPS

Several architects and planners have worked vigorously to develop graphic communication methods, making it possible for the public to understand and enter into the design process. One of the innovators in this trend was Lawrence Halprin:

> *I am concentrating on the issue of people's interactions with their environment both as individuals and in groups.... both aspects are important. We have been searching for archetypal relationships... in workshops which take place primarily out in the field. These taking part workshops allow people the opportunity to discover and articulate their own needs and desires for themselves and for their communities.... They discover ways of communicating with each other and arriving at creative decisions based on multiple input.*[5]

Jim Burns, planning consultant and former Halprin associate with wide experience in organizing workshops, described the workshop process as having four basic steps:

1. *Awareness*—Community members get a better experience of those things that form the community environment and how those things are interconnected. Awareness is achieved principally by going out into the community and looking and taking notes.
2. *Perception*—Citizens begin to understand their community and their personal relationship to it by modeling the collective experience of what exists and their hopes for what could exist.
3. *Decision-making*—Based on awareness and perceptions, the community describes what they would like done and when it should be done.
4. *Implementation strategies*—Devised to assure that the projects adopted by the community are realized.[6]

To complete these four steps, workshops have developed a number of graphic aids (see Figures 13-7 through 13-11) to involve the community members in the design process.

Figure 13-9 By Steve Levine.

Figure 13-10 By Steve Levine.

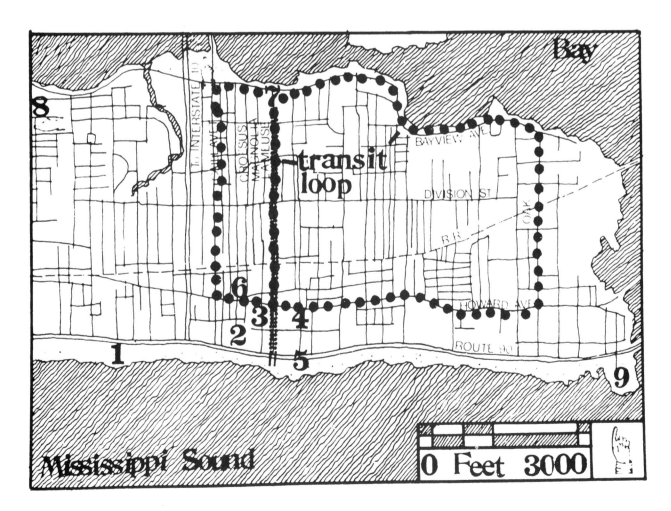

Figure 13-11 By Steve Levine.

Figure 13-12 By John J. Desmond. Phoenix study.

Figure 13-13 By Peter Hasselman. Atlantic City study.

AMERICAN INSTITUTE OF ARCHITECTS REGIONAL/URBAN DESIGN ASSISTANCE TEAM

For decades, the American Institute of Architects has been sending teams of professionals into communities to conduct urban design studies. These teams, which include architects, economists, urban designers, sociologists, managers, and lawyers, work with resource persons from the community to analyze problems and develop strategies. An important part of the Regional Urban Design Assistance Team (R/U DAT)[7] process is the report they give to the whole community on the findings of the joint professional-citizen team. It is critical to the future progress of community development that the public understands that the report is only a suggestion for an approach to development and not the description of a final product. The sketches used in the report to the community attempt to give general images of environmental objectives without proposing specific design solutions. They provide us with models for public design communication.

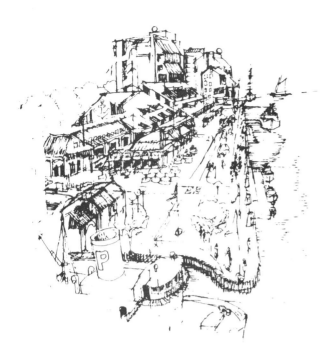

Figure 13-14 By William Durkee and Roy Mann. Portsmouth study.

Figure 13-15 By William Durkee and Roy Mann. Portsmouth study.

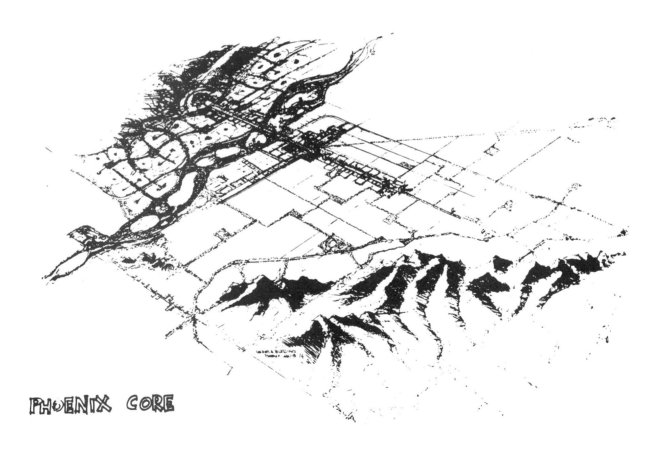

PHOENIX CORE

Figure 13-16 By Charles A. Blessing. Phoenix study.

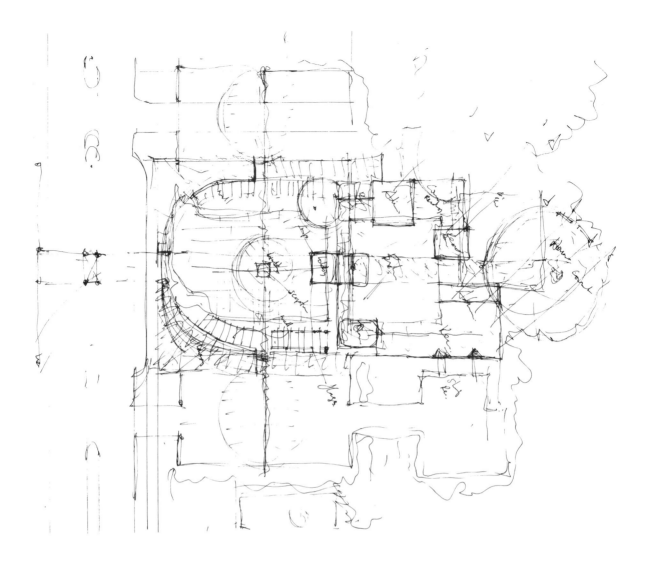

Figure 13-17 By Harry Eggink. Spatial zoning study.

Figure 13-18 By Harry Eggink. Site form investigation.

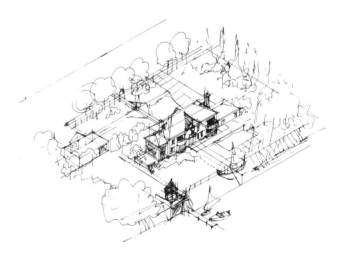

Figure 13-19 By Harry Eggink. Site study.

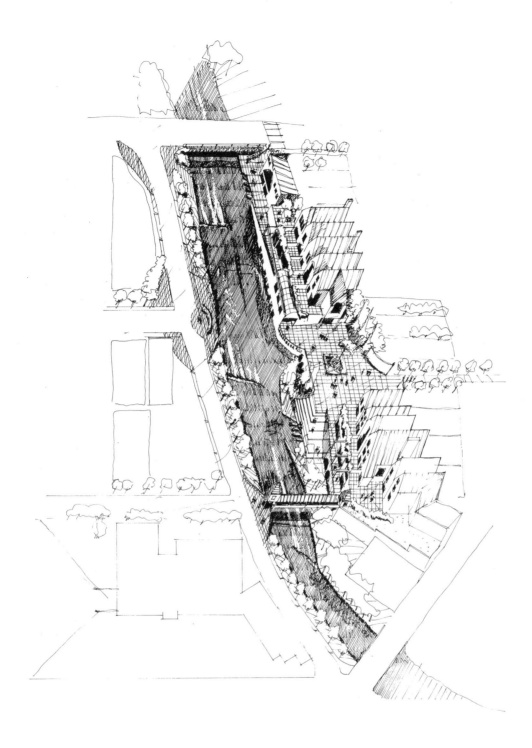

WORKING SKETCHES

In an attempt to involve community members in the design process, designers often develop ideas and drawings in a public, accessible space. Exploratory drawings can be an effective means of informally eliciting the participation of the community. These sketches may use familiar drawing conventions while staying loose in style.

Figure 13-20 By Harry Eggink. Elkhart, Indiana, urban design study.

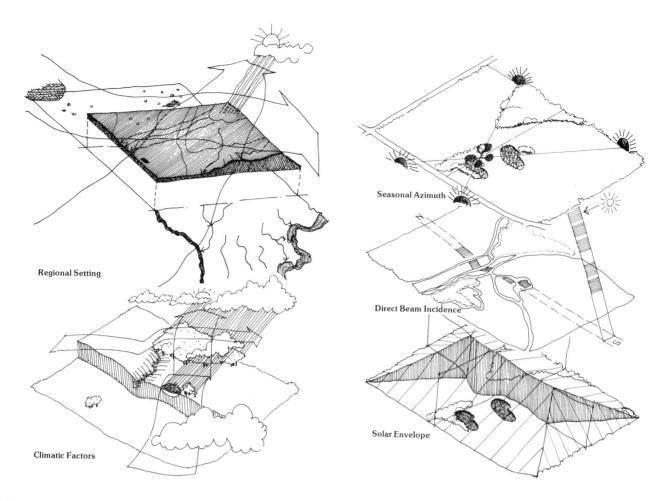

Regional Setting

Climatic Factors

Seasonal Azimuth

Direct Beam Incidence

Solar Envelope

Figure 13-21 By Harry Eggink. Climate and solar site studies.

Drawings published in reports or community newspapers usually need to be more carefully planned. To avoid the boredom or intimidation of confronting the public with too many drawings, each drawing must clearly and economically communicate the relationships among many design concerns. Axonometric or bird's-eye perspective views, such as those shown on these two pages, appear to be the most easily understood by the public. Although often based on carefully constructed underlay drawings, these illustrations are rendered in freehand so that they appear less formal and invite public discussion.

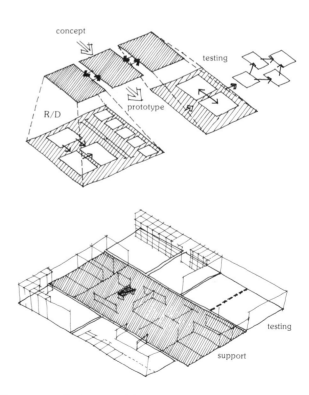

concept

testing

R/D

prototype

testing

support

Figure 13-22 By Harry Eggink. Programming diagrams.

Figure 13-23 By Harry Eggink. Program development studies.

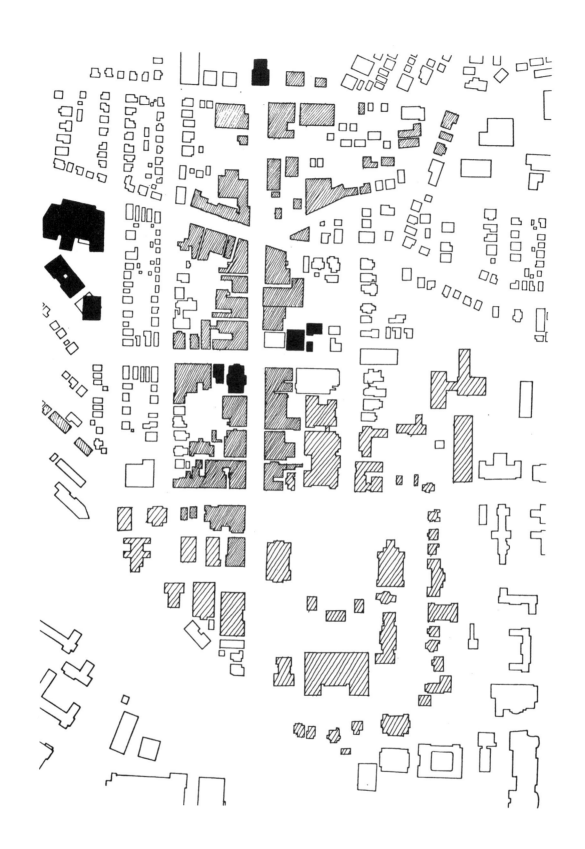

Figure 13-24 Urban analysis, Athens, Ohio.

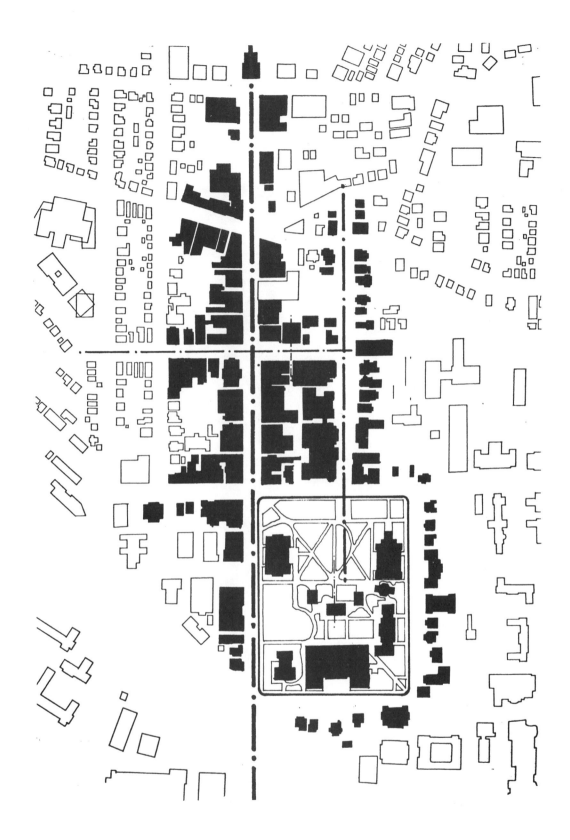

Figure 13-25 Urban analysis, Athens, Ohio.

Figure 14-1 By Nathan Moore. Computer model view.

14 Conclusion

Architecture and the other arts hold a vital place in the future of our culture, creativity being one of the most important factors. Looking over this book, it occurs to me that most of what I have written deals with how or what could be done and not so much with why.

The importance of the arts to national survival was pointed out clearly in the 1951 Massey Report commissioned by the Canadian government:

When Mr. Churchill in 1940 called the British people to their supreme effort, he invoked the traditions of his country, and based his appeal on the common background from which had grown the character and the way of life of his fellow countrymen. In the spiritual heritage of Great Britain was found the quickening force to meet the menacing facts of that perilous hour. Nothing could have been more "practical" than that appeal to thought and emotion.... Canada became a national entity because of certain habits of mind and convictions which its people shared and would not surrender. Our country was sustained through difficult times by the power of this spiritual legacy. It will flourish in the future in proportion as we believe in ourselves. It is the intangibles which give a nation not only its essential character but its vitality as well. What may seem unimportant or even irrelevant under the pressure of daily life may well be the thing that endures, which may give a community its power to survive. But tradition is always in the making and from this fact we draw a second assumption: the innumerable institutions, movements, and individuals interested in the arts, letters and sciences throughout our country are now forming the national tradition of the future.[1]

Architects are problem solvers, but the problems of architecture, like the problems of our society, run much deeper than the so-called practical level. A building should reinforce the spirit as well as provide safety and security. Architecture must still be an art as well as a science.

Visual communication is in the midst of sweeping changes in both methodology and scope. Computer and video technologies are obviously providing the designer with new graphic tools of amazing power and speed: computer-aided drawing systems that cut production time to a third of conventional drafting; expert or semi-expert systems that bring to bear the powerful memory of the computer; video simulation of the experience of moving through an environment proposed by the designer. These same technologies are revolutionizing the role of visual communication in the public domain; graphic techniques once held as skills of the specialist are becoming available to anyone with a computer; early exposure to computer graphics and television will provide future generations with unprecedented visual literacy.

In these early stages of adopting new technologies, it is common to focus on how we can accomplish various tasks with these machines. We become fascinated with developing hardware and software that can do more and do it faster. As I suggested at the opening of this conclusion, in order to gain for ourselves the full benefits of science, we must be equally focused on why we are using these technologies. A deeper understanding of the purposes of design is the key to developing new capabilities that are truly supportive of our aspirations. As Lewis Mumford wrote:

No matter how completely technics relies upon the objective procedures of the sciences, it does not form an independent system like the universe: it exists as an element in human culture and it promises well or ill as the social groups that exploit it promise well or ill. The machine itself makes no demands and holds out no promises: it is the human spirit that makes demands and keeps promises.[2]

Figure 14-2 By Nathan Moore. Computer model view.

Figure 14-3 By Nathan Moore. Computer model view.

Figure 14-4 By Nathan Moore. Computer model view.

THE CHALLENGES

In architectural education the temptation to focus on
the contrasts between traditional and digital media
seems irresistible. On the one hand is the belief that
digital media will not only provide new opportunities
but render other media obsolete. On the other side is
an equally strong commitment to the importance of
the qualitative impacts of traditional media. The resolution of these contrasting positions lies in two critical perspectives—the question of appropriateness of
media and the concept of media integration.

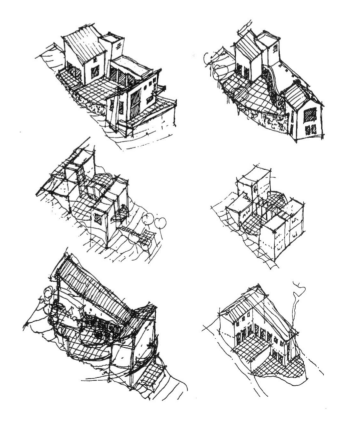

Figure 14-5 Development sketches, Hammonds Residence, House
+ House, architects.

Figure 14-6 Computer-rendered view, Hammonds Residence, House + House, architects.

Appropriateness

When Ludwig von Bertalanfy, a pioneer in general systems theory, was asked whether systems philosophy rendered scientific philosophy obsolete, he offered an analogy that would apply equally well to the evaluation of communication media. He pointed out that sail-powered ships had long since been replaced by diesel- and atomic-powered ocean liners for intercontinental cargo transport. However, this did not invalidate the principles of sailing. Sailboats continue to play an important role in sport and recreation, while fuel-powered ships continue to be developed to meet a range of commercial tasks.

In graphic communication, freehand drawing continues to be an evocative, comfortable, and effective support for ideation for individual designers or design teams. Sketching helps one to take in and "digest" environmental experiences. The differences between media such as charcoal, paper, clay, or paint promote different perceptions of the development of a design and afford a tactile, kinesthetic stimulus for thought.

But computer graphics have a decided edge for ease and speed in the application of conventions such as orthographic, paraline, or perspective projection. Three-dimensional modeling applications have developed to a point where models of spaces can be defined, illuminated and virtually traversed concurrent with design studies.

Integration

The more promising perspective exploits the complementary functionalities of traditional and digital media. If we focus on the link between the media—human thought—significant possibilities begin to emerge. Revisiting the process of graphic thinking discussed at the outset of this book, we can see the image on the computer screen as only one component of that process. In itself the digital perspective view is meaningless. It is the meaning the designer attaches to the image that matters, and the richness of that meaning varies depending on the depth or breadth of the designer's perception. Powers of perception, in turn, are related to the breadth of the designer's experience with relating a variety of experiences of architecture with visual representation. This train of dependencies brings us to freehand sketching and its role as a tool for gaining understanding of the roles of architecture and environment.

Ultimately, graphic thinking is about the marvel of human thought. Media come to life and reveal possibilities for design to the extent they reflect and provoke thought and imagination.

Figure 14-7 Computer model view.

SPACE OF
IMAGINATION

HERE ← → THERE

Figure 14-8 Sketched interpretations.

Notes

Preface to the Third Edition

1. Peters, Thomas J., and Waterman, Robert H., Jr. *In Search of Excellence.* New York: Harper & Row, 1982.

Preface to the First Edition

1. From "The Need of Perception for the Perception of Needs," keynote speech by Dr. Heinz Von Foerster delivered at the 1975 National Convention of the American Institute of Architects, Atlanta, Georgia.

Chapter 1

1. Broadbent, Geoffrey,. *Design in Architecture.* New York: John Wiley & Sons, Inc., 1973, p. 343.

2. Hamilton, Edward A. *Graphic Design for the Computer Age.* New York: Van Nostrand Reinhold Company, 1970, p. 16.

3. McKim, Robert H. *Experiences in Visual Thinking.* Monterey, CA: Brooks/Cole, 1972, p. 22.

4. Arnheim, Rudolf. *Visual Thinking.* Berkeley: University of California Press, 1969, p. 13.

5. Arnheim, Rudolf. "Gestalt Psychology and Artistic Form." In *Aspects of Form,* edited by Lancelot Law Whyte. Bloomington: Indiana University Press, 1966, p. 203.

6. McKim, *Experiences in Visual Thinking,* p. 40.

7. Arnheim, "Gestalt Psychology and Artistic Form," p. 206.

8. Levens, A. S. *Graphics in Engineering Design.* New York: John Wiley & Sons, Inc., 1962, p. 415.

9. Arnheim, Rudolf. *Art and Visual Perception: A Psychology of the Creative Eye.* Berkeley: University of California Press, 1954, p. 46.

Chapter 2

1. All of the successful architectural designers that I have interviewed stressed the importance of sketching ability in their work.

2. Perls, Frederick. *Ego, Hunger, and Aggression.* New York: Random House, 1969.

3. Downer, Richard. *Drawing Buildings.* New York: WatsonGuptill Publications, Inc., 1962, p. 9.

4. Cullen, Gordon. *Townscape.* London: The Architectural Press, 1961.

5. Gundelfinger, John. As quoted in *On-the-spot Drawing,* by Nick Meglin. New York: WatsonGuptill Publications, Inc., 1969, p. 62.

6. Folkes, Michael. *Drawing Cartoons,* New York: WatsonGuptill Publications, Inc., 1963, p. 19.

Chapter 3

1. *Webster's New World Dictionary,* 2d ed. New York: William Collins & World Publishing Co., Inc., 1976.

2. Arnheim, *Art and Visual Perception: A Psychology of the Creative Eye,* p. 33.

3. Lockard, William Kirby. *Design Drawing.* Tucson, AZ: Pepper Publishing, 1974, p. 124.

4. Jacoby, Helmut. *Architectural Drawings.* New York: Praeger Publishers, Inc., 1965.

5. Gundelfinger, *On-the-spot Drawing,* pp. 61–62.

6. Lockard, *Design Drawing,* p. 262.

Chapter 4

1. Bonta, Juan Pablo. "Notes for a Semiotic Theory of Graphic Languages." Paper presented to the International Conference on Semiotics, Ulm, Germany, 1972.

2. McKim, *Experiences in Visual Thinking,* p. 129.

3. Bruner, Jerome. *On Knowing: Essays for the Left Hand.* Cambridge, MA: Belknap Press of Harvard University Press, 1962, p. 123.

4. Arnheim, "Gestalt Psychology and Artistic Form," p. 204.

5. Bruner, *On Knowing: Essays for the Left Hand,* p. 182.

6. McKim, *Experiences in Visual Thinking,* pp. 1-24–1-26.

Chapter 5

1. Larson, Tom. Personal communication.

Chapter 6

1. Best, Gordon. "Method and Intention in Architectural Design." In *Design Methods in Architecture,* edited by Geoffrey Broadbent and Anthony Ward. New York: George Wittenborn, Inc., 1969, p. 155.

2. Broadbent, *Design in Architecture,* p. 365.

3. McKim, *Experiences in Visual Thinking;* p. 105.

4. McKim, *Experiences in Visual Thinking,* p. 127.

5. Rittel, Horst. "Some Principles for the Design of an Educational System for Design." Part I, *DMG Newsletter.* Berkeley, CA: Design Methods Group, Dec. 1970.

6. Pena, William M. *Problem Seeking: An Architectural Programming Primer.* Boston: Cahners Books International, Inc., 1977, pp. 170-179.

Chapter 7

1. Koeberg, Don, and Bagnall, Jim. *The Universal Traveler.* Los Altos, CA: William Kaufmann, Inc., 1976. p. 9.

2. McKim, *Experiences in Visual Thinking,* p. 45.

3. Rowan, Helen. "The Creative People: How to Spot Them." *THINK.* New York: IBM Corp., Nov.–Dec. 1962, vol. 28, no. 10, p. 15.

4. *Webster's New World Dictionary.*

5. March, Lionel, and Steadman, Philip. *The Geometry of Environment.* London: RIBA Publications Limited, 1971, p. 28.

6. Beeby, Thomas H. "The Grammar of Ornament/Ornament as Grammar." *VIA III,* The Journal of the Graduate School of Fine Arts, University of Pennsylvania, 1978, p. 11.

7. Beeby, "The Grammar of Ornament/Ornament as Grammar," pp. 11–12.

8. Carl, Peter. "Towards A Pluralist Architecture." *Progressive Architecture.* Feb. 1973, p. 84.

9. Norberg-Schulz, C. *Existence, Space and Architecture.* New York: Praeger Publishers, Inc., 1971, p. 109.

10. Hanks, Kurt, Belliston, Larry, and Edwards, Dave. *Design Yourself.* Los Altos, CA: William Kaufmann, Inc., 1977, p. 112.

Chapter 8

1. Rowan, "The Creative People: How to Spot Them," p. 11.

2. Rowan, "The Creative People: How to Spot Them," p. 13.

3. Pye, David. *The Nature of Design.* New York: Reinhold Publishing Corporation, 1964, pp. 65–66.

4. McKim, *Experiences in Visual Thinking,* p. 47.

5. Broadbent, *Design in Architecture,* p. 341.

6. Broadbent, *Design in Architecture,* p. 343.

7. Alexander, Christopher, Ishikawa, Sara, and Silverstein, Murray. *A Pattern Language.* New York: Oxford University Press, 1977, pp. xliii–xliv.

Chapter 9

1. Lockard, *Design Drawing,* p. 119.

2. Pena, *Problem Seeking: An Architectural Programming Primer,* p. 165.

Chapter 11

1. McKim, *Experiences in Visual Thinking,* p. 31.

2. Kubie, Lawrence. *Neurotic Distortion of the Creative Process.* Garden City, NY: Farrar, Straus & Giroux, Inc. (Noonday Press), 1961.

3. McKim, *Experiences in Visual Thinking,* p. 127.

4. Cherry, Colin. *On Human Communication.* Cambridge, MA: MIT Press, 1966, p. 4.

5. Jencks, Charles. *LeCorbusier and the Tragic View of Architecture.* Cambridge, MA: Harvard University Press, 1973.

Chapter 12

1. Broadbent, *Design in Architecture,* p. 358.

2. Caudill, William W. *Architecture by Team.* New York: Van Nostrand Reinhold Company, 1971.

3. For a description of brainstorming methods, see Gordon, William J. *Synetics: The Development of Creative Capacity.* New York: Macmillan Publishing Co., Inc., 1968.

Chapter 13

1. Drucker, Peter F. *The Age of Discontinuity.* New York: Harper & Row, 1968. Toffler, Alvin. *Future Shock.* New York: Random House, 1970. Bennis, Warren G., and Slater, Philip F. *The Temporary Society.* New York: Harper & Row, 1968.

2. These two renovation projects adapted large older structures for use as shopping complexes in the waterfront area of San Francisco. They have both been very successful socially, aesthetically, and economically.

3. Burns, Jim. *Connections: Ways to Discover and Realize Community Potentials.* Stroudsburg, PA: Dowden, Hutchinson & Ross, 1979. p. 13.

4. Dowling, M. I., Eggink, H. A., Leish, B., and O'Riordan, J. *East Cambridge Study.* Cambridge, MA: Graduate School of Design, Harvard University, 1976.

5. Halprin, Lawrence. *From Process: Architecture No. 4 Lawrence Halprin.* Edited by Ching-Yu Chang. Tokyo: Process Architects Publishing Company Ltd., 1978.

6. Burns, *Connections: Ways to Discover and Realize Community Potentials,* pp. 21–30.

7. The American Institute of Architects established the Regional/Urban Design Assistance Team Program several years ago as a service provided by the profession for the public. In its short history, the program has served cities throughout our country with a combined population of over 10 million people.

Chapter 14

1. *Report of the Royal Commission on National Development in the Arts, Letters and Sciences.* Ottawa, Canada: King's Printer, 1951.

2. Mumford, Lewis. *Technics and Civilization.* New York: Harcourt, Brace & World, Inc., 1962. p. 6.

Bibliography

I. DRAWINGS AND GRAPHICS

Atkin, William Wilson. *Architectural Presentation Techniques.* New York: Van Nostrand Reinhold Co., 1976.

Beittel, K. *Mind and Context in the Art of Drawing.* New York: Holt, 1972.

Bellis, Herbert F. *Architectural Drafting.* New York: McGraw Hill Book Co., 1971.

Bowman, William I. *Graphic Communication.* New York: John Wiley & Sons, Inc., 1968.

Ching, Frank. *Architectural Graphics.* New York: John Wiley & Sons, Inc., 1975.

Collier, G. *Form, Space, and Vision.* Englewood Cliffs, NJ: Prentice-Hall Inc., 1972.

Czaja, Michael. *Freehand Drawing, Language of Design.* Walnut Creek, CA: Gambol Press, 1975.

DaVinci, Leonardo. *Notebooks.* New York: Dover Publications, Inc., 1970.

DeVries, Jan Vredeman. *Perspective.* New York: Dover Publications, Inc., 1968.

Downer, Richard. *Drawing Buildings.* New York: WatsonGuptill Publications, Inc., 1962.

Dubery, Fred, and Willats, John. *Drawing Systems.* London: Van Nostrand Reinhold Co., 1972.

Goldstein, Nathan. *The Art of Responsive Drawing.* Englewood Cliffs, NJ: Prentice-Hall Inc., 1973.

Goodban, William I., and Hayslett, Jack. *Architectural Drawing and Planning.* New York: McGraw-Hill Book Co., 1972.

Guptill, Arthur Leighton. *Drawing with Pen and Ink.* New York: Reinhold Publishing Co., 1961.

Hanks, Kurt, and Belliston, Larry. *Draw! A Visual Approach to Thinking, Learning, and Communicating.* Los Altos, CA: William Kaufmann, Inc., 1977.

Hanks, Kurt, Belliston, Larry, and Edwards, Dave. *Design Yourself.* Los Altos, CA: William Kaufmann, Inc., 1977.

Hayes, Cohn. *Grammar of Drawing for Artists and Designers.* New York: Van Nostrand Reinhold Co., 1969.

Hill, Edward. *The Language of Drawing.* New York: Prentice-Hall Inc., 1966.

Hogarth, Paul. *Drawing Architecture: A Creative Approach.* New York: Watson-Guptill Publications, Inc., 1973.

Jacoby, Helmut. *New Architectural Drawings.* New York: Praeger, 1969.

Jacoby, Helmut. *New Techniques of Architectural Rendering.* New York: Praeger, 1971.

Kemper, Alfred. *Presentation Drawings by American Architects.* New York: John Wiley & Sons, Inc., 1977.

Kliment, Stephen A. *Creative Communications for a Successful Design Practice.* New York: Watson-Guptill Publications, Inc., 1977.

Lockard, William Kirby. *Drawing as a Means to Architecture.* New York: Reinhold, 1968.

Lockard, William Kirby. *Design Drawing.* Rev. Ed. New York: Van Nostrand Reinhold, 1982.

Lockard, William Kirby. *Design Drawing Experiences.* Tucson, AZ: Pepper Publications, 1974.

Lockwood, Arthur. *Diagrams.* New York: WatsonGuptill Publications, Inc., 1969.

McGinty, Tim. *Drawing Skills in Architecture.* Dubuque, IA: Kendall/Hunt Publishing Co., 1976.

Mendelowitz, David M. *A Guide to Drawing.* New York: Holt, Reinhart and Winston, 1976.

Murgin, Mathew. *Communication Graphics.* New York: Van Nostrand Reinhold Co., 1969.

Nicolaides, K. *The Natural Way to Draw.* Boston: Houghton-Mifflin, 1941; Paperback ed., 1975.

North Carolina University. State College of Agriculture and Engineering. School of Design. *The Student Publication of the School of Design.* Vol. 14, Nos. 1–5, 1964–1965.

O'Connell, William I. *Graphic Communications in Architecture.* Champaign, IL: Stipes Publishing Co., 1972.

Pedretti, Carlo. *A Chronology of Leonardo DaVinci's Architectural Studies after 1500.* Geneva: E. Droz, 1962.

Rottger, Ernst, and Klante, Dieter. *Creative Drawing: Point and Line.* New York: Van Nostrand Reinhold Co., 1963.

Stegman, George K. *Architectural Drafting.* Chicago: American Technical Society, 1966.

Steinberg, Saul. *The Labyrinth.* New York: Harper & Brothers, 1960.

Thiel, Phillip. *Freehand Drawing, a Primer.* Seattle: University of Washington Press, 1965.

Thurber, James. *Thurber and Company.* New York: Harper & Row Publishers Inc., 1966.

Walker, Theodore D. *Plan Graphics.* West Lafayette, IN: PDA Publications, 1975.

Weidhaas, Ernest R. *Architectural Drafting and Construction.* Boston: Allyn and Bacon, 1974.

White, Edward T. *Concept Sourcebook.* Tucson, AZ: Architectural Media, 1975.

II. DESIGN AND PROBLEM-SOLVING

Adams, James L. *Conceptual Blockbusting.* New York: Scribner, 1974.

Alexander, Christopher. *Notes on the Synthesis of Form.* Cambridge, MA: Harvard University Press, 1967.

Alexander, Christopher, Ishikawa, Sara, and Silverstein, Murray. *A Pattern Language.* New York: Oxford University Press, 1977.

Alger, J., and Hays, C. *Creative Synthesis in Design.* Englewood Cliffs, NJ: Prentice-Hall Inc., 1964.

Archer, L. Bruce. *The Structure of Design Processes.* London: Royal College of Art, 1968.

Bender, Tom G. *Environmental Design Primer.* New York: Schoken, 1976.

Best, Gordon. "Method and Intention in Architectural Design." *Design Methods in Architecture.* Edited by Broadbent and Ward. New York: George Wittenborn Inc., 1969.

Broadbent, Geoffrey. *Design in Architecture.* New York: John Wiley & Sons, Inc., 1973.

Broadbent, Geoffrey, and Ward, Anthony, eds. I. *Design Methods in Architecture Symposium.* New York: G. Wittenborn, 1969.

Burns, Jim. *Connections: Ways to Discover and Realize Community Potentials.* Stroudsburg, PA: Dowden, Hutchinson & Ross, Inc., 1979.

Duffy, Francis, and Torrey, John. "A Progress Report on the Pattern Language." In Moore, Gary T., *Emerging Methods in Environmental Design and Planning.* Cambridge, MA: MIT Press, 1970.

Environmental Design: Research and Practice. Environmental Design Research Conference. Los Angeles: University of California, 1972.

Garrett, L. *Visual Design, A Problem Solving Approach.* New York: Reinhold, 1967.

Halprin, Burns. *Taking Part.* Cambridge: MIT Press, 1974.

Halprin, Lawrence. *RSVP Cycles.* New York: George Braziller Inc., 1969.

Heimsath, Cloris. *Behavioral Architecture.* New York: McGraw-Hill Book Co., 1977.

Jones, John Christopher. *Design Methods.* New York: John Wiley & Sons, Inc., 1920.

Jones, Owen. *The Grammar of Ornament.* London: B. Quaritch, 1910.

Koberg, Don, and Bagnall, Jim. *The Universal Traveler.* Los Altos, CA: William Kaufmann, Inc., 1972.

Manheim, Marvin L. *Problem Solving Processes in Planning and Design.* Cambridge, MA: School of Engineering. MIT, 1967.

Moore, Charles Willard, Lyndon, Donlyn, and Allen, Gerald., *The Place of Houses.* Berkeley, CA: University of California Press, 2000.

Moore, Gary T. *Emerging Methods in Environmental Design and Planning.* Cambridge, MA: Design Methods Group. MIT Press, 1968.

Mumford, Lewis. *The City in History.* New York: Harcourt, Brace & World, Inc., 1961.

Nelson, George. *Problems of Design.* New York: Whitney Publishers, 1957.

Pena, William M., with Caudill, William W., and Focke, John W. *Problem Seeking.* Houston: Caudill Rowlett Scott, 1969.

III. VISUAL COMMUNICATION AND PERCEPTION

Alexander, H. *Language and Thinking.* New York: Van Nostrand Reinhold Co., 1967.

Arnheim, Rudolf. *Visual Thinking.* Berkeley: University of California Press, 1969.

Bach, M. *Power of Perception.* Garden City, NY: Doubleday, 1966.

Bartlett, F. C. *Remembering.* New York: Cambridge University Press, 1977.

Bartley, S. *Principles of Perception.* New York: Harper, 1972.

Block, H., and Salinger, H. *The Creative Vision.* Gloucester, MA: Peter Smith, 1968.

Bois, J. *The Art of Awareness.* Dubuque, IA: W. C. Brown, 1973.

Bry, Adelaide, and Bair, Marjorie. *Directing Movies of Your Mind: Visualization for Health and Insights.* New York: Harper and Row, 1978.

Chomsky, Noam. *Language and Mind.* New York: Harcourt Brace Jovanovich, 1972.

Chomsky, Noam. "Review of B. F. Skinner Verbal Behavior." *Language Magazine,* Jan–Mar 1959.

Cunningham, S., and Reagan, C. *Handbook of Visual Perceptual Training.* Springfield, IL: Thomas, 1972.

Feldman, Edmund Burke. *Art As Image and Idea.* Englewood Cliffs, NJ: Prentice-Hall Inc., 1967.

Gibson, J. *The Senses Considered as Perceptual Systems.* Boston: Houghton-Mifflin, 1966.

Gibson, James. *The Perception of the Visual World.* Boston: Houghton-Mifflin, 1950.

Harlan, C. *Vision and Invention.* Englewood Cliffs, NJ: Prentice-Hall Inc., 1970.

Hayakawa, S. *Language in Thought and Action.* New York: Harcourt Brace Jovanovich, 1978.

Huxley, A. *The Art of Seeing.* Seattle, WA: Madrona Publishers, 1975.

Janson, H. W. *The Nature of Representation: A Phenomenological Enquiry.* New York: New York University Press, 1961.

Jeanneret-Gris, Charles Edouard. *New World of Space.* New York: Reynal and Hitchcock, 1948.

Kepes, Gyorgy. *Language of Vision.* Chicago, IL: Paul Theobold and Co., 1944.

Luckiesh, Matthew. *Visual Illusions, Their Causes, Characteristics and Applications.* New York: Dover, 1965.

McKim, Robert H. *Experiences in Visual Thinking.* Monterey, CA: Brookes/Cole, 1972.

The Notebook of Paul Klee. Vol. 1: The Thinking Eye. New York: Wittenborn, 1978.

Paramenter, Ross. *The Awakened Eye.* Middletown, CT: Wesleyan University Press, 1968.

Pitcher, G. *A Theory of Perceptions.* Princeton, NJ: Princeton University, 1971.

Robertson, T. *Innovative Behavior and Communication.* New York: Holt, 1971.

Samuels, M., and Samuels, N. *Seeing with the Mind's Eye.* New York: Random House, 1975.

Summer, Robert. *The Mind's Eye.* New York: Dell Publishing, 1978.

Vygotsky, Lev S. *Thought and Language.* Cambridge, MA: MIT Press, 1962.

Walker, Theodore D. *Perception and Environmental Design.* West Lafayette, IN: PDA Publishers, 1971.

Whitehead, Alfred North. *Symbolism, Its Meaning and Effect.* New York: Macmillan Co., 1959.

IV. CREATIVITY

Banker, W. *Brain Storms,* New York: Grove, 1968.

Barrett, W. *Time of Need: Forms of Imagination in the 20th Century.* New York: Harper, 1972.

Batten, M. *Discovery By Chance.* New York: Funk and Wagnalls Co., 1968.

Berrill, N. J. *Man's Emerging Mind: The Story of Man's Progress Through Time.* New York: Fawcett World Library, 1965.

Boas, G. *History of Ideas.* New York: Scribners, 1969.

Bourne, L. *Human Conceptual Behavior.* Boston: Allyn and Bacon, 1966.

Brown, R. *The Creative Spirit.* Port Washington, NY: Kennikat, 1970.

Bruner, J., Goodnow, I., and Austin, G. *A Study of Thinking.* New York: Wiley, 1956.

Burton, W., Kimball, R., and Wing, R. *Education for Effective Thinking.* New York: Appleton, 1960.

Chang, C. Y. *Creativity and Taoism.* New York: Harper, 1970.

Cobb, S. *Discovering the Genius Within You.* Metuchen, NJ: Scarecrow, 1967.

DeBono, E. *Lateral Thinking.* New York: Harper, 1972.

DeBono, E. *New Think.* New York: Basic Books, Inc., 1968.

Dyer, F., and Dyer, J. *Bureaucracy vs. Creativity.* Coral Gables, FL: University of Miami, 1965.

Eberle, R. Scamper: *Games for Imaginative Development.* Buffalo: D.O.K., 1972.

Garfield, Patricia. *Creative Dreaming.* New York: Ballantine Books, 1974.

Gombrich, F. H. *Art and Illusion.* New York: Phardon/Pantheon, 1960.

Gordon, W. J. J. *Synectics: The Development of Creative Capacity.* New York: Macmillan, 1968.

Greene, Herb. *Mind and Image.* Lexington, KY: University Press of Kentucky, 1976.

Gruber, Howard E., ed. *Contemporary Approaches to Creative Thinking.* New York: Atherton Press, 1963.

Koestler, Arthur. *The Act of Creation: A Study of Conscious and Unconscious in Science and Art.* New York: Dell Publishing, 1973.

Korner, S. *Conceptual Thinking: A Logical Inquiry.* New York: Dover, 1959.

Krippner, S., and Hughes, W. *Dreams and Human Potential.* Paper presented to American Association of Humanistic Psychology, 1969.

Maslow, A. H. *The Farther Reaches of Human Nature.* New York: The Viking Press, 1973.

McKellar, Peter. *Imagination and Thinking: A Psychological Analysis.* Norwood, PA: Norwood Editions, 1978.

Osborn, A. F. *Applied Imagination: Principles and Practices of Creative Thinking.* New York: Scribners, 1957.

Pikas, A. *Abstraction and Concept Formation.* Cambridge, MA: Harvard University, 1966.

Pollock, T. *Managing Creatively.* Boston: Cahners Books, 1971.

Prince, George M. *The Practice of Creativity.* New York: Harper & Row (paperback, Collier Books, 1972).

Reed, F. *Developing Creative Talent.* New York: Vantage, 1962.

Rieser, Dolf. *Art and Science.* New York: Van Nostrand Reinhold, 1972.

Rowan, Helen. "The Creative People: How to Spot Them." *THINK.* New York: IBM Corp. Nov.–Dec., 1962, pp. 7–15.

Samples, Robert. *Introduction to the Metaphoric Mind.* Reading, MA: Addison-Wesley Publishing Co., 1976.

Watson, James D. *The Double Helix.* Pasadena, CA: Atheneum Press, 1969.

Illustration Credits

1-1, 8-29: By permission of Biblioteca Ambrosiana, Milano. From the *Codex Atlanticus,* figures 37 and 86 in *Leonardo DaVinci: The Royal Palace at Romarantin* by Carlo Padretti. Cambridge, MA: Harvard University Press, 1972.

1-2, 1-3: Reproduced from the *Catalogue of the Drawings Collection of the Royal Institute of British Architects, volume 9,* Edwin Lutyens, published by Gregg International, an imprint of Avebury Publishing Company, England, 1973.

1-4, 7-3, 7-33, 11-1: Reproduced from *Alvar Aalto: Synopsis,* edited by Bernhard Hoesli, published by Birkhauser Verlag, Basel, 1970.

1-5, 5-11, 5-15: Courtesy of Thomas N. Larson, FAAR, The Architects Collaborative.

1-6, 7-34, 11-10: Courtesy of Thomas H. Beeby, Hammond, Beeby, Babka, Architects, Chicago.

1-7, 2-6, 5-4: From Atkin, William W. *Architectural Presentation Techniques.* © 1976 by Litton Educational Publishing, Inc. Reprinted by permission of Van Nostrand Reinhold Company.

1-8: From Erman, Adolph. *Life in Ancient Egypt.* New York: reprinted by Benjamin Blom, Inc., 1969. Distributed by Arno Press, Inc.

1-17: From *Cybernetic Serendipity: The Computer and the Arts.* New York: Praeger Publishers, Inc., 1968.

1-24, 5-2, 11-2: Courtesy of David T. Stieglitz, Stieglitz Stieglitz Tries, Architects, Buffalo, NY.

1-27: Reprinted from the July 1978 issue of *Progressive Architecture,* copyright 1978, Reinhold Publishing Company.

2-2, 5-20, 5-22, 5-23, 7-29: Reproduced by permission of Lisa Kolber.

2-3, 7-18: Reprinted with the permission of Process Architects Publishing Company Ltd., Tokyo, and Lawrence Halprin. Copyright 1978. From *Process: Architecture No. 4 Lawrence Halprin.*

2-4: Reproduced by permission of Karl Brown.

2-5: Reprinted with the permission of Design Publications, Inc. From the March 1975 issue of *Industrial Design Magazine.*

2-7, 5-21, 5-26, 5-27: Reproduced by permission of Patrick P. Nall.

2-38: Reproduced by permission of Todd Carlson.

3-1: Rendering of the Student Union Housing, University of Alberta at Edmonton, Architects: A. J. Diamond and Barton Myers in association with R. L. Wilkin, Architect, and Barton Myers, Partner-in-Charge. Rendering by A. J. Diamond.

3-21: Courtesy of Thomas P. Truax. From a research study, Ohio University School of Architecture and Planning, 1974.

3-24, 3-25: Reprinted from *Helmut Jacoby Architectural Drawings.* New York: Praeger Publishers, Inc., 1965.

3-26: Reprinted from *Freehand Drawing: Language of Design,* by Michael Czaja. Walnut Creek, CA: Gambol Press, 1975.

3-27, 5-14: Courtesy of Michael F. Gebhart, The Architects Collaborative.

3-28: Reproduced by permission of Bret Dodd.

5-5, 7-5, 8-30: Reprinted from atelier rue de Sevres 35, by Guillermo Jullian de la Fuente and Anthony Eardley, a catalogue from an exhibition of project sketches and notes from LeCorbusier to Guillermo Jullian de la Fuente published by the College of Architecture in collaboration with the University Art Gallery, University of Kentucky, Lexington.

7-6: From Richard Saul Wurman and Eugene Feldman. *The Notebooks and Drawings of Louis I. Kahn.* Cambridge, MA: MIT Press, 1962.

5-1: By courtesy of Architectural Publishers Artemis, Zurich. Published in *Louis I. Kahn.* Copyright 1975.

5-3, 5-9: Courtesy of Edwin F. Harris, Jr., '59. From *The Student Publication of the School of Design,* vol. 10, number 2, North Carolina State University, Raleigh, NC.

5-6: From Papadaki, Stamo. *The Work of Oscar Niemeyer.* New York: Van Nostrand Reinhold Company, 1950.

5-7, 5-19: Courtesy of James W. Anderson and Landplus West, Inc., Land Planners/Landscape Architects.

5-8: Reprinted with the permission of Lawrence Halprin. From *The RSVP Cycles: Creative Processes in the Human Environment.* New York: George Braziller, Inc., 1969.

5-10, 5-12, 7-7: Courtesy of Gerald Exline. From Williams, A. Richard. *The Urban Stage* (Study Draft). Champagne-Urbana, IL, 11:1976.

5-13: Reprinted with the permission of Process Architects Publishing Company Ltd., Tokyo, and Romaldo Giurgola, Copyright 1977. From *Process: Architecture No. 2* Mitchell Giurgola Architects.

5-17: Drawing by architect Hugh Stubbins, from his book *Architecture: The Design Experience.* New York: John Wiley and Sons, 1976.

5-25: Reproduced by permission of Thomas A. Cheesman.

5-24: Reproduced by permission of James A. Walls.

7-11, 7-12: From "The Grammar of Ornament/Ornament as Grammar" by Thomas H. Beeby, published in *VIA III,* The journal of the Graduate School of Fine Arts, University of Pennsylvania. Reprinted with the permission of Thomas H. Beeby.

7-28: Reprinted from Norberg-Schulz, C. *Existence, Space & Architecture.* New York: Praeger Publishers, Inc., 1971.

7-32: Courtesy of Thomas P. Truax. From master's thesis project, Ohio University, 1975.

8-14: Courtesy of Mark S. Sowatsky. From Atlantis 2, thesis project, College of Architecture and Planning, Ball State University, Indiana, 1977.

10-12, 10-13, 10-14, 10-17: Reproduced by permission of Raymond Gaetan.

10-15, 10-16: Reproduced by permission of Tim Treman.

12-3, 12-4: Reprinted with the permission of William W. Caudill, FAIA, Caudill Rowlett Scott, from his book *Architecture by Team.* New York: Van Nostrand Reinhold Company, 1971.

13-5, 13-6: Drawn by Harry A. Eggink. From the *East Cambridge Study,* by Michael Justin Dowling, Harry A. Eggink, Bruce Leish, and Joan O'Riordan, Urban Design Program, Graduate School of Design, Harvard University, 1976.

13-7, 13-8, 13-9, 13-10, 13-11: Reprinted with the permission of the publishers and Steve Levine from *Connections: Ways to Discover and Realize Community Potential* by Jim Burns. Copyright 1979 by Dowden, Hutchinson & Ross, Inc., Publisher, Stroudsburg, PA.

13-13: Reprinted with the permission of Peter Hasselman, AIA, from the Atlantic City Study. American Institute of Architects, Regional/Urban Design Assistance Team.

13-12: Reprinted with the permission of John Desmond, FAIA, from *Phoenix Study.* American Institute of Architects, Regional/Urban Design Assistance Team.

13-14, 13-15: Reprinted by the permission of W. P. Durkee, Urban Design Associates, Pittsburgh, and Roy Mann, Roy Mann Associates, Cambridge, MA, from *Portsmouth Study.* American Institute of Architects, Regional/Urban Design Assistance Team.

13-16: Reprinted with the permission of Charles A. Blessing, FAIA, from *Phoenix Study.* American Institute of Architects, Regional/Urban Design Assistance Team.

13-17, 13-18: Drawn by Harry Eggink. Preliminary sketches for Basketball Hall of Fame at New Castle, IN.

13-19: Drawn by Harry Eggink. Rogan House, Elkhart, IN.

13-20: Drawn by Harry Eggink. East Bank Development for Elkhart, IN.

13-21, 13-22, 13-23: Reprinted with the permission of Harry Eggink from *Aleph Park,* a computer-based, high-tech, industrial site planning case study (Harry A. Eggink and Robert J. Koester, project directors; Michele Mounayar, principal consultant). Muncie, IN: Ball State University, College of Architecture and Planning and Center for Energy Research/Education/Service, 1984.

14-1, 14-2, 14-3, 14-4: Reproduced by permission of Nathan Moore.

14-5: By David Thompson Design. Reproduced by permission of House + House Architects.

14-6: Computer rendering by Shawn Brown. Reproduced by permission of House + House Architects.

Index